# THE  Trust BUSINESS

JOHN M. CLARKE

JACK W. ZALAHA

AUGUST ZINSSER III

EDUCATION POLICY & DEVELOPMENT

 AMERICAN
BANKERS
ASSOCIATION

1120 Connecticut Avenue, N.W.
Washington, D.C. 20036

This publication is designed to provide accurate and authoritative information in regard to the subject matter covered. It is sold with the understanding that the publisher is not engaged in rendering legal, accounting, or other professional service. If legal advice or other expert assistance is required, the services of a competent professional person should be sought.

*—From a Declaration of Principles jointly adopted by a Committee of the American Bar Association and a Committee of Publishers and Associations.*

Library of Congress Cataloging-in-Publication Data

Clarke, John M., 1947-
    The trust business / John M. Clarke, Jack W. Zalaha, and August Zinsser III.
        p.   cm.
    Includes index.
    ISBN 0-89982-350-5 : $37.50 (est.)
    1. Trust companies.   I. Zalaha, Jack W., 1939-      .  II. Zinsser, August, 1941-      .   III. Title.
HG4309.C48  1988
332.1'78—dc19                                                                     88-10345
                                                                                         CIP

Printed in the United States of America.

1991 Printing

# Contents

Cover illustration: *A Bureau of the Procuratori di San Marco,* (detail).

A manuscript illumination of the late fourteenth century depicts the Procuratori paying a legacy to the monastery of San Maffeo di Murano. The background calligraphy is from a 1397 ledger consigned by the executors of the estate of Domenedo da Pozzo to the Procuratori for the administration of the estate for Domenedo's son, Andrea.

*Seminario Patriarcale, Venice, Catastico di S. Maffeo di Murano.*
*Photograph by Böhm.*

# Preface

This edition of *The Trust Business* marks the most recent effort to update a text that was first published by the American Bankers Association in 1927. The text, like the business it deals with, continues to evolve. The services bank trust departments offer to individual and institutional clients, and the operational activities required to provide those services, continue to change as banks strive to serve the financial needs of the public more effectively and profitably.

The text, divided into four sections, provides a foundation on which the beginning student of trust can build. Key concepts and terms shown in bold in the text are defined in the glossary.

Section 1 introduces the most important elements of the trust industry, their historical origins, and their application to modern trust practices. The reader will learn the basic terminology of trusts and agencies, the principal trust services, and the meaning of fiduciary responsibility. Trust departments have combined traditional skills and modern practices to operate as profit-making centers in their banks. This has required that trust departments recognize and adapt to a constantly changing environment that is influenced by such factors as competition from new sources, heightened consumer expectation, and changing government regulations. The section concludes by focusing on what people own—assets—and how they own them. The type of asset and the form of ownership have important implications for trustees.

This broad view of trusts is reinforced and expanded in the following sections. Section 2 is devoted to trust services for individuals. The reader is introduced to the basic reasons why people use trust services. The remainder of the section offers an in-depth look at personal trusts and agencies. In particular, how trust departments handle guardianships and estate settlements, areas where human relations skills are as important as business expertise, are examined.

Section 3 turns the focus from the individual to corporate and institutional trust services. Employee benefit trusts, a rapidly growing area of trust business, is explored. The intricacies of the bank's role as trustee are revealed in the following chapter, when a discussion of how corporations and government bodies issue bonds to raise capital is presented. Other institutional clients of trust departments are charitable organizations. The variety of trusts available to such organizations is identified, along with suggestions of how these services may be marketed.

The final section of *The Trust Business* highlights trust department operations, from managing securities issues to selecting an investment portfolio that best meets a client's asset management objectives. The volume and extent of operational procedures are subject to close scrutiny. The section, and the text, concludes with a look at how trust departments are responding to the challenge of a deregulated environment that has spawned a host of new competitors offering trust services. No longer content to rely on referrals as the primary source of new business, trust departments are beginning to develop effective sales and marketing strategies to provide customers with cost-effective services.

This provides but a brief glimpse at the scope of this text. The trust business is an exciting and challenging area of banking that is on the threshold of entering new and previously forbidden investment markets—if the banking lobby is successful in easing the limitations on the types of investments trust departments may make.

# Acknowledgments

*The Trust Business* is the result of the collective efforts and wisdom of several individuals. Particular thanks go to the authors of this text—John M. Clarke, West Coast Director, Portland Office, The Rankin Group, Ltd., Beaverton, Oregon; Jack W. Zalaha, Vice President and Manager, U.S. Bank of Washington Trust Group, Vancouver Branch, Vancouver, Washington; and August Zinsser III, Executive Vice President, Asset Managment Group, First American Bank, Washington, D.C. They devoted considerable time and energy to organizing, reviewing, and revising the manuscript at various stages of completion. George W. Cowles, Senior Vice President, Bankers Trust Company, New York, New York; Ronald G. Wilson of Robbins & Green Law Offices, Phoenix, Arizona; and Cheryl Williams, Trust Officer, Crestar Bank N.A., Washington, D.C., also provided invaluable assistance in reviewing the manuscript. The authors gratefully acknowledge the writing contributions of David H. Buzzell and Tom Bisky.

SECTION  The Fundamentals of the Business

"Trust people have always known how to manage assets
profitably and prudently, no matter how diverse the
assets. In the thirties, we handled real estate; in the fifties,
chiefly stocks. Today, a trust officer must understand such
unusual investments as art and gold—but asset
management is still the name of the game."

—Van R. Gathany, *former chairman,*
*ABA Trust Executive Committee*

# A History of Trust Relationships

## INTRODUCTION

Four decades ago, when today's most seasoned commercial bankers were still in their formative professional years, banks handled almost 70 percent of the nation's financial resources. Now they handle about 30 percent. Why?

Largely because, in the intervening years, money market funds, comparatively unregulated "nonbanks," and other new, entrepreneurial competitors emerged. With technological innovation and aggressive marketing strategies, they gradually encroached upon many of commercial banking's most time-honored lines of business.

In the 1980s, with interest rates more volatile, profit margins narrower, and customer loyalty to specific institutions ever thinner, the better-managed banks began adopting bold coping strategies. They shifted toward lower-cost production, leaner staffing, and computerized basic services. To retain current customers and attract new ones, the most enlightened banks began to use **relationship management.**

What is relationship management? Medicine offers a good analogy. In a medical center, the internist is a top-notch professional who adds value to basic services. He or she sees the patient at the beginning—to determine whether, say, an X ray or blood testing is needed. Then after the tests are performed by others, the internist sees the patient again to evaluate results and prescribe treatment. In short, the internist assumes overall responsibility for the patient relationship and takes a personal interest at every point.

Similarly, in contemporary commercial banking, the officer who practices relationship management, or relationship banking in this context, is an experienced professional. He or she brings together specialists throughout the bank on the customer's behalf. While the officer does not execute every transaction, he or she does ensure that the customer is well served at every turn. When the customer needs or requests a new variety of service, the officer extends the relationship by making a smooth referral—with follow-up as needed—to a colleague in the appropriate area of the bank. Thus relationship banking responds directly to the often heard customer plea: "I don't want just a bank—I want a banker."

The trust business is relationship banking at its best—and oldest. The business began in Egypt nearly 4,000 years ago. Ever since then, the trust officer's job has been holding, managing, and caring for the property of others. Indeed, because officers on the personal side of the trust business tend to become privy to secrets of their customers' professional and private lives, the officer is nearly accorded the status of a family friend.

Property owners may be individuals (**personal trust** business) or organizations (corporate and **institutional trust** business). Traditionally, the trust departments in commercial banks have served the wealthiest individuals and the biggest institutional clients, but this is changing today.

As an introduction to the trust business, this chapter examines how the trust function developed from English common law and how it has flourished in the twentieth century. We will then look at the place of trust in contemporary relationship banking. The chapter closes by considering the basic functions of a trust department and defining such terms as trust, trustee, agency, fiduciary, and guardian.

## MILESTONES IN THE HISTORY OF THE BUSINESS

The trust business is as old as the Great Pyramids and as new as the latest piece of computer software, as the following chronology shows:

### Twentieth Century B.C.

References to wills date back to the earliest civilizations. For instance, archaeologists have discovered three Egyptian wills, each nearly 4,000 years old. One of these is so modern in form, so plainly expressed, and so properly witnessed that it might almost be admissible in a modern probate court.

### Second Century A.D.

Ancient Rome recognized various prototypes of the trust institution. For example, after the time of Marcus Aurelius (A.D. 161–80), it was customary for Romans to leave gifts by will to fraternities or trade unions. These wills contained instructions on the use of the property, and as a result, the fraternal, professional, or other institution was in essence charged with the administration of a trust.

### Eighth Century

The office of the executor was recognized to some degree in England from the beginning of the eighth century. The role of the English executor evolved over the centuries until the turn of the nineteenth century when British courts finally recognized the executor as a trustee and not the *owner* of the assets.

### Tenth Century

In Europe at this time, men often left their wills for safekeeping with the church or a monastery and named a clergyman as executor. The person thus named acted as a representative of the church.

### Twelfth Century

Between 1118 and 1312, the Order of Knights Templars was the most powerful financial organization in Europe and was engaged extensively in the banking business. The order's treasurers were frequently named as executors of wills, and some evidence suggests that they also held and invested funds for annuities. Thus the Knights Templars were in many respects pioneers in the trust business as settlers of estates and administrators of trusts.

### Middle Ages

In England from the twelfth century through the early part of the fourteenth century, common-law courts were the prevailing seats of justice. Common law is the legal system that, even today, underpins the administration of justice in the English-speaking countries—that is, the United States and the nations making up the British Empire and the Commonwealth of Nations. (Common law differs from civil law, the legal system that prevails in the European, Asiatic, Central American, and South American countries. These countries inherited their legal systems from Rome; the common-law nations, from England.)

Historians say that if the common-law courts had continued to exercise "equitable" powers, the Court of Chancery never would have developed. The Court of Chancery, presided over by the monarchy's chancellor and keeper of the Great Seal, became an established "court of the realm" by the end of the reign of Henry V (1413–22). It captured equity jurisdiction from the common-law courts, which by then had become rigid and inflexible.

Before the Court of Chancery took over, equity was equity and law was law. That is, equity was administered in somewhat "practical and rough-and-ready fashion" by the earliest of the English chancellors. These, according to Scott's *Law of Trusts,* (3d ed., Little, Brown & Co., 1967), "were ecclesiastics and not lawyers."

Despite the famous injunction in Shakespeare's *Henry VI, Part 2* ("The first thing we do, let's kill all the lawyers"), until men who were trained in the law were entrusted with the Great Seal, both justice and equity were imprecise and unevenly dispensed.

In truth, the entire basis for the theory of the trust business stemmed from a fifteenth century accident—the development of the dual justice system. The system recognized a split between property's **legal ownership** and **equitable ownership** (equity). According to Scott, "It was possible . . . for one person to have the legal title to property and for another to compel him to exercise his legal rights for the other's benefit. There would be nothing extraordinary about the trust if the matter had stopped there. But the courts of equity went further. . . . They gave the beneficiary an interest in the property and gave him protection in the enjoyment of that interest. The result is something unique, a double form of ownership. Down beneath is the trustee who holds the legal title; above him is the beneficiary who has the equitable ownership."

### Sixteenth Century

By the reign of Henry VIII (1509–47), equity in England had begun to assume the shape of law. Sir Thomas More, a trained lawyer, succeeded Cardinal Wolsey as chancellor in 1529. Although More held the Great Seal for only 3 years, equity took a quantum leap forward during his administration. With few exceptions, the Great Seal has been in the hands of lawyers until the present day.

The English use of the trust is clearly the predecessor of the modern trust—although some would argue that personal trusts are of Roman or English-German origin. An English law, the **Statute of Uses** (1536), sought to eliminate the concept of holding property for the use of another. However, the apparently common practice of giving property to one person for the use of another—the **use upon a use**—remained as a means of evading debts, especially taxes. For instance, a property owner would convey property to someone for a third person's use—usually the relative of the owner—to avoid encumbrances and other financial difficulties. From the use upon a use, the modern trust developed.

### Seventeenth Century

A **ward** is a person who by reason of mental incompetence, some other incapacity, or status as a minor is under the protection of a court—either directly or through a guardian. In the seventeenth century, so-called **guard-**

**ianships in chivalry** usually proved disastrous for the ward. The guardian's profit, rather than the ward's best interests, was the overriding concern. Because the guardian's interest in the property could be sold and transferred to the highest bidder, the guardian usually sold the ward in marriage to get the best financial settlement of the property for himself. Charles II (1660–85) abolished guardianships in chivalry.

## THE TRUST BUSINESS IN THE UNITED STATES

From the preceding chronology, it is apparent that the *personal* side of the trust business—encompassing wills, guardianships, and so forth—developed over many hundreds of years in many different lands.

Not surprisingly, perhaps, *corporate* aspects of the trust business—with institutions as both purveyors and consumers of trust services—have come into fullest flower in the United States.

### Eighteenth-Century Precursors

The idea of corporations handling trust business may have come to the United States from India. As early as 1774, a public official known as an **ecclesiastical registrar** was given legal authority to settle the estates of British subjects who died in India. In effect, the registrar was a one-man corporation.

**Agency houses** also developed in India during this period. These were organized to transact business for trustees and individuals, to receive money on deposit, and to administer estates.

### Nineteenth Century

In the main, the history of trust institutions in the United States extends just over a century and a half. The first part of the nineteenth century witnessed the transition from an agricultural and mercantile society to an industrial nation. During the same period, the locus of economic growth shifted from the countryside to the cities.

These changes in society brought a change in the form of business organizations from proprietorships and partnerships to corporations that could finance manufacturing enterprises. Corporations also were created to handle the estates of those whose wealth consisted of stocks and bonds. With the advent of manufacturing and the formation of corporations, successful businesses could easily be passed intact from one generation to the next. Unlike passing on a farm to heirs, only stocks and bonds were involved.

Increased demand for trusts and trustees stemmed from the need to keep property from minors and some other heirs. Little by little, many U.S. corporations became involved in the trust business.

## The Earliest Trust Charters

In 1822, Farmer's Fire Insurance and Loan Company of New York became the first institution chartered to engage in the trust business. During this era, the business was dominated by life insurance companies. By 1840, several kinds of institutions were involved in both corporate trusteeships and the performance of personal trust services.

For American capitalism, 1853 was truly an *annus mirabilis*—a year of wonders. Commodore Perry opened Japan as a rich new market for the wares of Andrew Carnegie, Henry Clay Frick, and other U.S. entrepreneurs; the Gadsden Purchase opened a huge new tract of western land to Cornelius Vanderbilt's railroads; and in New York City, a banker's dozen of the town's leading politicians, financiers, and industrialists opened a new kind of banking institution. Chartered by New York State to serve as executor and trustee of corporate and personal funds, the United States Trust Company of New York City became the first American institution devoted exclusively to trust services.

During the next half century, the number of institutions engaged in the trust business proliferated rapidly. In most of these institutions, a department devoted exclusively to trust services functioned apart from the firm's general business. Informally, this distinction foreshadowed the so-called **Chinese Wall** that arose decades later—through force of federal regulation and fiduciary-law precedent—to forbid the commercial and trust departments of a bank from sharing customer credit or investment information.

## Trust in the Modern Era

In 1896, representatives of trust companies asked the American Bankers Association (ABA) to amend its bylaws to permit the organization of a trust company section. The section held its first meeting the following year. However, national banks were not allowed to engage in the trust business until the 1900s.

From 1906 to 1918, as a result of action by the U.S. Congress, the U.S. Supreme Court, and the Federal Reserve Board of Governors, national banks won authority to engage in the trust business. By 1920, about 1,300 national banks offered trust services.

Today, more than 4,000 American banks have charters authorizing them to engage in the trust business. Together, these institutions hold, manage, and care for more than $800 billion in customer assets, both retail and corporate. In a single 5-year period—from 1982 to 1987—the total amount of assets under management more than doubled.

### Changes Since 1930

Wealth is the impetus of the trust business. Traditionally, trust services were designed for the wealthy and refined into quasi-personal services for them. In the first few decades of this century, even though trust services were available and benefited many who were not truly wealthy, the public mind identified trust as an elitist service appropriate only for people with great sums of money.

After the 1930s, however, the trust business changed dramatically. The Great Depression significantly influenced public attitudes toward the accumulation, preservation, and disposition of wealth. As a result, the trust business began to encompass increasingly larger segments of American society. For example, the growth of **employee benefit funds** managed by trust institutions has enabled millions of Americans to feel that their employee benefit plans, including Social Security, will provide enough financial security at retirement. They have less need to accumulate assets from their discretionary funds for their retirement, and people are more likely to save to satisfy current wants and to meet unexpected emergencies.

Changes in the tax laws over the years, and new investment approaches and reporting methods have brought about changes in the trust business. For instance, the **Tax Reform Act of 1986** has had significant effects on bank trust departments, according to the Taxation Committee of ABA's Trust and Investment Management Division in the association's Trust and Private Banking Center in Washington, D.C. In enacting the law, Congress did not "meddle with the basic structure of income taxation for trusts and estates; however, the tax law has created many problems for trust departments, including increased paperwork and customer confusion," according to an article by the ABA committee's chairman in the *ABA Banking Journal.* Some tax accountants say that the Tax Reform Act of 1986 has not taxed income as many previous statutes did, but nonetheless has discouraged the use of trusts and estates as devices to accumulate income.

Of course, previous tax laws also had a major effect on the process of wealth accumulation, preservation, and disposition. Tax laws enacted in the 1940s prevailed through the 1950s—but there were major tax law changes in 1962, 1969, 1976, 1981, and as we have seen, in 1986. Some forms of income and transactions were penalized by the laws, thus encouraging some ways of obtaining, holding, and distributing wealth and discouraging others. However, the direction of the various tax law changes has been anything but consistent, and one intent of the Tax Reform Act of 1986 was to limit the alternatives available.

Tax law changes have paralleled changes in how trust departments report activity in trust accounts and how they manage cash. For example, since the late 1960s, most trust departments have automated their entire accounting systems. Automation enables trust departments to give clients detailed statements of account activity and status with minimal delay. Tax information can be produced in a form that a client or a client's tax advisers can easily understand. The use of automated systems has improved trust services, helped trust departments handle increasing volume, and stabilized future costs.

Steady inflation—along with the advent of employee benefit plans and changes in tax laws—has for decades proved a major influence on the trust business. In the 1970s, for instance, a long period of inflation at higher rates than ever seen before caused people to reorient financial planning from long to short range and to reevaluate traditional ways of accumulating and preserving wealth.

The high interest rates of the 1970s produced widespread demand for a better return on cash investments. Trust departments responded to this demand by initiating cash-management programs for their accounts, using a wide variety of money market instruments.

In addition to traditional U.S. Treasury bills and commercial paper, trust departments began using variable-rate notes, time-open certificates of deposit, money market funds, and short-term investment trusts, which are common trust funds. Each choice of investment vehicle that a trust department makes is a function of the department's size, its degree of automation, and the needs of its clients. With the product explosion in the trust industry of the 1970s, trust assets became significant (see exhibit 1.1).

Unfortunately, costs kept pace with revenues, putting increased emphasis on profitability for trust departments and customers alike. Deposits of individuals and corporations previously left on demand or in low-yielding accounts (thus providing "cheap" money for the banks) were rapidly shifted to high-yielding money market investments. Automation, although essential, has demanded a large commitment of resources. Increased regulation of trust departments has also required additional outlays. And trust departments have had to compete with other financial institutions for staff, which has led to increases in salary levels.

In summary, a bank by the 1980s could no longer provide trust services as a personalized service to the wealthy without regard to the profit margin.

## AGENCIES VERSUS TRUSTS

Let's examine the basic terminology of trusts and agencies. Basically, a **trust** is an arrangement in which one person—the **trustor**—transfers legal title to property to another—the **trustee**—who manages the property for one or more other people—the **beneficiaries.** In an agency account, the client, called the **principal,** engages the **agent,** the bank, to perform an **agency** or a specific service for the principal.

*What is the difference between a trust and an agency?* First, as noted, with a trust the title of the property involved passes to the trustee; with an agency

EXHIBIT 1.1   Trust Asset Growth, 1980–86

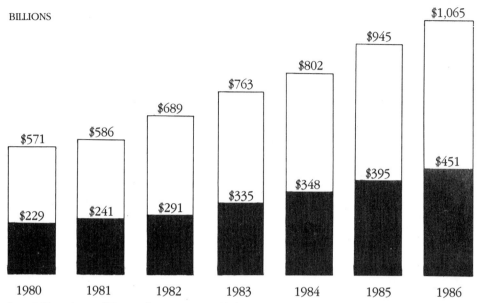

BILLIONS

Source: *Trust Assets of Financial Institutions,* published by the Federal Financial Institutions Examination Council. Only discretionary assets are shown. The shaded areas represent the value of employee benefit accounts.

account, the title of the property does not pass to the agent. An example of each instance might be helpful.

Widower Arthur Richardson, a successful small business entrepreneur, sold his business at a considerable profit and invested in real estate. Arthur now plans to pursue his lifelong interest in archaeology by exploring several areas in South America and the Middle East. He decides to establish a trust for his children with the bank that had served him well when he was in business. When the trust is established, Arthur deeds the property that he wants included in the trust to the bank as trustee.

Likewise, his friend Dr. Bill Thomas has many investments that he no longer has the time to manage properly. Bill established an investment management agency account with his bank's trust department. The bank, as agent, manages Bill Thomas's investments. But, in establishing the agency, the doctor does not deed the property to the bank and, thus, retains title to all the investments involved in the agency.

The *first* fundamental difference between trusts and agencies is that, with a trust, title passes to the trustee. This does not occur with an agency. The *second* fundamental difference between trusts and agencies is that, ordinarily, a trust cannot be closed by either the beneficiary or the trustee and does not have to be ended by the death of the individual or the dissolution of the institution. An agency account, however, can be terminated by either the principal or the agent and always ends with the individual's death or the institution's dissolution. Thus Arthur Richardson's children could not decide, unilaterally, to end the trust when it becomes effective at Arthur's death. Bill Thomas or the bank could end the investment management agency at any time.

## HOW TO RUN A TRUST DEPARTMENT

Although separated from the commercial side of banking, trust departments historically functioned as a service arm of the commercial department and offered a range of services including settling estates, managing trust accounts, and providing investment management. In recent years, as the pressure for profitability has become more and more critical, trust departments are being viewed as independent profit centers of commercial banks that serve individual, corporate, and institutional clients. The future of the trust business depends on its ability to offer profitable services to meet the trust and financial needs of these respective market segments.

### A Trust Department's Responsibilities to Clients

Banks and other trust institutions have **fiduciary** relationships with their clients, which essentially means that trust officers, as representatives of their banks, must always act in the best interest of all the other parties on issues within the scope of their relationship. It is important to emphasize that the bank is the fiduciary and that the trust officers act as representatives of the bank. A trustee has a fiduciary relationship with a beneficiary and an agent has a fiduciary relationship with a principal (client). The bank, not the trust officer or the trust department, is the trustee or the agent.

### The Foundation of Trust Services

Exhibit 1.2 shows that the fundamental trust service blocks of agency accounts, employee benefit accounts, trusts, and estate settlements rest on a foundation of operational, personal, and investment services.

In brief, operational services consist of the safekeeping, receipt, disbursement, accounting, and reporting activities. The investment services involve all activities related to managing investments.

Referring to exhibit 1.2, the types of accounts from left to right are

- agency accounts
- employee benefit accounts

EXHIBIT 1.2   The Foundation of Trust Services

| Types of Accounts | Agency Accounts | Employee Benefit Accounts | Trusts | Estate Settlements |
|---|---|---|---|---|
| **Foundation** | Investment Services | | | |
| | Operational Services | | | |
| | Personal Services | | | |

- trusts

- estate settlements

These are the four basic types of accounts a trust department maintains for its clients. Some types of accounts are created for personal, corporate, and institutional clients alike. Let's take a brief first look at each of a trust department's most basic products.

## PRODUCTS FOR INDIVIDUALS

The bank's trust department is able to provide services for individuals that have a wide range of financial management needs. The fiduciary relationship obligates the trust department to act in the best interests of the client.

### Personal Agencies

The principal kinds of personal agencies a bank trust department performs for individuals are those in which the trust institution acts as safekeeping agent, custodian, managing agent, attorney-in-fact, and escrow agent. In each case, the client (the principal) authorizes the trust department (the agent) to perform a range of clearly specified duties involving the principal's property. It is important to bear in mind, though, that title to the property does not change in an agency relationship.

### Custody Accounts

These agency accounts provide the basic operational services of safekeeping, receipts and disbursements, and recordkeeping. Sales and purchases are made by instruction, and cash disbursements are prearranged or as instructed. Custody accounts involve no investment supervision and no discretion.

Individuals or organizations who make their own investment decisions or retain the services of a third party for investment supervision use this basic service.

### Management Agency

These agency accounts offer full investment supervision services in addition to custody services. The client using this type of account is paying for professional investment management. Currently, most trust departments' investment management services are limited to publicly traded securities and improved real estate. Some departments offer management services for agricultural investments, timberlands, mineral interests, and other specialized businesses.

## Trust Accounts

Trust accounts offer management services for assets. The income from the assets may benefit either the trustor or some other person or organization. Under certain conditions, the trustee may have the discretion to invade the trust assets to meet the needs of the beneficiary. A trust is unique in that, like a will, it also may provide for the disposition of a person's assets held in the trust.

These special features of trust accounts allow trusts to meet a variety of client needs. Individuals who want their assets managed and used for their benefit in the event of incapacity select a trust account. Clients who want to provide for their dependents, who, because of age, level of maturity, state of health, or financial sophistication are not considered capable of handling the assets, may establish a trust. The trust account allows a person to provide for a succession of beneficiaries—for example, first for a spouse until death, then for the children during their lifetime, and finally for grandchildren.

### Guardianships

A trust department may serve as guardian of a minor or a mental incompetent, caring for the property and, in rare cases, the person. As a guardian, a trust department has duties similar to those of a trustee. The estate of the ward must be well managed for the sole benefit of the ward, and the courts are uncompromising in their determination that the best interests of the ward must be the primary consideration of the guardian. This modern attitude and practice differs markedly from the medieval guardianships in chivalry.

*Estate Settlement Accounts*

Trust department services involved in settling estates are different from other accounts. Personal, operational, and investment services are provided immediately after death. **Estate settlement** involves securing and valuing all assets, settling the decedent's obligations, paying all taxes due, and distributing all assets in accordance with the will or, if the person died without a will, in accordance with the state laws governing distribution. An individual who has a bank trust department as personal representative will have his or her estate settled by a professional organization that will be available when needed, will act with integrity and impartiality, and will complete the settlement without unnecessary delay.

In settling estates, trust departments follow the instructions in a decedent's will, when there is one. A **will** is a legally enforceable declaration of instructions about the distribution of an individual's assets after his or her death. Wills are viable only in societies that recognize the right of the individual property owner to decide who will obtain his or her property. Nearly all English and American wills name a personal representative, an **executor,** to carry out the terms of the will. In some Western countries, however, an executor is the exception rather than the rule.

## PRODUCTS FOR INSTITUTIONS AND CORPORATIONS

Corporate trusts and agencies serve three basic needs: to raise capital for businesses, to reward employees, and to provide income for retired employees. In addition, trusts for charitable purposes and institutions offer accountability for public donations and sound investment management.

### Corporate Agencies

The trust institution acts as an agent in discharging specific duties with regard to the property. Two types of corporate agencies are common today—transfer agencies and registrarships. Transfer agencies have their origins in a mid-nineteenth-century fraud case in which the court held the New York and New Haven Railroad Company liable for the damages resulting from fraudulent certificates the company's transfer agent issued. To prevent similar occurrences, trust companies were formed to serve as agents for transferring and registering stocks and bonds. To protect companies further—and in compliance with an 1869 New York Stock Exchange regulation requiring registration of active stocks at an approved agency—the agency of registering stock developed in addition to and separate from the transfer service.

## Corporate Trusts

When a corporation decides to borrow money for several years, it may prefer to borrow from the investing public by issuing bonds or other obligations. As it would be impractical to enter into separate agreements with hundreds of lenders, the corporation executes an agreement, called an **indenture**, with a trust institution that acts as trustee for all the lenders. The first recorded instance of a corporate trust indenture occurred in 1830 in the United States, and other indentures were agreed to throughout that decade. These financial arrangements were a major factor in the rapid industrial development of the United States.

### *Employee Benefit Accounts*

This general term is applied to all forms of trusts and agencies established to provide full custody services, compliance reporting, investment management, and special recordkeeping of each participating employee's interest in pension, profit-sharing, and other benefit accounts.

Employee benefit trusts are the newest type of trust account, with few existing before the twentieth century. After 1940 the number of employee benefit plans increased considerably, and trust companies began bidding actively for employee trust business. In 1974, Congress enacted the **Employee Retirement Income Security Act** (ERISA) that defined the responsibility of parties managing employee benefit funds.

## Charitable Trusts and Agencies

A bank's trust department offers trustee and agency services to charities and charitable institutions freeing them from the responsibilities of investing and managing assets. This enables those involved to concentrate on the philanthropic goals of their charity.

## SUMMARY

The trust business is centuries old. Its primary function always has been holding, managing, and caring for the property of others. It is an example of relationship banking at its best. Trust officers often develop close personal ties with clients—usually, the more complex the relationship, the closer the officer-client tie. Owners of property placed in trust may be individuals or organizations (including business enterprises and nonprofit institutions).

Trusts are agreements in which the trust department receives title to property or assets and manages them in the best interests of the beneficiaries. Among the trust functions performed by bank trust departments are settlement of estates, personal and corporate trusteeships, guardianships, and employee benefit trusts. Trust departments also perform agencies or specific services for both individual and corporate customers in which legal title is not passed to the trust department. The range of personal agency services available includes those of custodian, management agent, attorney-in-fact, and probate agent. Two corporate agencies are those of transfer agent for stocks and bonds and registrar for stocks.

In recent decades, widespread growth of such important accounts as employee benefit trust funds and the need for their management has enlarged bank trust departments. They are now no longer seen as the exclusive preserve of the wealthy. Although trust assets have grown steadily, with assets under management multiplying rapidly among the nation's more than 4,000 bank trust departments, revenue has not kept up with the costs of providing trust services.

This is a time of dramatic transition for banks in general and trust services in particular. New technology is changing the way business is done. Now, for example, such services as accounting and reporting are automated, allowing the trust department to standardize its products while providing the flexibility to tailor services to the client's needs. By adapting its methods, expanding its services, and creating a higher profile, the trust department can compete in today's financial marketplace.

### QUESTIONS FOR REVIEW

1.  Define the concept of use upon a use. How did the modern trust arise from this practice?

2.  What effect did the inflation of the 1970s have on the trust business?

3.  What is a fiduciary relationship?

4.  Do you think that trust departments primarily serve aging, wealthy clients?

5.  What are the major types of personal accounts?

6.  What is the principal difference between a trust and an agency?

CHAPTER 2 Trust Markets and Their Regulators

## INTRODUCTION

The business of commercial banking has involved managing clients' deposits to return a profit to the bank. Traditionally, the commercial and trust departments of banks have been clearly separated with little or no interaction between them. While their operations must remain separate to comply with regulations, an understanding of the other's products and services can benefit both areas of banking.

The bank's role is undergoing radical change in today's competitive market for investment funds. Banks must respond creatively to this changing atmosphere by developing innovative ways to meet clients' needs. As banks attempt to unify the delivery of financial services, the public's perception between the banking and trust business probably will diminish. The trust business, then, need no longer be a mysterious aspect of the banking industry but can become an integral part of a bank's roster of total services available to several markets.

This chapter considers how the four basic accounts in a trust department relate to "service blocks" customarily offered by the department in its chosen markets. We will explore the current environment in which trust departments operate and close the chapter by examining how the trust business is chartered and regulated.

## THE CHANGING TRUST ENVIRONMENT

The environment for the trust business is changing at an accelerating pace and the business will continue to be regulated to some degree. Several factors currently affect the environment of the trust business, such as legislation, competition, client perception, and level of bank profit. Legislation in the field of tax and banking laws is creating new business opportunities and reducing current ones.

Competition in the financial services business has increased rapidly in the last decade. Brokerage firms have entered the investment management business and extended these services from institutional to individual clients. A few savings institutions have opened trust departments and others are studying the possibility. Money market funds and mutual funds provide the potential client with a highly satisfactory investment alternative, thus diverting some potential business from the trust industry. Financial planners have emerged as recognized professionals competing with banks as they develop additional services to complement the financial counseling they now provide their clients. Another source of competition are the emerging financial conglomerates. These groups and other new competitors are not subject to the same regulatory constraints as the trust business; therefore, their business opportunities and costs differ from those of the trust industry.

The public's perception of trust departments and how the potential client sees the industry's role in the financial services business has considerable effect on the business environment. The industry has had a difficult time establishing its public identity, and the entry of competition compounds the problem. With the rapid expansion of financial opportunities and services available, the client probably will have an even more difficult time identifying the trust industry's services.

From the early 1970s, banks have become aware that trust departments should be profitable in their own right. Trust department revenues, which in many cases depend on the market value of publicly traded securities, have not kept pace with costs that were driven up by the extended period of inflation. Thus the traditional methods of pricing trust services are being questioned.

The pricing problem will not be resolved merely by identifying costs. Competitors that offer a comparable service—or one perceived to be comparable—may enjoy cost advantages enabling them to price services lower than trust departments could. For example, a broker holding securities performs a custody service seemingly similar to that of an established trust department. However, the client's cash held by the broker may not be backed by as much reserve as that held by a trust department. Often the services these new competitors offer are completely standardized packages. If a client's needs fit into the pattern, then the service could be less expensive than that of a trust department. Bank trust departments tend to offer somewhat more personalized services and tend to be managed by people experienced in the field.

## HOW TRUST DEPARTMENTS
## PERSONALIZE BASIC SERVICES

Let's expand now on the account chart introduced in chapter 1 by adding a series of trust services. (See exhibit 2.1.) When delivered in combination, by

EXHIBIT 2.1   Building Blocks of Trust

**TYPE OF SERVICE**

| TYPE OF ACCOUNT | Safekeeping | Receipts and Disbursements | Accounting and Reporting | Investment Supervision | Compliance | Exercise of Discretion |
|---|---|---|---|---|---|---|
| Custody Accounts (Agencies) | | | | | | |
| Investment Management Accounts (Agencies) | | | | | | |
| Employee Benefit Accounts | | | | | | |
| Trust Accounts | | | | | | Partial to Full Discretion |
| Estate Settlements | | | | | | Full Discretion |

mixing and matching service blocks, these services can be personalized. (An American Bankers Association survey of bank trust departments in the early 1980s found banks managing individual and corporate clients' assets for profit with more than 80 types of financial services.)

Let's examine each service block, left to right. Each block consists of several major activities.

## Safekeeping

Traditionally, this service consisted of holding securities and notes in the trust department vault. To reduce the movement of certificates, in the 1970s the securities and trust industry started using depositories to keep certificates centrally located for easy transfer of ownership. Today, safekeeping involves holding securities in accounts with Federal Reserve Banks, in accounts with a depository either as a direct participant or through an intermediary, and in departments' vaults. In estates and trusts where the assets might include land

and tangible personal property in addition to securities, safekeeping also involves adequate insurance and protection of assets by alarm systems, house-sitters, or removal to secure storage.

## Receipts and Disbursements

This service encompasses both cash and securities and involves collecting all income and distributing it regularly by transferring funds to the client or beneficiary. If payments are not received, steps are taken to locate and obtain the payment. Purchases and sales are executed by delivering or receiving the security or cash. Again, most certificates involving publicly traded corporations are kept at a depository and are traded by transmitting instructions and cash to a remote facility. In today's business when many purchases of money market investments require settlement on the day of purchase, electronic facilities and experienced staff can avoid costly errors.

## Accounting and Reporting

Accountability is one of the fundamental responsibilities of a trustee or personal representative to its trustors and beneficiaries. Further, it is an absolute requirement for all court-appointed fiduciary relationships, such as executors or **conservatorships.**

As part of that accountability, every receipt and disbursement, cash or security, is recorded chronologically so that a continuous record of activity and the current status of each account are available. Such recording originally was done manually; later, mechanical accounting machines were used. Today, most departments have a computerized accounting system that facilitates the production of reports to the client. These reports of activity and current status are an important part of the trust business, because they represent a continuous communication link that is vital to a satisfactory relationship.

## Investment Supervision

This service block, which represents a significant element of many trust department accounts, involves three distinct activities: identifying investment opportunities through analysis, selecting specific investments for each portfolio based on a client's objectives, and buying and selling securities. These highly visible activities are of major concern to trust customers. The results achieved in investment supervision have a significant impact on the reputation of the institution's trust department.

## Compliance

This service prepares and submits reports to third parties required by law. It includes preparing tax returns of all types, accountings and inventories to courts, reports to employee benefit plan participants, and any other reports the account requires. With the enactment of the Employee Retirement Income Security Act (ERISA) in 1974, the compliance service block has acquired a much greater significance and forms an important part of trust services in many accounts.

## Exercise of Discretion

This service is the most unique aspect of trust services and the most difficult to understand. Exercise of discretion should not be confused with the limited discretion granted to an agent in selecting specific securities for a portfolio. All trustees by the nature of their position have the authority to exercise some discretion. The trust instrument can expand this discretionary authority to the point that, in effect, the trustee becomes the alter ego of the person who established the trust. The trustee makes all decisions on the investment and use of the funds in trust for the beneficiaries. This includes decisions involving investment objectives, expenditures on behalf of beneficiaries, and distributions and invasions of principal for beneficiaries.

## THE CHALLENGE OF MARKETING

No business is justified unless it satisfies the needs and desires of its customers. So keeping the service blocks, the foundation services (operational, personal, and investment), and the types of accounts in mind, let us discover how a trust service can be tailored to meet a customer's particular needs.

## Customer Profile: Petroleum Engineer Working Abroad

Petroleum engineer Robert Marshall, a widower, has two children, aged 18 and 20. He has just been hired for a 2-year field assignment in a Southeast Asian country. The salary is substantial and all his living expenses will be paid by his employer. Unfortunately, he will be out in the field most of the time and communications will be poor. Mr. Marshall must make arrangements for the next 2 years covering his household in the United States, his security investments and cash flow, the financial needs of his two children who are now in college, his taxes, and his own financial needs.

Robert Marshall has sought the help of a trust department, which can do the following to help him:

- hold his securities, collect the income, and make all investment decisions based on his objectives

- receive his salary and invest it temporarily pending disposition

- receive and pay all expenses related to his U.S. household, such as mortgage, taxes, utilities, and maintenance costs

- pay his children's education and living expenses, disburse their allowance, and exercise discretion with respect to covering any other financial needs they have

- prepare his income tax returns, file them, pay the taxes due, and represent him if his returns are audited

- wire funds to his bank overseas on either a predetermined basis or on request

- send him periodic reports on all receipts and expenditures and on the current status of his portfolio

The trust department will perform all these services as a trustee under an agreement with Mr. Marshall, which he can revoke at any time. The agreement will further provide that, if he should die during his overseas assignment, the trust will continue for his two children until they reach a specific age.

In this example, all of the service blocks from safekeeping to exercise of discretion are used to build a comprehensive service that meets Robert Marshall's particular needs. The service has the foundation, form, and flexibility to respond to a variety of needs and contingencies.

The trust business continues to address the diverse needs of individuals and organizations. Although the case above demonstrates how the service-block approach can be used to deliver trust services that meet specific needs, a trust department need not "reinvent the wheel" in each customer relationship. Many accounts in trust departments will have one or more features tailored directly to the needs of a particular customer. However, a substantial segment of the service provided is the same for each account of that type. Discerning a client's needs, and altering a product's mix to meet those needs in a cost-effective manner, is a guaranteed formula for success in the trust business.

## THE LEGAL ENVIRONMENT OF THE TRUST BUSINESS

"If we were asked what is the greatest and most distinctive achievement performed by Englishmen in the field of jurisprudence I cannot think that we should have any better answer to give than this—namely, the development, from century to century, of the trust idea."

So proclaimed one Professor Maitland to generations of law students, recounts Scott's *Law of Trusts*, adding: "The purposes for which trusts can be created are as unlimited as the imagination of lawyers."

Still, trust departments and trust services are supervised by state or federal agencies. These regulators help set outer limits for "the imagination of lawyers" and others involved in the trust business by issuing rules governing both the scope and conduct of the business.

### Charters and the Powers They Confer

Who can be in the trust business? Actually, any person or legal business can "act in trust" for another. However, most trust business is performed by

- family members who often are asked to handle the business of caring for the money or property of relatives

- law firms, which in certain parts of the country have a large market share of the trust business

- financial institutions

This book concentrates on financial institutions—specifically, on commercial banks and **trust companies,** corporations that act like banks by engaging in trust business for both individuals and business organizations.

A bank planning to engage in the trust business must either receive a separate permit or charter or meet certain requirements of a general state banking statute. In most states an administrative branch of the state government grants trust powers. The Comptroller of the Currency is authorized to grant a national bank the right to act as trustee, executor, administrator, registrar of stocks and bonds, guardian of estates, committee of property of incompetents, assignee, receiver, managing agent, or in any other fiduciary capacity in which state banks and trust companies are permitted to act under state laws.

In granting an application from a national bank for a trust charter, the Comptroller of the Currency considers the following factors:

- the bank's financial capacity to exercise the trust powers applied for

- the community's needs for trust services and the probable volume of trust business available to the bank

- the general condition of the bank

- the general character and ability of the bank's management

- the type of supervision that the proposed trust activities will receive—including the qualifications, experience, and character of the trust department officers

- the availability of legal counsel competent to advise the bank on trust issues

## Penny History of Trust Regulation

In 1934, the Federal Reserve Board put into effect its Regulation F, "Trust Powers of National Banks." Regulation F marked the beginning of comprehensive and effective government supervision of the trust business. As adopted, it applied to national banks only. Fortunately, the Federal Reserve Board decided that state banks should meet requirements substantially similar to the regulations governing national banks. Soon most state member banks were voluntarily operating their trust departments in harmony with Regulation F. In 1963, when authority to supervise the exercise of trust powers of national banks was transferred from the Federal Reserve to the Comptroller of the Currency, Regulation F became Regulation 9 without major changes. Regulation 9 applies to all national banks and to state banks in their administration of common trust funds.

The official name of the regulation is Title 12, Chapter 1, Part 9, Code of Federal Regulation (12 C.F.R. § 9). The Comptroller of the Currency issues periodic opinions, or interpretations, on Regulation 9, which change from time to time and can be just as important as regulations themselves for governing the daily scope and conduct of the trust business.

In addition to Regulation 9 and state regulations governing the conduct of trust business, the trust business is also subject to securities laws and to the state laws of the jurisdiction in which they conduct business.

## Who Examines Trust Departments?

The primary method of trust department supervision is the periodic—approximately annual—examination of the department by experienced examiners from the federal or state supervisory offices. For budgetary reasons, state and federal regulatory agencies share examination results to avoid duplication.

| Trust departments in | Are examined by the |
|---|---|
| • state banks | • state banking authority |
| • state banks and members of the Federal Reserve System | • Board of Governors of the Federal Reserve through Federal Reserve banks |
| • state banks and nonmembers of the Federal Reserve System | • Federal Deposit Insurance Corporation |
| • national banks | • Comptroller of the Currency |

The trust examination evaluates a trust department's condition in relation to that of the entire bank. One objective is to improve trust service standards in the interest of the clients and the entire trust business.

Trust department examinations have acquired an established place in the bank examination program. As examiners familiarize themselves with the administration and operation of highly developed trust departments, they are able to make constructive suggestions to departments that do not have the advantage of an extensive organization. Because they see many trust departments, examiners can distinguish between good and undesirable policies and practices. Their suggestions are favorably received by most trust officers.

Some executives in the trust business believe that, because relationship banking may combine banking and trust products in unfamiliar ways, bank examiners will have to understand relationship banking too. In mid-1982, the Comptroller of the Currency decided to combine trust examinations with examinations of the other areas of the bank. While some trust business observers dismissed this as merely a cost-control move on the comptroller's part, others noted that it might in fact help develop a new breed of examiner—one who can correctly appraise banking infrastructures that may be unprecedented but are manifestly right for today's trust marketplace.

In early 1987, the Office of the Comptroller of the Currency (OCC) announced it would institute a compliance program to accompany its traditional program of examinations. The Deputy Comptroller for Trust and Securities said the program would enable the agency "to deal with bank systems and less with bank mechanics." He said the program involves OCC examiners looking at recognized or suspected problems, giving "customized" examinations of narrowly selected areas, and then conducting thorough examinations for compliance in selected banks each year.

Separately, two other federal agencies made announcements in early 1987 that could have significant impact on the trust business.

The Federal Reserve Board said it was researching the need for a standard ratio for capital-to-trust discretionary assets. Bank trust accounts were estimated at the time to contain $1.1 trillion in corporate trust assets and $4.1 trillion in trust discretionary and nondiscretionary assets. Because the banking industry itself has only $2.7 trillion in assets, trust departments may represent "a huge off-balance sheet risk for banks," said a Fed official explaining the rationale for the agency's research initiative. One thorny complexity, he added, is how to quantify risk for a trust department that excels at creating innovative products. However, in March 1987 the Fed released their proposed regulations on risk-based capital, and trust department guidelines were excluded.

The Federal Deposit Insurance Corporation (FDIC) announced a new direction in bank supervision with possible implications for trust departments in the state bank nonmember universe it regulates and examines. To stretch its examination force, the regulator will "rent" auditors from independent accounting firms. Observers saw the need for the FDIC to deal with differences in methodology and emphasis between its own "auditors," whose prime role is to gauge asset quality, and their counterparts in certified public accounting (CPA) firms, who have traditionally stressed verification of figures by selective sampling. To deal with the difference in examination techniques, FDIC said it would provide the auditors with additional training. The agency added that perhaps its examiners, many of whom were not trained as CPAs, might benefit from exposure to outside auditors "in a kind of cross-fertilization," in the words of the director of the FDIC Division of Bank Supervision.

### The Chinese Wall

Obviously, an institution with a fiduciary duty to manage its clients' investments profitably does not exist in a vacuum. Inside the same bank that makes commercial loans to corporate customers is a trust department that trades those customers' securities.

Over the years, regulators have seen a potential conflict of interest when a bank that engages in both commercial and trust activities acquires, in the former, some knowledge of so-called "material insider information." To continue trading in securities of its corporate customers on the basis of information about their confidential business plans could render a bank liable under federal securities law, some authorities have said. On the other hand, traditional fiduciary principles may in theory impose on the bank a duty to use such information for the advantage of its clients' investments.

So is a bank to be sued as a fiduciary for failing to break a federal law? Hardly. But to minimize the possibility of liability under either body of law, banks have devoted considerable attention over the years to developing and implementing procedures and policies to prohibit and prevent transmittal of "insider" information on corporate secrets from the commercial department to the trust department. Collectively, the procedures and policies by which a bank segregates its commercial department from its trust department have come to be known as the Wall or the **Chinese Wall.**

In extreme cases, large banks have erected separate dining rooms for their commercial and trust executives. But even when physical changes have been impractical—as in much smaller institutions—most banks have gone somewhat beyond the regulators' demands for written policies by instituting administrative changes to create an actual and effective separation of trust department functions from the other functions of a bank.

The Chinese Wall has split the industry into two camps. In one are strict adherents to the letter of securities and fiduciary law. They debate, for example, whether the Wall should be "impermeable" or "semipermeable"—that is, should all information received by the commercial department concerning a banking customer be withheld from the trust department (the "Impermeable Wall"), or only all inside or material inside information (the "Semipermeable Wall")?

The other camp is peopled with entrepreneurial relationship managers, trust marketers, and others who believe that, as a practical matter, the Chinese Wall has been extended far beyond its original purpose and effectiveness. In fact, when surveying the current marketplace for financial services, these observers seem to share the perspective of the small boy who admitted that he could not see the emperor's nonexistent new clothes—that is, they simply do not see a Chinese Wall left standing in the marketplace *de facto* (in fact), even if strict constructionists continue to insist that one stands *de jure* (in law).

In a 1982 study, *Synergy in Banking in the Eighties,* the American Bankers Association and the international accounting firm of Coopers & Lybrand concluded that the Chinese Wall had been extended in a manner that had put bank trust departments at a disadvantage in competing with comparatively unregulated nonbank providers of financial services. The 500-page study recommended that banks and their trust departments integrate as many functions as possible, searching for ways to exploit nontraditional opportunities.

## The Prudent-Man Rule

In addition to the Chinese Wall, the **prudent-man rule** is a venerable precedent in the legal and regulatory environment of the trust business. The term refers to a rule laid down by statute or judicial decision that authorizes a fiduciary to apply the standard of a prudent investor—rather than select investments for the client merely on the basis of a list prescribed by statute or some government agency. The rule also has been called the American rule or the Massachusetts rule because it dates from the landmark opinion of Justice Putnam of the Massachusetts Supreme Judicial Court in the case of *Harvard College v. Amory* (1830):

> All that can be required of a trustee to invest is that he shall conduct himself faithfully and exercise a sound discretion. He is to observe how men of *prudence*, discretion, and intelligence manage their own affairs, not in regard to speculation, but in regard to the permanent disposition of their funds, considering the probable income, as well as the probable safety of the capital to be invested. (*Italics for emphasis.*)

Most state legislatures have adopted the prudent-man rule.

## Fiduciary Duty to Minimize Taxes

Because the prudent-man rule permeates the law of fiduciaries, it is not surprising to discover that it is the standard that controls a trust department's handling of its customers' tax affairs. According to Professor Mark L. Ascher of the University of Arizona, almost all of the recent tax cases expressly embrace the rule "and none is inconsistent with it."

Later chapters will take a closer look at certain tax implications and other accounting implications of a trust department's investment choices on behalf of its clients. In passing, though, let us examine the impact of the latest sweeping change in tax law—the Tax Reform Act of 1986—on a trust department's business development.

In the January 1987 edition of the *ABA Banking Journal*, J. Stoddard Hayes, Jr., then vice-president and trust counsel of Wilmington Trust Company, Delaware, and chairman of the Taxation Committee of ABA's Trust and Investment Management Division, noted that trust officers have "often focused on income tax savings as a way to sell trust business. Now, with no jazzy tax benefits to point to, they must learn new sales strategies."

The Tax Reform Act of 1986, according to Hayes, "abolishes Clifford Trusts and Spousal Remainder Trusts—devices that shifted income into *current* tax dollars, as beneficiaries usually prefer. Although these devices have never been the mainstay of trust departments' business, they were attention-getters.

"By the end of 1988, less than 2 percent of all deceased persons' estates will be subject to the federal estate tax system, according to U.S. Treasury predictions. As a result, complex estate plans with long-term trusts are dinosaurs."

For most people, Hayes concludes, "convenience and common sense are more important attributes of trusts than is sophisticated tax planning. This is a marked contrast to the attitude just a decade ago. As a result, the trust department's approach to marketing must change. Trust departments that only provide traditional trust services may soon find that there is little or no market for their services."

## SUMMARY

Today, the trust business sees itself as a financial services business that is operated for profit. It combines traditional skills and modern practices to deliver high quality services responsive to clients' needs. In developing a profit-making business, trust departments must be properly managed. Trust managers must not only know the services being provided, they must also be skilled in planning, organization, service design and delivery, marketing, and pricing.

As governments charter banks and permit them to enter the trust business, governments have some responsibility in ensuring that the business is conducted properly. The ability of the banking system to function properly directly affects most businesses and the prosperity of the entire country. Since the trust business has become an important segment of many banks, trust is a proper subject of government regulation and supervision.

Bank trust departments, their clients, and the general public have benefited from government involvement in the trust business. A new environment has developed, however, that was created by changing legislation, competition from new sources, and the need for increased profitability within trust departments. Bank trust departments must find a way to make their services even more attractive and clearly identifiable to the public. Developing services with the commercial banking side of the business could be the most innovative approach.

With increased public awareness of investment opportunities—such as money market funds that are available without significant loss of liquidity—the traditional role of the bank is undergoing a radical change. Clients' rising expectations will encourage banks to become involved to a much greater extent in the delivery of a host of financial services for a fee. Banks could have significant advantages over their competitors in the future by increasingly blending the commercial banking and trust business to provide the public with expanded, easily delivered financial services. The trust business will continue to evolve rapidly and will require employees to be innovative during the challenging era ahead.

## QUESTIONS FOR REVIEW

1. Briefly describe how the environment for the trust business is changing.

2. What are the principal types of trust services?

3. Can any bank engage in the trust business? What factors does the OCC consider before granting a permit or charter?

4. What federal or state supervisory office oversees your bank's trust activities?

5. Briefly explain the concept of the Chinese Wall.

6. How did the term prudent man find its way into the terminology of the trust business?

CHAPTER *3* Key Concepts:
Assets and Ownership

## INTRODUCTION

As the old saying goes, possession is nine-tenths of the law. Indeed, in the early laws governing the trust business, the conception of ownership or title was hazy—what mattered was *seisin* or possession. Of course, English common law afforded certain remedies if the person holding **chattels** (any kind of property, except an inheritable piece of real estate) on behalf of another abused the confidence placed in him.

Only in modern times has it been common to convey money or securities in trust for another and for a person's wealth to consist mostly of personal property rather than land.

This chapter examines historical and modern distinctions between real and personal property. We consider how assets (property types) are classified, how the trust business handles assets under these classifications, the ways assets can be owned, and how ownership can be transferred.

## TYPES OF ASSETS

In this chapter, the term "asset" refers to what an individual owns and "property" signifies a specific type of asset.

### Real Property

**Real property** is land and anything attached to the land that is intended to become or can be considered a fixture. These fixtures are referred to as improvements to the land that could include buildings, walls, bridges, and surfaces such as roads, parking lots, and patios. Trees, bushes, and crops on the land are also usually classified as real property.

The concept of real property stems from the fact that land is immovable and a legal action to recover land—the thing itself—was also possible. The Latin word for thing is *res*, which is the basis of the English word real. Actions for the recovery of land, therefore, became known as real actions, and the property that was the subject of these actions was called real property. Real property, thus, meant property that might be recovered in an action because it cannot be moved.

### Personal Property

Essentially, personal property is movable; it is not fixed to the land. Personal property may be **tangible**—property of physical substance, such as an automobile—or **intangible**—property that gives evidence of value or of a right—such as a certificate of stock.

Traditionally, property that was not real property could not be recovered in an action—because it could have been removed or destroyed. However, damages could be sought against the individual who might have removed or destroyed it. The property that was subject to this action was called personal property.

### Distinctions Between Real and Personal Property

The distinction between real and personal property is mostly of historic significance in the United States. Land was the chief source of wealth in the colonial and postcolonial periods. Specific laws of the state in which the land—or real property—was located prevailed when an owner died **intestate**, without a will. These specific laws, the **canons of descent**, represented a separate system from the system that governed the distribution of personal property, goods that are not land related. The **statutes of distribution** of the state that the owner regarded as a permanent home (his **domicile**) governed the transmittal of personal property from an intestate's estate. Since two systems governed the distribution of a decedent's assets, the same people did not always receive both the real and the personal property. Real property descended to the intestate's heirs; personal property usually was distributed among the owner's next-of-kin.

Today, many states have passed new probate codes that overhaul existing descent and distribution statutes eliminating the distinction between real and personal property. State laws vary, however. Some states have merely modified their laws, and others retain the traditional canons.

The historical basis for the distinction between real and personal property has lost its meaning. Actions are now brought for damages to real property and for recovery of personal property. However, assets still are classified as real and

EXHIBIT 3.1  Assets

| Real Property | Personal Property | |
| --- | --- | --- |
| | *Tangible Personal Property* | *Intangible Personal Property* |
| • Land | • Vehicles, including boats | • Cash in banks |
| • Improvements on land, including buildings | • Household furnishings | • Stocks |
| | • Jewelry | • Bonds |
| • Trees and bushes | • Tools and equipment | • Notes |
| • Growing crops | • Unincorporated business equipment and inventory | • Accounts receivable |
| | | • Partnership interest |
| | • Harvested crops | • Insurance contracts |
| | | • Employee benefit interests |
| | | • Mineral interests |
| | | • Options |
| | | • Deferred compensation contracts |
| | | • Patent rights |
| | | • Copyrights |
| | | • Royalties |

personal property, and the concept of land as real property and goods as personal property survives.

## TYPES OF ASSETS MANAGED BY TRUST DEPARTMENTS

This section describes those assets, particularly types of personal property, that trust departments most frequently manage. Exhibit 3.1 lists types of property most familiar to trust officers by category of asset.

Managing assets requires considerable knowledge of several kinds of property and experience in dealing with them. For example, anyone managing commercial real estate should know property management and have an appreciation of those factors that enhance rental value. Certainly, trust officers cannot be experts in all types of property listed in the exhibit; however, most have experience in the major types of property. In some areas of the country, trust officers develop expertise in specialized fields that are important to the localities they serve. Mineral interests, livestock, and crop specialties are good examples.

## Real Property

Few people have difficulty recognizing real property after learning that the basic concept involves land and its fixed attachments. Three types of real property are described briefly here as a sample of the kinds of real property trust officers handle in managing assets for others.

### Residential Real Property

Whether a primary residence, vacation home, or rental property, the distinguishing feature of residential real property is its use as a dwelling. This type of asset frequently requires a decision on whether the property should be retained in a trust for use by a beneficiary and, if so, under what conditions.

For example, John Roberts, the decedent, has named in his will two primary beneficiaries who are unrelated. His brother Carl is to receive income from the trust and, at Carl's death, John's close friends, the Bartons, are to receive the assets in the trust. The primary asset is a large, comfortable home in a neighborhood that is slightly declining; Carl and his wife like the place and would like to live there. However, the high cost of maintaining the house with Carl and his wife living in it would rapidly use up more than the income generated by the trust. The trustee must consider the Barton's as well as Carl's financial interests in deciding whether to retain or sell the house. The local housing market and Carl's alternatives must also be weighed carefully. Under the circumstances the trust department decides, after discussion with Carl, that it would be better to sell the house. The proceeds from the sale will go to the trust to be reinvested in securities and Carl will receive the income produced.

### Commercial Real Property

Any real property of any size that is used for retailing or other business is considered commercial real property. Larger properties with multiple tenants require extensive property management services. If a trust department does not have the personnel with expertise in this area, it will retain the services of a property management firm.

*Agricultural Real Property*

Management of real property used for any agricultural purpose generally involves either leasing the property or actively managing a farming business.

## Intangible Personal Property

These assets cannot in themselves be touched or realized with the senses. A certificate of stock is classified as intangible, because it is only an evidence of a right. That the certificate as a piece of paper is a tangible thing is irrelevant. The right is the stockholder's claim on the profits and assets of the company. If the certificate were lost, destroyed, or stolen, the stockholder would not lose his or her right but would have to take clearly prescribed steps to prove that right. The same logic applies to notes, bonds, and other evidences of debt; they are valuable not in and of themselves but only as evidence of an owner's rights.

Assets classified as intangible personal property represent some 90 percent of the assets held and managed by most trust departments. In addition to cash, stocks, bonds, and notes, intangible personal property that trust departments manage includes limited partnership interests, life insurance contracts, and mineral interests.

### Cash

Monies in demand deposit accounts and monies invested in short-term investments of minimal risk qualify as cash. Such investments would include Treasury bills, short-maturity certificates of deposit, commercial paper, money market funds, and other money market types of obligations.

### Stocks

Stock is the evidence of ownership of a share of an incorporated business. Referred to as an equity interest, common stock entitles the owner to share in the profits of the business. Much publicly issued stock has a well-developed market in which the price of the stock reflects the buyers' and sellers' expectations about the current and future prospects for the company. Publicly traded common stocks represent a substantial portion of the assets trust departments manage.

### Bonds

Bonds include, regardless of name, all publicly issued debt obligations of corporations and of federal, state, and local governments. By issuing bonds, corporations and governments finance their businesses. Bonds have a set maturity date and either a set or floating interest rate. At maturity the issuer is obligated to pay the holder the amount shown on the face of the bond. Before maturity they can be traded; however, their value will depend on their rating and the interest rates prevailing at the time of the trade.

### Notes

Notes are promises to pay that may be secured by a lien on some collateral—for example, a note secured by a mortgage on real property. Such notes must be distinguished from those that are publicly issued, such as U.S. Treasury notes. Unlike bonds, no established market exists for notes. Thus sales must be negotiated directly between the buyer and the seller.

### Limited Partnership

These assets are similar to stock in that they represent a share in the equity of a partnership in which the owner's liability for the debts of the partnership is limited. Limited partnerships often offer special tax benefits not available by owning stock and frequently are used for investments in real property, oil and gas exploration and development, and investment in equipment for lease.

### Insurance

Life insurance contracts are widely held throughout the United States and often have a dual purpose. A contract exists to pay a sum of money on the death of the person whose life is insured. Also, if the terms of the contract so provide, the contract can become the means of borrowing against the paid cash value of the contract. As an asset, insurance contracts occur in trusts, in some employee benefit accounts, and in estates.

### Mineral Interests

These are property interests in oil, gas, and other minerals that are retained by the seller on the transfer of the real property involved. Separating mineral interests from real property is a common practice in many parts of the United States. In retaining mineral interests, the holder maintains the right to explore the land for minerals by mining. Generally, mining rights are leased out, and the owner of the mineral interests receives rent plus a royalty or a percentage of the revenues from the sale of any oil, gas, or minerals extracted.

## Tangible Personal Property

As the term implies, tangible personal property means physical assets that can be touched and have an inherent value in themselves. The typical tangible personal property encountered in the trust business is the assets of decedents whose estates the trust department is settling. Automobiles, jewelry, furniture, silverware, and other household goods are tangibles. In most cases trust departments dispose of personal property from an estate by either distributing the property to the beneficiaries or selling it.

Recently, however, certain tangibles have gained wide acceptance as investment assets rather than as "use" assets. These items include precious metals, gems, stamps, and some antiques—which some people are acquiring instead of other forms of financial assets. In states where the more traditional canons of descent prevail, how assets are classified can determine which assets will be used first to settle a decedent's debts. Furthermore, the classification may have substantial effect on which beneficiary of a given estate gets a particular asset.

For example, suppose the decedent, William Harrison, made a will leaving all his tangible personal property to his sister and the rest of his assets to his son. Among Harrison's assets are 1,000 silver quarters. As currency, the quarters are worth $250 and would form part of the remainder of the estate that would belong to his son. But because of the value of silver at the time the estate was settled, their content value far exceeds their monetary exchange value. Thus, they may arguably be classified as tangible personal property and be distributed to the decedent's sister.

This kind of problem, of course, can be avoided if, when drafting the will, those items that might be subject to more than one type of classification are pinpointed. Clients should be asked how they want any potentially troublesome tangible items classified in their estate.

## HOW TO CONVERT ASSETS

The most obvious conversion of an asset from one property category to another would be to sell either real property or tangible personal property for cash, thus converting the asset to intangible personal property. Less obvious forms of conversion also occur. An owner may change an asset from real property to personal property or from personal property to real property.

For example, a tree standing in the forest is real property, but when it is cut down for firewood, the resulting logs are personal property. A person who dies intestate may not have enough personal property to pay his or her debts, and the administrator may have to sell some of the real property to obtain enough cash to pay the debts. Sometimes all the real property may be sold, leaving a cash surplus after the debts have been paid. This cash surplus is considered real property in states where the canons of descent prevail and would be passed to the decedent's heirs.

## FORMS OF OWNERSHIP

In this context, property rights are those that a person has to property that he or she owns or has an interest in. The rights involved depend on the kind or degree of ownership. An absolute owner has the exclusive rights of possessing, using, enjoying, and disposing of property. In a limited ownership one or more of those rights are absent or reduced. Property rights can be classified in two ways: legal ownership and equitable ownership, and estates and interests.

## Legal Ownership and Equitable Ownership

The classification of rights in assets that is important in the trust industry involves splitting ownership in two parts, with legal ownership vested in one person and equitable ownership in another.

For example, Horace Carlson transfers stock to the trust department of the Downtown National Bank to act as trustee by holding the stock, collecting dividends, and paying income to his wife, Sylvia Carlson, during her lifetime, and then transferring the stock to their son, Henry Carlson, at Sylvia's death. This typical trust illustrates the two kinds of ownership. Horace Carlson parted with his legal right, title, and interest in the stock by transferring the shares to the bank trust department, which then became the legal owner of the stock. On the company's books the stock is transferred to the trust department, whose representative can attend and vote at stockholders' meetings. The trustee receives the dividends and has the right to sell, trade, or otherwise dispose of the stock. As owner of the stock the trustee can sue or be sued, just as Horace Carlson could have sued or been sued before the transfer was made.

As the legal owner of the stock, the bank does not become entitled to enjoy or use the dividends for its own purposes. The trustee does not receive the benefits of ownership. Sylvia Carlson has the right to receive the income, and Henry Carlson has the right to receive the principal eventually. The trust department is the legal owner of the stock, and Sylvia and Henry are the equitable owners of the stock. Sylvia is the equitable owner of the income and Henry is the equitable owner of the principal. Together, they are referred to as the beneficial owners or the beneficiaries.

Both real property and personal property are divisible into legal ownership and equitable ownership. That is, anyone may convey real property or deliver personal property to another to hold in trust for others. In each case the trustee becomes the legal owner and the others, the equitable owners.

## Estates

An **estate,** in this context, refers to the **right, title,** or **interest** an individual has in real property. It is accurate to call a person's interest in real property an estate.

The three legal estates in land are fee simple estates, fee tail estates, and life estates. In the eyes of the law these estates constitute real property. The law of the state in which the real property is located controls whether a given estate may be used.

### Fee Simple Estates

These are the highest form of estates in land. A person who holds land in **fee simple** owns the land outright. If the individual dies without leaving a will, the land goes to his or her heirs. If there are no heirs, the land escheats, or reverts, to the state. In most states, a deed that conveys land to an individual is enough to transfer a fee simple estate.

### Fee Tail Estate

On the death of the owner, called the tenant in tail, the estate descends to the children whom the owner physically parented or their issue whether or not the owner leaves a will. If the owner has no physical descendants, the estate reverts to the original grantor on the theory that the individual who granted the **fee tail** is still the fee simple owner of the remainder.

### Life Estate

Two kinds of **life estates** are possible: an estate for the life of the person holding the estate (the tenant) or an estate for the life of a person or persons other than the tenant. Although life estates generally are used for land, they can also involve tangible personal property.

For example, George Sloan, an elderly gentleman, conveys his residence and all its furnishings to his widowed younger sister, Marcia, for her lifetime. Marcia has all property rights involving use but not disposal of the home and the furnishings. She does not have the right to sell the estate, take the proceeds, and move to a Caribbean island. George's will states that after Marcia's death his son, Hugh, will receive the property.

### Leasehold Estates

In addition to the three legal estates in land just described, lesser interests in land exist. The most common is a tenancy for years, which is a tenancy for a specified time; it could be in effect for a day or for 99 years. This property interest is known as a **leasehold.** The instrument creating the interest is a lease.

## Undivided Interests

Three types of undivided interests in real property usually are possible under law: **tenancy in common, joint tenancy,** and **tenancy by the entirety.** In some states, particularly in the Southwest and Pacific Coast areas, **community**

**property** laws prevail that give both a husband and a wife an undivided one-half interest in their property due to their marital status.

### Tenancy in Common

An estate is owned by tenants in common when two or more people own an interest in a property that does not pass to the surviving owner(s) when one owner dies. Each owner is said to have an undivided interest in the place.

For example, Mr. Browning devises his farm to his niece, Jane, and to his stepson, Jon. (A **devise** is a gift of real property established by a will.) Jane and Jon take possession as tenants in common. Unfortunately, Jon is killed in an avalanche while skiing. Jon's undivided interest in the farm passes to his heirs or devisees and not to Jane.

### Joint Tenancy

When two or more people own property that passes to the surviving tenants at the death of a tenant, these people are joint tenants. For example, if Mr. Browning devised his farm to Jane and Jon as joint tenants with **right of survivorship,** after Jon's death, the farm would become Jane's property exclusively as the sole tenant. Usually, unless the intention to create a joint tenancy is expressed, a transfer of real property to two or more people creates a tenancy in common in the absence of a governing statute. (Two or more people may also own personal property jointly; on the death of one, the other(s) receives the property. This situation is analogous to their being joint tenants with right of survivorship.)

### Tenancy by the Entirety

When real property is conveyed to a husband and wife in states that recognize this form of tenancy, the property goes to the survivor at the death of the spouse. Unless they both agree to sell or otherwise dispose of the property, neither spouse has a disposable interest in the property during the lifetime of the other. Therefore, neither spouse's individual creditor may reach the property, either before or after death. Where tenancy of the entirety is recognized, its rights apply even when the spouse is not named in the title to the property—for example, "to Joan Thomas and her husband."

In a state that recognizes estates by the entirety in personal property, a gift of personal property made to a husband and wife without any reference to survivorship would probably vest them as tenants by the entirety, which would give the surviving spouse the right to take all the property.

## Nominee Ownership

**Nominee ownership** is a means of registering securities in the name of a person, partnership, or corporation especially designated to hold title to the securities. Nominee ownership is used extensively in the trust business to facilitate management of accounts. When many accounts in a trust department hold shares in the same company, the nominee method makes collecting interest and dividends, selling securities, and managing capital changes an easier task.

## Transfer of Ownership

The most frequent form of transfer of ownership of an asset is by sale or bargain in which both parties give something referred to as consideration. Usually, one side gives money for the asset or service being acquired; the transfer may also involve service for an asset, or an asset for an asset. The trust business is involved extensively with the transfer of ownership of assets without consideration, that is, payment of some form.

This section discusses the various methods of transferring assets without consideration, followed by a discussion of the sales of assets normally held in accounts in trust departments. These discussions will not include the extensive tax implications involved in transfers.

### *Outright Gifts During Life of Donor*

When a gift of an asset is made during the life of the giver (donor), all that is necessary to complete the transfer is the giver's intention to make the gift and the effective delivery of the asset. The gift of 100 shares of stock by a mother to a daughter during the mother's lifetime by the delivery of the certificate for the shares with the assignment executed to the daughter is an example of such a gift.

### *Survivorship Under Joint Tenancy*

Registering or titling an asset in the names of two persons as joint tenants with right of survivorship means that ownership passes entirely to the surviving tenant when one tenant dies.

### *Will*

One of the most important means of transferring assets without consideration is by will. Though not an inherent or inalienable right, since it was granted by the state and may be taken away by the state, the statutory right to dispose of assets by will exists in almost every country. That right does not necessarily extend to all assets that a person owns at the time of his death. For instance, in states that have community property, a husband or wife cannot by will dispose of more than his or her half of the community assets. In most states a husband cannot dispose of all his assets by will to the total exclusion of his wife's rights if she objects, and in some states a wife cannot dispose of her assets by will to the exclusion of her husband's rights if he objects.

### In Trust

A trust is a transfer by agreement or deed during a person's life, or by will after his or her death, of assets to a trustee. The trust instrument states the terms under which the trustee is to hold the asset, and to whom and when the income and principal of the trust is to be paid, delivered, or conveyed. Trusts can also be established by corporations and are commonly used to manage funds in employee benefit plans.

### Intestate

When a person dies without leaving a will, the real property descends according to the laws of descent in the state where it is located, and the personal property is distributed by the administrator according to the laws of distribution in the state where the decedent had his or her residence. In some states all property passes according to certain rules that apply to real and personal property alike. The estate of the heirs in the real property and the interest of the distributees in the personal property are subject to the rights of the surviving spouse.

## SALE OF TRUST ACCOUNT ASSETS

Market and liquidity are two major considerations in selling assets commonly found in trust department accounts. The market involves finding a buyer for the asset; liquidity refers to the price in relation to the length of time necessary to locate a purchaser. For example, if a trust department is selling a piece of unimproved commercial real estate, the search for a buyer should be focused on the commercial real estate market, not the residential real estate market. The asking price should be a figure that will attract potential purchasers; if the price is set too high, the property will remain unsold for an indefinite period.

The key factors of market and liquidity are discussed in this section in relation to specific assets generally held in accounts that trust departments manage.

## Common Stock

Most of the common stock held in trust departments is publicly held and actively traded on one of the national or regional exchanges. The exchange offers both the market and the liquidity. Price is established through the bidding of buyers and sellers. Selling publicly traded common stock requires the services of a stockbroker. Except in the disposal of very large holdings, selling stock merely involves placing an order to sell at the price then being bid for that stock.

**Closely held** stock, however, poses unique problems and liability for a trust department. The liquidity and marketability of closely held stock may be particularly difficult to assess.

## Bonds

Corporate and government bonds are sold on an exchange basis usually through a broker or, in the case of government agency issues, a correspondent bank. Generally, there is an active and precise market, and liquidity does not present a problem. Municipal bonds issued by states, counties, and cities present a different problem. Generally, these bonds are purchased by brokers for resale. The broker receives the difference between the purchase price and the sales price. In times of volatile interest rates, brokers face extensive risk. Therefore, they will either not buy municipal bonds or only buy them at prices substantially below the present market. These factors make municipal bonds generally less liquid than common stock.

## Real Estate

The market for real estate whether it is residential, commercial, or agricultural is much narrower than for stocks and bonds. Real estate is generally sold through the services of a real estate broker. The liquidity of the property is affected by the price asked, current interest rates, and national or regional economic conditions. Consequently, while the price asked may be right, other financial considerations may make the property temporarily unsellable.

## Real Estate Notes

Notes secured by real estate have a limited market. No established brokerage system exists for such assets and there is a limited number of purchasers. Sales of real estate notes generally result from direct negotiation between the buyer and seller. The final price usually reflects a discount in excess of what a comparable bond would sell for. As a result, real estate notes are not considered highly liquid.

## Limited Partnership and Mineral Interests

These assets are similar to real estate notes in that the markets are small and the liquidity is low.

### Tangibles

As most trust departments do not acquire tangibles for accounts they manage, the sale of tangibles usually occurs only in connection with the settlement of an estate. Normal household furnishings have a fairly wide market, but liquidity tends to be relatively low. The normal method of sale is by auction either on site or by consignment to an auction house. An auction sale, which is considered a public sale, theoretically realizes the best price. Special items such as art, antiques, and collections may be sold through a dealer or consigned to an auction house specializing in the items.

### SUMMARY

This chapter focuses on what people own—assets—and how they own them. Assets may be classified primarily as real property and personal property. Real property is land and fixed attachments to it, such as buildings, roads, and trees. Personal property is essentially movable—that which is not attached to land. Personal property may be tangible, such as furniture, or intangible, such as stocks or bonds. Real property and personal property were passed down to future generations on the basis of two separate systems of law—the canons of descent and the statutes of distribution. Thus the two types of property have been treated differently with regard to succession. Also legal actions that could be brought against those violating the two forms of property were different; however, this is no longer the case. The two classifications of real and personal property remain: land is still considered real property, while goods are considered personal property.

Trust departments hold and manage both real and personal property for their customers. This chapter discusses many of the ways that trust departments relate to the types of property they manage as trustee—from residential real property to insurance contracts. In drafting a will, for example, property classification should be clearly defined to avoid misunderstanding and perhaps ill will among the beneficiaries when dual classification of an asset is possible.

Assets may be converted from one type of property to another—by selling or changing the use. The ways that trust departments sell the various assets they hold relate to the key factors of market and liquidity.

Forms of ownership are discussed in two ways: legal and equitable ownership, and estates and interests. When a trust department becomes a trustee of a given property, it becomes the legal owner although the equitable ownership is retained by the beneficiaries. The equitable owners may have different interests in the property: one may be the equitable owner of the income and the other may be the equitable owner of the principal. Both real and personal property may be divided into legal and equitable ownership.

People may hold land in fee simple, fee tail, or for life. The three kinds of undivided interests in real property recognized by law are tenancy in common, joint tenancy, and tenancy by the entirety. Other relevant estates and interests—such as community property provisions, leasehold estates, and nominee ownership of securities are also noted.

The chapter closes with a section on how ownership is transferred, particularly the major ways of transferring property without a fee, which represent a considerable segment of ownership transfers in the trust business.

## QUESTIONS FOR REVIEW

1. How do real property and personal property differ? List five types of tangible and intangible personal property.

2. Using an example, explain the distinction between legal and equitable ownership of property.

3. What are the three types of undivided interests in real property?

4. Define intestate.

5. Discuss the relative liquidity and marketability of stock, real estate, and tangibles.

SECTION *2* Services to Individuals

"A social benefit should flow from what we do—never harm.

"If you can conceive of something, and think toward it hard enough, it can happen. The people you influence can do the same—but only if they discover how themselves.

"The impossible in the trust business is a permeable wall. Besides, it's fun.

"I'd never cheat a competitor—but I might outsmart him."

—J. Richard Boylan, *former chairman,*
*ABA Trust Executive Committee*

CHAPTER *4* The Consumer
Marketplace

## INTRODUCTION

Trust services are much easier to understand when the needs these services address are also understood. The most significant services that trust departments offer their individual accounts usually involve investment management of all kinds of property. This includes stocks, bonds, real estate, insurance proceeds, accumulated pension benefits, and other forms of personal property.

Clients usually are concerned about their ability to manage their own property. Examples include an individual worried about his or her failing health; a spry retiree more interested in travel than in clipping investment coupons; a minor inheriting wealth from a relative; a recent widow whose husband always managed the family investments; young parents concerned about their family in the event of their deaths; or even a client, with his or her own successful investment program, who cannot keep the records straight. The key to determining who needs trust services is simple: find an individual with a present or potential financial management problem.

This chapter, begins with a profile showing how the financial management needs of a business executive were fulfilled by a business development officer for a trust department. We will then look at how personal trust services respond to three basic human needs—security, peace of mind, and control of one's assets. Finally, the chapter considers how banks are responding to the needs of the contemporary marketplace.

### Customer Profile: A New Client
### with Complex Needs

Roger Kirkland, a financial planning and business development officer for a large bank's trust department, was driving across town to meet Stan Lynott for a luncheon appointment. Lynott had called earlier in the morning to arrange the appointment and had informed Roger that Alan Lynott, Stan's father, had recently passed away. Although Stan's bank was not involved with the estate settlement, he was confused about several issues and had many questions. The local branch manager of Stan's bank had suggested he contact the trust department, so he made the luncheon date.

Roger Kirkland knew that the death of a family member or close friend frequently triggered an appointment with a trust department representative. Often the bank trust department is involved with settling the estate and other financial details. At other times, as in this instance, the trust department was asked to provide counseling and guidance. Kirkland was keenly aware that the death of a family member often motivates people, through an unpleasant form of shock therapy, to arrange their own affairs. As he pulled into the restaurant parking lot, Roger Kirkland knew he must listen attentively.

Stan Lynott was waiting for Roger when he arrived. Lynott was in his early forties and appeared to be a successful businessman. During the lunch, Kirkland gleaned the following information.

Alan Lynott had named Stan as personal representative, or executor, under his will. Stan Lynott had no idea how to fulfill this task. Clearly, he felt obligated to his deceased father to administer the estate according to his father's wishes. Stan was already concerned about tensions developing among his brothers and sisters that were directly related to some of his early decisions regarding the estate. He wanted to see those difficulties resolved.

Stan's mother now owned the stock portfolio, valued at approximately $500,000, that she and her husband had owned jointly. Mrs. Lynott had concentrated on her nursing career and never paid much attention to the family finances. Although Stan had attempted to help his mother with management of the investment portfolio, he found the time demands overwhelming.

As Roger Kirkland had suspected, Stan confessed that he and his wife had neglected to make their own wills. Stan Lynott is now 40 years old and his wife is 38. They have two small children, aged 7 and 10. Lynott believed his father's estate had been well planned, but in view of the difficulties the family was now having, he wondered if there were a better way to plan his own estate.

Roger Kirkland thought he detected a reservoir of other problems troubling Stan. As dessert was being served, he gently guided the discussion toward Stan Lynott's business activities. Roger's hunch was correct.

Stan had originally purchased a small network of independent service stations with a partner whom he had recently bought out. Although the partners agreed to end the partnership, serious disagreement existed about the value of the business and the corresponding price Stan Lynott should pay his former partner. Litigation appeared imminent.

Stan also remarked that he would like to establish a profit-sharing fund to reward and motivate his employees. The complexity of the task, however, and his attorney's $3,500 bid to draw up the plan had dampened his enthusiasm.

As they were finishing their coffee, Stan mentioned that, with all his other current problems, his own security portfolio had fallen into disarray. Some stocks were at home, others were at the broker's, and he had even misplaced one certificate completely. He had 3 month's worth of unopened dividend checks stacked up on his desk at home. His records were in such horrible shape, he said, that he could not look his accountant in the eye at Rotary luncheons.

Roger had indeed listened intently. He assured Stan that reliable help was available, and that he would contact him before the end of the week with his proposal.

Can Roger Kirkland's trust department help Stan Lynott? Yes. Several services offered by most trust departments would immediately relieve Stan and his family. Roger would probably propose that Stan take advantage of a number of services:

- As an agent for the personal representative, the bank could act for Stan in managing his father's estate in a way that would best serve the family's interests and also adhere to his father's wishes.

- The estate and tax planning service would help the Lynotts use their estate most effectively. Through the process of analyzing their estate, the Lynotts would have to arrange in the order of importance their family needs, objectives, and goals. What they would want done with their property in the event of either or both of their deaths would be carefully reviewed, perhaps with an attorney and an accountant present. A will would be drawn up by the Lynott's attorney to reflect their preferences, possibly with the bank trust department named as personal representative. A testamentary trust, a trust established by a will for those whom the decedent names, could be established in the will for the surviving spouse and children.

- A custodial account (sometimes called a custodial agency) would provide Stan with the recordkeeping he needs to keep his financial dealings in order.

- A living trust would free Stan's mother from worrying about managing her money and would give her additional protection in case of sudden physical or mental incapacity. A living trust also would make estate settlement without probate possible at her death. If she would prefer not to have a living trust, Roger would recommend a management agency for her investments.

- A profit-sharing retirement fund would benefit the employees of Stan's service stations. The fund would be an excellent way to retain good workers and to reward them for their service. By using prototype plans that the trust department had drafted and approved, Stan would save the expense of having a custom-tailored plan drawn by his attorney.

- The trust department's business advisory services could provide an unbiased third-party valuation of what Stan's business is worth, to be used in the possible litigation with his former partner.

Notice that many of the services have repercussions far into the future. When Stan and Roger had lunch, Stan probably had no idea that many of these proposed services existed. He certainly did not ask for an agency for another fiduciary—the personal representative—or a prototype profit-sharing plan. Stan presented Roger with his current situation; underlying that situation were problems that could be solved with a minimum of effort—by his bank's trust department.

### MEETING HUMAN NEEDS

Personal trust services respond to three basic human needs—security, peace of mind, and control of assets. Trust department clients do not simply buy trusts, agencies, and custodial accounts; they are buying the security, peace of mind, and sense of control these services bring them.

### Security

Undoubtedly, the most basic of the three needs is security. Lack of security was at the root of Stan Lynott's request to visit with Roger Kirkland. Although he was concerned about his father's estate and his mother's investment dilemma, he was primarily motivated by the realization that he had not adequately provided for his family and for himself in the event of his own incapacity or death. His father's death had reminded him of his own mortality and made him aware that he had not given enough thought to his own family's security.

Clients obtain security involving their possessions by making wills and providing for estate administration so that property can be transferred smoothly when they die. Living trusts include the benefits yielded by a will and a testamentary trust, combined with the added security of professional financial management and financial protection during a person's lifetime. Security can also be assured for an incompetent person by a guardianship, also called a conservatorship, that protects the incompetent's property.

## Peace of Mind

Peace of mind is an extension of security. Once personal security needs are satisfied, most people strive to extend that satisfaction to those they love and care for. When the effort succeeds, people experience a rewarding peace. Notice that Stan Lynott was anxious to extend the security he sought for himself and his nuclear family to his brothers and sisters, his mother, and even to the employees of his business.

Young adult clients enjoy peace of mind from knowing that their young children will be cared for by a testamentary trust in the event of their mutual deaths. Elderly clients feel relieved that their financial affairs are in order and that they will be cared for by a living trust if they become incapacitated. Individuals who know little about the stock and bond markets can feel at ease by having professionals manage their investments with a management agency or a living trust account. Trust services also offer increased peace of mind to a client when other family members and loved ones are successfully encouraged to prepare for their financial future with whatever trust services may be applicable.

## Control

People do not always realize that they need management services to keep their property organized so that they actually have more control of it.

An orderly investment program is the best way to obtain control of income. When clients manage their investments, a custodial account is all they need. When clients choose not to manage their investments, a management agency account meets their needs. Wills and testamentary trusts also provide the client with control. For example, a testamentary trust can provide for the long-term controlled care of handicapped children. Taxes can be controlled by special types of trust accounts, and tax planning can maximize income with both living and testamentary trusts.

## SERVICES THAT MEET NEEDS

Let's look at the type of services trust departments offer individuals in relation to specific family and financial needs. The matrix (exhibit 4.1) shows the range of individual needs that the corresponding trust department services are designed to meet.

From protecting minor children to tax minimization and recordkeeping, trust department clients can find a way to solve many of their personal financial problems. The services that are probably most unfamiliar are the guardianship (or conservatorship), the standby trust, and the power of attorney.

Usually, the court appoints an individual or an institution as guardian (conservator) of a minor's property or that of an individual who is declared to be incompetent. For example, if the parents of a minor child die intestate, then the probate court will appoint a guardian to manage the property of the young person until he or she comes of age.

In a standby trust, the trustor—the individual establishing the trust—essentially goes through the initial step in setting up a trust. The assets, however, remain in the name of the client until one of the following three events occurs:

- The client instructs the bank to take over.

- The client becomes incapacitated and is unable to function or to manage the assets.

- The client dies.

The standby trust allows the client to retain control of the assets or switch the control back and forth. Thus the tax savings of a trust can be obtained without any loss of control unless the client requests it.

The **power of attorney** is a witnessed document authorizing the individual named to act as attorney-in-fact for the person who signed the document. In financial transactions, the power of attorney usually involves power to take only certain specific actions.

A testamentary trust can only be created through a will; a living trust transfers title of the trustor's property to the trustee during an individual's lifetime. A living trust is particularly appropriate for someone who has little interest in managing his or her finances. Stan Lynott's mother is a good example.

## LIFE STAGES

Stages of human development can be helpful as a guideline to understanding the needs that trust services address. For example, young clients, to approximately age 25, usually have their financial security provided for as beneficiaries of testamentary and educational trusts or by guardianships. These clients either

EXHIBIT 4.1.  Service Matrix

**TYPE OF SERVICE**

| Nature of Need | Estate Settlement | Trusts | Agencies | Guardianship (Conservatorship) |
|---|---|---|---|---|
| Protection of Minor Children | · | Educational trust Testamentary trust | | Yes—when no other arrangements have been made. |
| Protection from Financial Incapacity | | Living trust Standby trust | Power of attorney | Yes—when no other arrangements have been made. |
| Family Protection from Untimely Death | A will at least avoids intestate succession. | Testamentary trust Living trust Standby trust | | |
| Investment Management | | Living trust | Management agency | |
| Tax Minimization | | Charitable trusts Living trust Standby trust Testamentary trust Other specialized trusts | Management agency for tax-exempt securities. | |
| Controlled Distribution of Wealth at Death | A will is always an essential ingredient to control property distribution. | Living trust Standby trust | | |
| Charitable Giving | | Charitable trusts Testamentary trusts | | |
| Recordkeeping and Asset Control | | | Safekeeping accounts Custodial accounts Escrow accounts | |

cannot legally hold title to property as minors or have not reached the age that their parents or guardians established for them to receive the assets.

In the 25 to 50 age bracket, trust services provide security and peace of mind with wills and trusts designed to protect families in the event of the death of one or both parents. For those fortunate enough to have had a financial head start in life, trust departments frequently provide professional investment management while the individuals are busy with their careers. Most employed people during this age span are also covered by a pension and a profit-sharing plan that frequently are handled by bank trust departments.

The control element is probably strongest in the 50 to 65 age group. In this age category most wealth accumulation and stabilization takes place. The client's children are usually grown and launching their own careers, which significantly lessens a client's financial responsibilities to the family. Professional investment management involving either a management agency or a living trust is common for individuals in this age group. Sophisticated estate and tax planning, encompassing living and testamentary trusts and wills, must be skillfully developed to minimize current tax liabilities and eventual tax liabilities at death. Custodial accounts keep the investment portfolios of busy clients who are rapidly accumulating wealth under control. Although they may manage their investments, these people seldom have the time or the experience to maintain accurate and current records and to keep securities organized and safe. Many other business services that trust departments offer also are attractive to people in this age category.

Security and peace of mind dominate the needs of those who are 65 and older. Since their children are generally well established, older people return to a concern for their own financial and physical well-being. Again, professional investment management is provided with management agencies and living trusts.

In this age category, however, clients with personal agency accounts are frequently encouraged to change their service to a trust. A trust account is more flexible in providing for financial needs in the event of incapacity and for the testamentary powers it offers. Estate planning to avoid unnecessary taxation, and the corresponding use of wills and trusts to accomplish minimal taxation, is an important service.

Many clients choose to travel or to take up other endeavors during their retirement. Professional investment management with a trust or a management agency is often essential when the customer is engaged full time in these other activities. Clients with substantial wealth may also turn their attention to charitable donations in substantial amounts. They may also wish to establish trusts for grandchildren and other relatives. Several different trust account formats are also available that are highly sophisticated and are designed to yield tax advantage.

## A CHANGING MARKET

In the previous discussion, the focus was on traditional services that trust departments offer, which had previously been the preserve of the exceptionally wealthy. The market is no longer merely traditional, however. More people are looking for a wide range of financial services that will enable them to make maximum use of their money. Recent legislation and broader regulations are encouraging investors to hunt for new opportunities that will offer the best return on their resources. The trust industry is now finding itself in a business that is competitive with services offered by brokerage houses and insurance companies.

Meeting people's financial needs in this environment requires determining what those needs are and how they can best be met. Designing services for these carefully defined groups—such as the newly affluent—is the clear challenge of the eighties for trust departments.

## SUMMARY

This chapter examines the financial and underlying human needs that trust services meet. Clients are looking for security, peace of mind, and control of their property. The entire range of trust services meets these needs at different levels in a variety of ways. The customer profile showed that a newcomer to personal trust services might have several problems that can be solved easily by services housed under the trust department roof. Stan Lynott and his family certainly had their choices—options that Stan would not have known to ask for directly. He would be sold on the services when he saw that they actually did meet his needs and addressed his problems.

Trust department roles in serving individuals span the gamut from keeping items safe in vaults to legally owning and managing large and complicated trust funds for sizable families. Across a life span, individuals' needs for trust services change as their educational, career, and family situations shift. In a time of changing legal and regulatory restrictions, trust services to individuals have considerable potential for expansion to reach several new and profitable markets, each representing different sets of needs.

## QUESTIONS FOR REVIEW

1. What basic human needs do personal trust services fulfill? Can these needs be tapped in young adult clients, or are they unique to elderly clients? Why?

2. Name some trust services that may fulfill a client's objective of protection from financial incapacity, tax minimization, recordkeeping, and asset control.

3. What is a standby trust? What three events can trigger a change in control over trust assets?

4. What are the primary human needs of clients in the 25 to 50 age bracket? In the 65 and older age group?

*5* Personal Agencies
and Other Services

## INTRODUCTION

The American Bankers Association defines an agency as follows: "An account in which the title to the property constituting the agency does not pass to the trust institution but remains with the owner of the property, who is known as the principal, and in which the agent is charged with certain duties with respect to the property."

In this chapter we will look at agencies—or services—that trust departments perform for individual clients, rather than those that are offered corporations or other institutions. The chapter defines an agency and the process involved in setting up one, briefly traces the origins of an agency, distinguishes between general and specific agencies, examines an agent's powers and duties, and discusses in detail four typical agencies that trust departments offer.

## AGENCY RELATIONSHIPS

An agency is a relationship in which one person or institution, the agent, acts for or represents another, the principal, in a matter involving the principal's property. Thus the bank trust department is the agent, and the trust department's client is the principal. An agency relationship is generally a contractual one that usually involves a written agreement in the form of a letter of instructions, an agency agreement, or a letter of attorney. Although agencies may be created by oral agreement, few banks would enter into an agency relationship without the benefit of a written agreement.

Agencies almost always are ended at the death of either party. The only exception to this is an "agency coupled with an interest" in which the agent has a legal interest in the property. This agency remains in effect until the agent can realize his or her legal interest. Either the client or the bank can terminate an agency relationship. Throughout the life of the agency, however, the agent is always subject to the authority and control of the principal. Agents should be selected carefully because they may subject the principal to personal liabilities. Bank trust departments represent less risk to the client than some individual agents might because bank trust officers understand clearly the nature of the agency relationship and have the resources and experience to perform the task.

Laws relating to agencies and trusts evolved from English common law and date from the Middle Ages. The concept of trust and agency appears to have been synonymous for several hundred years. Gradually, however, the concepts of trust and agency were differentiated. Trusts involved split titles to property; with agencies, one person retained title. Eventually, the trust relationship evolved into a more extensive fiduciary relationship than an agency.

## General Agencies

When principals authorize, through a power of attorney, an agent to represent them in every way and in every business transaction that may arise, they have made a **general agency** agreement. In this general agency relationship, the agent may virtually perform any legal act that the principal could. Usually, a bank trust department will encourage a client who wants to enter into a general agency relationship with the bank trust department to use a trust instead. A trust will accomplish the same purpose with many additional benefits.

Some banks, however, will accept standby general powers of attorney to the bank trust department, which the bank cannot exercise until the clients request it, or until the client is incapacitated. Use of standby powers requires that the state accept the durable concept of an agency relationship, in which the agency relationship is not terminated by the incapacity of the principal. Most but not all states currently recognize durable forms of agency.

Many banks and estate lawyers recommend that clients lodge with their original will, kept by the nominated personal representative (executor), a general power of attorney and letter of instructions. The letter of instructions directs the bank or individual holding the general power of attorney not to act unless the client becomes incapacitated. Then the holder must use the power of attorney in good faith and judgment after consultation with the family, the client's attorney, and the client's doctor. This is used as a way of protecting assets so that a conservatorship need not be imposed on the person. Many prefer this to a standby trust as protection against incapacity.

## Specific Agencies

In specific agencies, the principal authorizes the agent to do one or more clearly defined things. Specific agencies are the type of agency relationship most often established between bank trust departments and their clients. For example, the safekeeping of assets constitutes a specific agency. Although a management agency implies a more general power, it too is a specific form of agency because the agent's duties are limited to investment management of the assets deposited to the agency account.

The simplest form of agency to imagine is that of a mother giving money to her young son and instructing him to go to the store to purchase a loaf of bread. This example has all the elements of a modern agency. The son, acting as agent, has accepted the transfer property—the money—with the authority and instructions of his mother—the principal—to carry out a lawful act—the purchase of a loaf of bread. This simplified example of a specific agency can be used to analyze the duties and powers of agents.

## AN AGENT'S POWERS

The authority of an agent to act on behalf of a principal is an aggregate of the expressed, implied, and apparent powers involved. The expressed powers of an agent are those contained in a formal agreement creating the agency. An agent's implied powers are those that grow out of its expressed powers.

In our simplified example, the expressed power is to purchase a loaf of bread. The implied powers would include the power to examine various loaves of bread to select the best one; the power to accept a receipt for the money spent in purchasing the bread; and the power to request a bag to carry it home in. Each expressed power contained within the agreement gives rise to a number of implied powers.

The apparent powers of agents are defined as those that the principal permits the agent to appear to have even though the agent does not actually possess that power. Assume in our simplified example that the youngster frequently buys items at the store for his mother and sometimes charges the items to his mother's account, which the mother promptly pays at the end of the week. One day, without the authority of his mother, the youngster charged a bag of licorice to the account. The mother had permitted the son to have apparent authority to purchase the licorice and charge it to her account. In this instance, the mother will have to pay for the candy, since apparent authority has the effect of real authority.

## AN AGENT'S DUTIES

An agent owes four basic duties to the principal—loyalty, obedience, care and diligence, and accountability. These are general duties of all agents regardless of the type of agency.

The first duty of every agent is loyalty to the principal. The legal concept of loyalty first involves adherence to law and then faithfulness. Loyalty is the highest of the agent's duties to the principal. The agent must act with good faith and loyalty to further the principal's interest in all dealings affecting the property the agency covers. If the agent fails to do so, the agent is responsible to the principal for any loss that results. To extend the example, if the youngster lost the money while attempting to catch tadpoles at the frog pond with his friends when he should have been purchasing a loaf of bread, he would be violating his duty of loyalty to his mother.

The second basic duty of an agent is to obey the principal's orders, provided they do not require actions that are illegal or contrary to public policy. With this exception, an agent must comply with the principal's command regardless of a personal opinion about the appropriateness or expediency of that command. If the agent exceeds, violates, or neglects such command, the agent is liable to the principal for any resulting loss or damage. Most lawsuits between agents and principals involve an alleged violation of obedience the agent owes the principal. The purchase of a bag of candy with his mother's money rather than a loaf of bread would be an obvious violation of obedience.

The third basic duty an agent owes the principal is the exercise of ordinary care, diligence, and skill in the performance of assigned responsibilities. If the agent fails in these duties, the agent is liable to the principal for any resulting loss or injury. Like many words with legal connotations, "care and diligence" have different shades of meaning; they are usually described as slight, ordinary, or great. An agent must exercise the same degree of care and diligence as a person of ordinary prudence would in conducting his or her own affairs. The agent must also handle the principal's business with reasonable skill. Reasonable skill is that which is ordinarily possessed and exercised by persons of similar capacity engaged in the same business or employment.

What amounts to the exercise of ordinary care, diligence, and skill depends on the circumstances of each case, including the kind of agency, the agent's responsibilities, and the nature of the property involved in the agency. Returning to our simplified example, the youngster will select a loaf of bread, properly wrapped, reasonably fresh, free of mold, and—if truly skilled—will look for a sale.

The fourth basic duty of an agent is to make a complete accounting to the principal. This includes an accounting for all property subject to the agency, complete with receipts and disbursements. If any subagents were appointed, an accounting of their activity is also warranted. An agent is also under a duty to account for property or funds it receives for a specific purpose. If the agent fails to apply the funds to the purpose for which the funds were received, the principal will be able to recover the funds from the agent. Again returning to the example, the youngster will present a receipt for the bread to his mother and return the appropriate change. The boy probably will be liable from his personal allowance for any of the money spent on bubble gum or other unauthorized frivolities.

Whether an institutional agent owes the principal higher standards of performance regarding the four duties than an individual agent is a pertinent issue. Generally, the courts seem reluctant to hold institutions to higher standards when agencies are involved. However, if a trust institution promoted a service as one that offered a higher standard, the court would hold it to that higher degree. Higher standards are required of trust departments than of individuals when trust agreements are involved, as bank trust departments essentially are considered to be the professionals in the trust business.

## KINDS OF AGENCIES

Bank trust departments offer their clients some agency accounts including **safekeeping, custodial, management,** and **escrow agencies.**

### Safekeeping Agency

A safekeeping agency, as the name implies, constitutes the placing of property, usually documents such as deeds, contracts, and securities, in a secure place. Although jewelry, keepsakes, coins, stamp collections, and other physical items may be securely stored, the safekeeping function in a bank trust department is usually limited to documents and securities. With the wide acceptance of safe deposit vaults, many banks retain the entire safekeeping function within the safe deposit area, rather than assigning the document and security segment to the trust department. Safekeeping used to be provided to the bank's customers free of charge. However, as bankers have become more astute in realizing their costs of doing business, most institutions now charge a reasonable fee for the service.

The duties of a safekeeping agent for documents and securities include receiving the property; maintaining it in the condition in which it was received, except for natural and unavoidable physical deterioration; and delivering the property to the principal when requested. In performing these duties, the agent must exercise proper care.

When serving as safekeeping agent, a trust institution has no responsibility with regard to the property until it has actually received it. When a bona fide representative of the trust department receives the property, whether on the institution's premises or not, the bank's safekeeping responsibilities begin. Once received, the agent must see that the property is held safely. It must not be stolen, destroyed, mutilated, lost, or embezzled.

With the modern conditions that are standard in trust department storage areas, physical destruction or mutilation of property seldom occurs without trust department negligence. The agent is, therefore, usually held responsible for the loss. If destruction occurs as a result of a natural event, however, such as a violent earthquake that destroys the property or so mutilates it that its value is lost, the agent is not liable.

If tangible property or securities included in the safekeeping account are lost through negligence while in the agent's possession, the agent is responsible for the value of the lost property. In such cases the agent first tries to recover the property. If that effort fails, the agent is responsible for making good its monetary value. If the lost property is an irreplaceable document, the agent is liable, not for the monetary value of the document, but for the amount of loss the client sustained by losing an irreplaceable document. If the lost item is a registered security, the agent must have a duplicate issued and must bear the cost of obtaining that duplicate.

An agent is liable for embezzlement, which in the banking context relates to inside thefts committed by officers and employees of the trust department. Some trust institutions have attempted to limit this liability by placing language in their agency agreements that relieves the agent of liability for acts of its agents and employees, provided that the institution uses due care in selecting and supervising them. Such a clause, however, could not be relied on to exonerate the trust department in the unlikely event of an internal theft.

When property is delivered from the safekeeping account to the owner or to the owner's order, the safekeeping agency ends. If the property is delivered to a wrong person, the safekeeping agent is liable. Even if delivery to a wrong person is made in good faith, the agent is still liable, since such a delivery would be a violation of its agency agreement.

## Custodial Agency

Custodianships are one of the most basic personal agency services trust institutions provide. Most bank trust departments have a simple form that the client completes and delivers, together with securities, to the trust institution. The duties of a trust institution as custodian include all those of a safekeeping agent, plus the following:

- to receive dividends and interest from the property and disburse or reinvest them according to the client's instructions

- to execute any ownership certificates required for the client's income tax or other purposes

- to notify the client of corporate actions, including bond calls, stock subscription rights, defaults in bond principal or interest, tender offers, class action suits, and the adoption of protective measures concerning the securities in the account

- to collect the principal of matured or called bonds and matured mortgage notes and to report all such collections to the client

- to buy, sell, receive, or deliver securities according to the specific instructions of the client

- to provide a periodic statement of account activity including receipts, disbursements of income and principal, and securities or other documents

The custodial service basically relieves the client of the need to make frequent trips to a safe deposit box to clip coupons and deposit them for collection, to redeem bonds that have matured or have been called, or to remove or deposit stock certificates that have been bought or sold from the client's security portfolio. The custodial service frequently will save the client losses that may occur because the individual failed to act promptly in clipping coupons or presenting securities for redemption.

When collecting the income, the custodian credits the amount to the account of the client, pays it to the client's order, or reinvests it in accordance with the client's instructions. If the custodian does not collect the income on time—for example, by failing to clip and deposit interest coupons—the custodian is responsible for the interest on the coupons between the due date and the date they were presented for payment. If the coupons become uncollectible because of failure to present them promptly for payment, the custodian is liable both for the value of the coupon and the interest after the due date.

The custodian presents matured bonds and matured mortgage notes for payment. When the proceeds are received, the custodian either notifies the client promptly or reinvests the funds in accordance with the client's established directions. If the custodian fails to collect the principal of bonds or mortgages on time, the minimum amount for which it will be charged is the loss of interest and principal sustained by the client because of the delay.

Under a standard agreement in custodial agencies, many trust institutions agree to notify the client of all calls, subscription rights, defaults, and other matters in connection with securities and mortgages in the account. A custodian who has made such an agreement and fails to notify the client of such matters will be responsible for any loss the client sustains as a result.

In addition to giving the client detailed receipts for securities when the account is opened and when additions are made to it, the custodian periodically provides statements of collections, disbursements, and securities held.

The client retains full control of the investment management of the property subject to the custodianship. The custodian buys, sells, and exchanges securities or makes other capital changes only at the express direction of the client. If the custodian fails to execute a client's order involving a security transaction, it is responsible for any loss traceable to such failure. This is assuming, of course, the transaction could have been made at the time the custodian failed to do so.

## Management Agency

To this point, the agencies discussed have not allowed the trust department serving as agent any discretionary responsibility. The management agency represents a further enlargement of the trust department's activities and responsibilities as agent because this agency involves latitude to make decisions based on the agent's sound judgment.

As managing agent for securities, real property, or both, the trust department provides a management or advisory service as complete as the client may request, in addition to safekeeping and custodial services. The duties that a trust department performs in the role of managing agent differ widely and are not yet fully standardized. Standardization would, in fact, be extremely difficult in view of the many forms a management agency may take and the types of property involved.

### Managing Securities

In addition to the safekeeping and custodial duties discussed earlier, a trust institution acting as managing agent for a client's securities will usually provide one or more of the following services:

- conducting periodic reviews and analyses of the securities in the account and making recommendations for retention, sale, exchange, or conversion of present securities, and for the purchase of new securities

- providing advance notice of the pending maturity of bonds, notes, and mortgages

- preparing an annual information statement for income tax purposes

- ensuring that necessary renewals of insurance policies accompany deposited mortgages, and that taxes on the mortgaged property are paid

- receiving income from sources other than deposited securities—for example, rents, royalties, or salaries

- paying bills for the client or making other remittances if requested to do so

- watching for advantageous opportunities to exchange convertible bonds for stock or to sell bonds to sinking funds, that is, funds that institutions set aside periodically to buy or redeem a specific class of securities

Some management agencies are fully discretionary, and the trust institution is free to buy, sell, and exchange securities within the portfolio without the client's consent. The client receives a monthly statement showing any changes the trust department made in his or her securities portfolio. Of course, a client also can make changes if he or she so desires. A trust department would undertake a fully discretionary management agency only after detailed counseling with the client to determine clearly the individual's investment objectives. Frequent follow-up contact between the trust institution and the client is necessary to ensure that the client's objectives are being met and to decide whether any changes in the investment approach are appropriate.

Other levels of discretion are possible in a management agency that involves securities. One step removed from full discretion is an arrangement that is sometimes called "keeping consultation," which essentially means informing the client as the transaction occurs.

At another level of discretion, trust officers make recommendations to the client about proposed investment changes based on the trust department's review and analysis of the security portfolio.

### Managing Property

As managing agent for real property—usually improved property that includes a house or other buildings—a trust department may handle all the details connected with the management of that real property. The following duties are typical:

- to obtain tenants

- to arrange, execute, cancel, or renew leases

- to collect rents

- to advise the client about the need for making repairs and alterations and to carry out instructions concerning those repairs and alterations

- to advise the client on the amount and kinds of insurance needed and to purchase that insurance

- to pay insurance premiums, taxes, interest on mortgages, and other assessments

Like the management agency for securities, a management agency for real property will have varying degrees of discretion assigned to the trust institution. Not all trust departments are prepared to manage real property. In that case, the department may effect an arrangement by which it accepts the management agency responsibility for real estate by obtaining the client's consent to use a rental or real estate firm. The firm would act as a subagent and would report to the trust department as agent for the client.

Management agencies may extend over a long period of time or may have a short life. A professional or retired person may desire to be permanently relieved of the management responsibility of his or her property, while also retaining title to and full control of it. But a person who is vacationing abroad for several months may want his or her securities attended to only during the interim. Whether the agency is of short or long duration, the managing agent must give vigilant attention to the securities or real estate subject to the account.

Until recently, trust institutions were generally loath to accept management agencies that did not permit an investment program to conform, at least generally, to the normal investment program it used for its trust accounts. In recent years, however, a virtual explosion of investment alternatives have become available to the investing public. Brokerage houses, insurance companies, and independent investment advisers have been much quicker than trust institutions to respond to their clients' desires for access to these widened investment opportunities.

Many banks therefore are responding to this challenge by accepting management agency business that 10 years ago would have been thought of as risky, off-beat, or too exotic. For example, many large banks now have an options expert on their staff and would now accept a client who wanted to invest in a nontraditional options program. Trust departments have been adding investment specialists with a wider range of expertise to tailor their services to client preferences. Also, with increased exploration for and discovery of natural resources such as oil and gas in many areas of the country, trust departments are adding experts in these areas to their staffs to serve clients better. Precious metals and various collectibles are other investment specialties that trust departments are incorporating.

The level of expertise a trust institution needs in order to offer management agencies is a decision that the managers of each trust department must address for their department. Obviously, the same degree of expertise will not be found in a small community bank trust department as in the trust department of a large New York City institution. Most trust departments still find that they cannot be all things to all people. It does appear, however, that more trust departments seek to be more things to more people in response to competitive challenges.

### Escrow Agency

An escrow occurs when two or more persons deposit money, securities, instruments, or other property with a third person (or institution) to be delivered on a certain contingency or the occurrence of a certain event. The person or institution with whom the assets or documents are deposited is called the escrow agent. An escrow has four basic features:

- a complete agreement between the parties to the escrow that no difference of opinion between the contracting parties remains

- a deposit of money, securities, instruments, or other property with the escrow agent

- an intentional surrender by each party of dominion over the money, securities, instruments, or other property deposited by each party

- definite instructions to the escrow agent, specifying the conditions under which the escrow agent delivers the money, securities, instruments, or other property to the party entitled to receive them to fulfill the agreement between the parties

The establishment of an escrow account is not complete until no disagreement exists among the parties about the duties and responsibilities of the escrow agent. Either a fixed time or a definite event that will terminate the escrow account must be agreed to. Escrow accounts usually are opened in connection with a real property transaction, although the property may also be patent rights, formulas, or other personal property rights as well as stocks, bonds, or other intangibles.

An escrow agent's main responsibility is to carry out instructions, not to exercise discretion. In most instances that escrow agents have been held liable for loss, they have failed to carry out instructions. They may well have done so with the best of motives. An escrow agent essentially is a stakeholder and should never deviate from the original instructions, even to the slightest degree. The deviation that most often leads an escrow agent into difficulty is the premature delivery of documents or money. An escrow agent assumes full liability for all losses resulting from deliveries not authorized by the instrument or the consent of all the parties.

As a practical matter, the escrow agent should supervise formulating and writing the instructions to make certain that the language in the agreement is unmistakably clear. The escrow agent should also insert the usual clauses that serve to protect the agent and to notify the other parties of the extent and the limit of the agent's liability.

The following profile shows how a trust department's agency services can benefit a particular customer's needs.

## Customer Profile: A Friend of the Family

Brad Kemple, a trust officer for a medium-sized Midwestern bank, chose his usual seat at church events on the aisle about two-thirds of the way back from the altar. Brad was attending the wedding of one of his favorite clients, Linda Albright. He smiled when he thought of the possibility of rewriting his job description to include the dozen or so weddings, graduations, funerals, and other events arising every year from his job.

But this occasion was special. For 12 years, Brad and Linda had a professional-client relationship that at times had seemed more like a father-daughter relationship. Linda, now a successful architect, was just minutes away from marrying her architectural business partner, John Mason.

Brad met Linda just after her parents had been killed in an automobile accident. They had made no will. Brad's bank had been appointed to administer the estate, of which Linda was the sole heir. Because she was still a minor, the court established a guardianship for Linda's benefit, and Brad's bank had been appointed guardian. Brad could not help reminiscing about their trials and tribulations over the years, as the organist was warming up the prelude to the bridal march.

Linda was 20 years old when the state in which she resided lowered the age of minority from age 21 to age 18. Linda had entered college 2 years earlier and had been disappointed that the bank had restructured the securities in the guardianship account from growth-oriented stocks to high-income-producing stocks and bonds. There was also a small apartment complex in the account that the bank continued to hold. When the guardianship terminated a year earlier than expected because the age of minority had been changed, Brad had attempted to encourage Linda to establish a management agency account. He felt this would be advantageous to Linda because the bank could continue to manage her investments while she channeled her energies into completing college. However, Linda had her own ideas for investing the assets that differed from what the bank had recently done with the security portfolio. When she left the bank the day she terminated her guardianship—stocks, bonds, and deed in hand—Brad had a hunch he might be seeing her again in the not too distant future.

Brad's hunch was right. Linda had sought the counsel of a stockbroker who had quickly restructured the portfolio back into growth-oriented investments. Linda had stock certificates, bonds, coupons, and dividend checks scattered all over her house and was rapidly losing track of where things were. When she sought Brad Kemple's counsel for this problem, he suggested a safekeeping account. The bank would keep the securities in its vault, would receive the securities from Linda, and would make them available to her or her designated representative. For a modest extra charge, the bank would also collect the dividend checks, clip the coupons, collect the rents from the apartment complex, and deposit them monthly to Linda's checking account.

This arrangement improved things greatly for Linda. However, the stockbroker bought and sold securities regularly, and Linda began to find the frequent trips to the bank to deposit or remove securities burdensome as she became more involved at college. At this point, Brad Kemple suggested a custodial account which, in addition to the features of the safekeeping account, would eliminate Linda's frequent trips to and from the bank. Under the custodial arrangement, the bank would work directly with the broker in executing buys and sells of securities. In addition, the bank would monitor the security portfolio for changes such as called bonds, stock splits, and other capital changes and would notify Linda or her brokers so a timely decision could be made. The bank would also temporarily invest the income produced by the securities and the apartments between the time it was collected and paid to Linda's checking account.

After Linda finished college and began her graduate studies, Brad received a telephone call one day from the bank's bookkeeping department. He was surprised to learn that Linda had developed a habit of overdrawing her checking account and was doing so increasingly. The bookkeeper had called Brad because he was aware of the trust department's monthly deposits to the checking account. When Brad brought this to Linda's attention, she was most embarrassed and admitted that it had been a problem. She indicated that with the increased tuition and other expenses of graduate school, the income from her securities and the apartments had not been sufficient for her needs. Brad had noticed that during the 3 years Linda and her broker had managed the account there actually had been little or no growth among the securities, and there seemed to be a steady pattern of liquidating securities from the portfolio.

Brad arranged an appointment for Linda and the officer who had been in charge of the investment aspects of Linda's guardianship account. The investment officer explained that the bank had shifted the orientation of the guardianship portfolio from growth to income-producing securities to provide for Linda's increased income needs during her college years. He explained that while Linda was living with her grandmother after her parents' death, the modest income provided by the growth securities had been sufficient to meet her needs. However, the additional expenses of room, board, tuition, and extracurricular activities at college had made necessary a security portfolio that generated more income. The stockbroker Linda had chosen to help her was genuinely attempting to fulfill her desires to structure a growth portfolio. The economy had performed sluggishly for the past several years, however, and Linda's needs for money to complete her education meant that some of the better securities had to be sold, negating what limited potential existed for growth.

Linda asked the investment officer what the bank would recommend now. He replied that it was imperative to restructure the portfolio immediately so that further liquidations would not be necessary. He felt that another short period of adverse economic activity was imminent and that this downturn would be followed by a long-term recovery. He suggested retaining those stocks that would weather the forthcoming economic storm and respond with better than average results to the economic recovery. He further suggested that the remaining securities be sold and reinvested in short-term bond obligations of the federal government and high quality corporations. This would provide for Linda's income needs during her graduate program. Also, since they would be maturing shortly after she completed her education, funds would be available for reinvestment in the growth-oriented securities Linda preferred. Brad Kemple also offered to counsel Linda on how to control her spending habits to get more spending power from the money currently available to her.

Linda realized that she really had never appreciated the service she received under her guardianship because she had been too young to understand. Now that she had seen both sides of the picture, she was eager to return the assets to the bank for management. Brad suggested that a management agency account be immediately arranged, and Linda readily agreed.

## SUMMARY

This chapter focuses on the specific services that trust departments provide for individuals with a range of financial management needs. These services, called agencies, involve a fiduciary relationship, meaning that the trust department as the agent of the client has the obligation to act in the best interests of the client, rather than in its own interest.

Principals, or clients, retain some liability in agency agreements, so it is important to select an agent who is professionally prepared for the job as trust department officers are.

Although general agencies exist—primarily in the form of standby general powers that are given in the event of incapacity—most agencies are specific in nature. The expressed, implied, and apparent powers of an agent are examined in the context of a young boy whose mother commissioned him to buy a loaf of bread.

There are four basic, general duties of an agent to a principal—loyalty, obedience, care and diligence, and accountability—regardless of the agency involved.

The chapter looks at the kinds of agencies trust departments offer. Although the simplest form of agency, the safekeeping agency, primarily involves storing property securely, considerable care must be taken by the agent in receiving and delivering the property to the client. Modern safekeeping processes are so advanced that, barring extreme natural disasters, the property is safely maintained.

With a custodial agency, the client receives all the benefits of a safekeeping agency and several additional services, including several routine and time-consuming activities involved in investment. Precise records of transactions are kept, and the client receives regular statements showing all receipts and disbursements.

The broadest form of agency is a management agency, which involves some degree of discretion on the part of the trust department. In regard to a securities management agency, levels of discretion range from full authority to manage the investments in the account—including buying and selling the securities—to recommending the best investments for the client's objectives. As management agent for real property, several specific duties usually are involved—from obtaining tenants to paying taxes, insurance, and assessments. When a trust department does not have the kind of expertise the client needs, the officers may decide to obtain the services of a subagent—such as a realtor—with the client's consent.

Recently, many trust departments have been expanding their expertise to include specialists in such areas as minerals, options, precious metals, and collectibles. These investment specialists are helping their departments to become more competitive with alternative investment opportunities that have become so popular in the last decade.

The final agency discussed is the trust department's role as escrow agent. The escrow agency requires trust department officers to hold assets or documents when two or more parties are involved. The officers cannot deliver the assets to either party unless a specific, clearly identified event or circumstance has occurred. In the escrow agency, no discretion is involved. The agent should follow orders precisely, because the trust department can be liable for any deviation from the agreement. The agreement itself should be prepared carefully to make certain that the trust officer and all the parties are truly agreed on the conditions, which should be stated as clearly as possible.

## QUESTIONS FOR REVIEW

1. Explain the difference between the principal and the agent in an agency relationship. What are the four basic duties owed by an agent to a principal?

2. What are the primary responsibilities of a safekeeping agent? Is the safekeeping agent usually responsible if property is lost in delivering it from the safekeeping account to the principal?

3. Aside from safekeeping responsibilities, what are the duties of a custodial agent?

4. Explain the difference between discretionary and nondiscretionary responsibilities of a managing agent.

5. Are an escrow agent's responsibilities primarily discretionary or nondiscretionary? What are the four basic features of an escrow account?

6. What are the typical duties of a managing agent for a trust account that has an apartment building as one of its assets?

 Trusts and Other
Fiduciary Services

## INTRODUCTION

This chapter explores the backbone service of all trust departments—the personal trust account. We will begin by looking at the characteristics of a personal trust: how it differs from a personal agency, the basic elements that are common to all trust accounts, and the primary types of trust accounts. With this basic understanding of personal trusts in hand, we will next consider the reasons for establishing a personal trust account, such as asset management and tax savings. Finally, the chapter takes an in-depth look at the trust agreement and explores the administration of trusts, including both the business and personal aspects. Guardianships, a close relative of the trust account, and the duties of a guardian also merit discussion.

## CHARACTERISTICS OF A TRUST

As many legal definitions of the word trust exist as authors offering definitions. A good legal definition, supplied in Scott's *Law of Trusts,* holds that a trust is

> A fiduciary relationship with respect to property, subjecting the person by whom the title to property is held to equitable duties to deal with the property for the benefit of another person, which arises as a result of a manifestation of an intention to create it.

Let's look at each element of this definition and apply it to redefining the concept of trust.

- *A fiduciary relationship* . . . A fiduciary is a person to whom property is entrusted to hold, control, and manage for another. Referring to the relationship as fiduciary also implies that it is one of confidence, reliability, good faith, and fairness.

- *. . . with respect to property, subjecting the person by whom the title to property is held to equitable duties to deal with the property for the benefit of another person . . .* As discussed earlier, property is defined as consisting of the thing itself and the many diverse rights in that property. With a trust, two of those property rights are divided between the two main participants of a trust. The first of those property rights is the legal title to the property that is held by an individual or a trust institution, not for its own use but for the benefit of another. The second of those property rights is the beneficial enjoyment of the property. Beneficial enjoyment may include actual use of the property itself, or merely the right to receive income generated by the property. In any event, although title or ownership in the property is transferred to the trustee, the right to enjoy the fruits of the property rests with the trust beneficiary.

- *. . . which arises as a result of a manifestation of an intention to create it.* Usually the various parties entering into a trust are aware of their actions and of their intent to create a trust relationship. These trusts are known as **express trusts.** Sometimes the parties involved are unaware that their actions constitute a trust, yet a trust is established as the presumed intention of the parties from the nature of the transaction. This is known as a **resulting trust.** At other times, a court of equity will impose a trust on several parties when there is no intention of creating a trust, but creating a trust is necessary to prevent a failure of justice. This is known as a **constructive trust.** Constructive trusts and resulting trusts will not be covered in this book. However, it is worth pointing out that there is not always a manifestation of an intention to create a trust.

Trusts are almost always created for two practical purposes: to solve a financial problem or to create a financial opportunity. Although trusts are sometimes viewed by the general population as being mysterious instruments of the rich, they are often created to meet the needs of ordinary people.

Having considered each element in Scott's definition of a trust, it can now be redefined as

> A business and personal relationship founded in confidence, reliability, good faith, and fairness through which one party assumes ownership of property and a separate party enjoys the benefits of that property for the intended purposes of solving a problem or creating an opportunity.

## Difference Between a Trust and an Agency

It is worthwhile to restate and expand earlier definitions of trusts and agencies. An understanding can be further aided by distinguishing a trust from an agency on two major points.

First, the legal title to property and the beneficial enjoyment of that property are always separated in a trust. Without this separation, no valid trust exists. In an agency, the principal always retains title to and control of the property. The agent merely acts in accordance with the principal's instructions; neither legal title to the property nor beneficial enjoyment of the property pass to the agent. The agent merely has certain powers with respect to the property, which are to be distinguished from rights in the property.

The second major distinction is that an agency relationship is always ended by the death of either the principal or the agent. A trust, however, does not necessarily close at the death of the beneficiary. Often, at the death of a primary beneficiary, the trust will continue for the benefit of one or more contingent beneficiaries. Also, the death of the trustee rarely terminates a trust. Until the purpose of the trust is fulfilled, the trust will not disintegrate for lack of a trustee. A court of competent jurisdiction will appoint a new trustee until the trust purpose is satisfied.

## Elements of a Trust

All trust accounts administered by trust institutions have five major elements: trustor, trustee, beneficiary, property, and trust agreement. Let's look at why each of these are essential to a trust.

*Trustor.* The trustor is the person who created the trust. Other terms for trustor include creator, grantor, and settlor. A nontechnical way of viewing this person would be to consider him or her as the client of the trust institution who establishes a trust relationship.

*Trustee.* The trustee is the individual or institution holding the legal title to the trust property. As used in this text, the trustee is a bank trust department.

*Beneficiary.* The beneficiary is the person who has the right to enjoy the benefits of the property held by the trustee. The beneficiary does not have to be an individual person; it could be a corporation, public institution, or charity.

*Property.* All trusts must have property subject to the trust. There must be some property, as discussed earlier in the text, in which the legal title and beneficial interest may be separated between the trust institution and one or more beneficiaries.

*Trust agreement.* Finally, there must be a trust agreement—the document creating the trust. In most cases, the agreement is a written contract between the trust institution (trustee) and the client (trustor). The introductory provisions to trust agreements usually are similar. The trustor and the trustee are identified, an express intention to create a trust is stated, and the property subject to the trust agreement is identified. The nature of the trust agreement will depend on the problem being solved by creating the trust. Often a trust is created in the will of a decedent: it is then known as a testamentary trust. On other occasions, an expression of trust is contained in a court order—for example, the court may impose a trust to achieve justice in a divorce settlement.

A person creating a trust may transfer property to a trustee and name himself or herself as beneficiary. In other words, one individual may be both the trustor and beneficiary. Historically, one individual could not be both the trustee and beneficiary because there would be no separation of the legal title and the beneficial enjoyment of the property.

Modern practice, however, recognizes the existence of a trust in which an individual can act as trustee and is also the beneficiary. For example, an individual would name himself as beneficiary during his lifetime and would, upon death or incapacity, provide for a bank to serve as successor trustee and dispose of assets. These trusts are established for continuity and to avoid delays in the disposition of assets. When the trustee and the beneficiary are the same person, the trust is almost always a revocable living trust. This type of trust can cause a great many problems if ownership in the property is not clearly changed from the trustee to the successor trustee. Revocable living trusts will be discussed later in this chapter.

## Types of Trusts

There are several kinds of trusts, depending on the nature of the problem being solved and the instrument used to create the trust.

## Active, Passive, and Standby Trusts

A trust can be active, passive, or standby, with the distinction being the nature of the trustee's duties. If the trustee is required to perform some duty, the trust is termed an **active trust.**

A **passive trust,** on the other hand, requires the trustee to serve only as titleholder without any specific function. A passive trust is sometimes referred to as a dry trust holding title or a naked trust.

A **standby trust** is a special kind of trust designed in response to trustors looking for financial protection from incapacity, avoidance of probate, or financial savings from a trust account, but who prefer to forgo investment management. When a standby trust is established, property is deposited in the trust, but the trustee has absolutely no responsibility in the management of the property. The trust agreement contains instructions to be followed in the event of the trustor's incapacity or death. Until the trustor instructs the trustee to assume management, becomes incapacitated, or dies, the standby trust remains passive.

## Revocable and Irrevocable Trusts

Another major characteristic of a trust that depends on the nature of the problem being solved is whether it is revocable or irrevocable. A **revocable trust** is one in which the trustor has reserved the power to terminate the trust if he or she so chooses. The trustor may have given this right to others also. On occasion, the beneficiary is even given this power of revocation.

An **irrevocable trust** is one in which the trustor does not possess the power of terminating the account. The trustor may, however, make a trust irrevocable for a given period of time only, after which it would become revocable. Or the trustor may make it revocable for a stated period, and if it is not revoked within that period, the trust would be made permanently irrevocable. The trust instrument should always state whether a trust is revocable or not. If the trust is silent, a presumption one way or the other will be made based on state law.

Trust departments exercise great care in accepting irrevocable trusts. Once created, they are extremely difficult, if not impossible, to terminate until the purpose of the trust has been fulfilled. Time and changing conditions may, in fact, alter or even eliminate the original purpose of the trust. If the trust agreement is worded without flexibility, the trust may be forced to continue, even though its original purpose has been diminished or negated. Legal counsel for both the trust department and the trustor always should review an irrevocable trust agreement to make certain that it is accurate and that all parties fully realize the ramifications of the trust's irrevocability.

## Living Versus Testamentary Trusts

By far the two most common types of trusts that trust departments administer are living trusts and testamentary trusts. The primary distinction between the two is the instrument used to create the trust. A **living trust** is created by a contract between a living individual and a trust institution. It is always an express trust since its creation involves a contractual agreement in which the intention to create a trust is specifically stated. Most living trusts are also active in that some current responsibility befalls the trustee. This is not always the case, however, and some exceptions will be discussed later in this chapter.

A **testamentary trust** is contained within the provisions of a decedent's will. A will has no legally binding effect until the writer of the will dies. Since the trust institution is not a party to the creation of the will, a testamentary trust is not a form of contract. The trust institution may or may not have been involved in the estate planning process that led to the drafting of the decedent's will. In either event the trust institution would not sign the will, and the trust institution's approval is not technically required. However, once the trust department accepts the trust, it has the same effect basically as the contractual relationship of the living trust.

Testamentary trusts normally constitute a large segment of a trust department's personal trust business. The provisions of the trust are contained within the **testator's** will and, therefore, do not come into effect until his or her death. The testamentary trust is activated during the estate settlement procedure, usually when the first distribution is made from the probate estate to the testamentary trust.

Testamentary trusts are almost always express trusts, since their provisions are contained in a will. Occasionally, the will is vague about whether a trust was intended, but the circumstances and language of the will make it apparent that a trust is the only way to fulfill the testator's wishes. This is known as an implied trust or a resulting trust and usually occurs in wills that are not professionally drawn.

Testamentary trusts are always active, requiring some form of trustee activity, and they are usually irrevocable, since the testator is deceased. Sometimes, however, a testator will grant the beneficiaries of the trust the power to withdraw a part or even all of the trust assets. Removing all the assets from the trust would, of course, terminate it. More frequently, the testator will grant the beneficiary the right to demand a change of trustees if unsatisfied with the performance of the original trustee or if the principal beneficiaries move to another area.

## REASONS FOR CREATING A TRUST

As established earlier in this chapter, a trust is a relationship "through which one party assumes ownership of property and a separate party enjoys the benefits of that property for the intended purposes of solving some problem or creating an opportunity." The benefits of a trust are numerous and varied. Some of the principal advantages are

- to obtain professional property management and investment service

- to alleviate concern over potential incapacity

- to avoid probate

- to obtain tax savings

- to provide financial protection for family members

- to hold property as a separate estate

As an introduction to some of the principal reasons for creating a trust, let's look at the following scenario.

### Customer Profile: Playing the Cards Right

"Six hearts . . . six spades . . . six no trump. . . ." The bidding in the bridge game was getting serious. Hazel, Gladys, and Beatrice had been getting together on Thursday afternoons for years to enjoy a game of bridge and keep abreast of the latest neighborhood happenings. Naomi had just joined the group about a month ago to replace the fourth long-time member of the group, Millicent. Millicent had suffered a stroke several weeks earlier and was now recovering in a nursing home. Unfortunately, Millicent's recovery probably would never be complete.

As the card game wore on, the conversation turned to Millicent. Gladys expressed some concern for Millicent's personal and financial affairs. She understood that a guardianship had to be established to take care of Millicent's financial affairs. Hazel added that Millicent's daughter, Jean, had come several hundred miles to initiate the court proceedings that would establish the guardianship. According to Jean, getting the guardianship established and then sorting out a month's worth of financial problems created by Millicent's medical problem had been quite a hassle. Apparently, Jean had had to return home before arranging everything, and she and the local attorney were trying to get everything straightened out long distance. Beatrice mumbled that there ought to be a better way to handle a situation like Millicent's.

Hazel said that, in fact, there was a better way. Several years ago she had established a trust account with her local bank trust department. Gladys gasped, alarmed that Hazel would turn complete control of her assets to a group of stuffy old men who would lock up her money and never give it back to her.

Hazel replied that she had thought the same thing before visiting one of the bank's trust officers.

Instead, Hazel had found a young, compassionate trust officer who endeavored earnestly to understand her concerns. The trust officer, Miss Prather, had recommended a trust account to Hazel to provide investment management, financial protection from her own possible incapacity, estate settlement at her death, and continued financial protection for Hazel's adult, learning-impaired daughter.

Beatrice was curious about the investment management and asked how Hazel's trust was performing. Hazel said her trust had earned a 5 percent return last year. Gladys snickered and remarked that 5 percent was a poor return considering how her savings account and money market funds were producing a 7 percent interest return. Hazel explained that she really did not need any more than a 5 percent return to meet her living expenses and that her trust had been growing nicely, thank you, having appreciated nearly 33 percent in the last 2 years. Combining her current income and the growth of assets, Hazel's total investment return had been around 20 percent per year. While the trust was producing sufficient money for her to live on, the growth of her assets enabled her to support her favorite charities and provide gifts to her grandchildren for their college educations.

Hazel added that should she become incapacitated as Millicent is, her bank trust department would immediately assume her financial affairs without appointing a guardian. The trust agreement empowered the trust officer to use her discretion to further Hazel's financial interests if Hazel became incapable of managing her own assets. The delays, expense, and confusion of a guardianship proceeding would be completely avoided. If her incapacity proved temporary, she could resume full control of her financial affairs when she felt up to it.

At her death, her estate would be settled through the trust agreement, rather than through her will. Since all of her property was in her trust account and her trust agreement contained instructions on what to do with her property, her will would not be submitted for probate. Hazel explained that the advantage of this form of estate settlement is that it requires less time than a probate proceeding, is much less formal, involves only about one-half the expense, and is completely private. Her trust agreement is a confidential arrangement between her and her bank. At her death, the estate would be settled in complete confidentiality, with only the people directly involved in her estate aware of the provisions of her trust. The trust agreement would not be filed in the public records as a will is when it is admitted to probate.

Finally, Hazel remarked that the trust would continue after her death for the benefit of her learning-impaired daughter during her lifetime. Hazel's daughter was able to function in the community and live on her own, but Hazel wanted to be sure after her death that her daughter would be financially protected. At the death of her daughter, the remaining trust assets would be distributed to Hazel's grandchildren by her son.

Gladys, who was still more inclined to believe the trust department horror stories, asked Naomi, who had remained silent, what she thought of Hazel's trust account. Naomi was a retired accountant and managed her own investments quite successfully. Naomi shared many of Hazel's financial needs, although she did not currently require investment management assistance. She had, however, considered the possibility of her own incapacity and was also aware of the advantages of settling an estate through a trust rather than a will. Naomi had visited her bank and established a standby trust that specifically addressed her concerns. The standby trust would only be activated to a management trust at her direction, by her incapacity, or by her death. She, too, had found the trust personnel friendly and geniunely concerned with providing a meaningful service to her.

Impressed by her friends' handling of their personal affairs, Beatrice announced that she would visit the trust department to see which of their services might benefit her. Gladys was thinking about it too, but she was not going to admit it to the group. She was thinking about it so hard, in fact, that she never even noticed that Hazel had successfully finessed the queen of diamonds out of her hand.

## Investment Management

Probably the most common reason for establishing a trust is the desire for professional or specialized investment management. Many individuals with substantial amounts of wealth do not have the necessary skills to manage their wealth in their own best interests.

A retired restaurant owner, for example, who sold his business for a sizable amount might not understand the intricacies of the financial markets in which he intends to invest the proceeds of his sale. Or a person who has recently inherited a fortune from a deceased relative may have no idea how to invest wisely. Others may not have the time to devote to investment management or have higher priorities. Doctors, dentists, and other professionals are frequently so immersed in their professional occupations that they do not have the time to effectively manage the substantial wealth they are accumulating. Another example is the retired couple who have spent their lives creating wealth and now want to enjoy a tour of the world rather than watch over their investments. In each of these cases, the principals may wish to establish a living trust for investment management.

Testamentary trusts are also often created for investment management purposes. For example, a business owner may set up a testamentary trust to carry on the business for the benefit of his or her family, until such time as a family member was capable of taking over the business or until the business could be sold at a profit. A farm owner could similarly provide that the farm continue operating for the benefit of his or her adult children, who may have chosen professions other than farming. In addition to the professional investment services offered by bank trust departments, the trust beneficiaries enjoy relief from the burdensome details of property management.

## Protection from Incapacity

Another common reason for establishing a trust account, particularly among the older population, is the concern about the individual's own potential incapacity. Since a trust relationship continues in the event of the incapacity of the trustor, he or she will be financially protected if a serious accident or an illness occurs. Should such misfortune befall the trustor, the establishment of a guardianship or other means of protecting the trustor's finances will be unnecessary.

## Avoiding Probate

Because the legal title to property held in a living trust is in the name of the trust institution rather than the name of the trustor, the property subject to the trust need not be distributed by the probate process. If the trust agreement contains instructions on what is to be done with the property at the death of the trustor, the trustee will retain that legal title to the property and follow the instructions contained in the trust instrument.

Only that property in the decedent's name alone is subject to the probate process and will be distributed in accordance with the decedent's will. If all of a trustor's property is subject to a trust account, probate becomes unnecessary because no property passes under the terms of the will. This does not mean individuals with all of their property in trust should not have a will. Conceivably, an individual could acquire property and either forget or not be able to place that property in the trust account. A will is therefore necessary to ensure that any such property would be handled according to the decedent's wishes.

Frequently, the will of a person with a trust account will leave all property to the trust so that the trust terms clearly control the disposition of all property. This type of will is sometimes referred to as a **pour-over will,** since the assets outside the trust pour over into the trust from the probate estate at the testator's death.

People try to avoid the probate process for many reasons. Because the process is often so little understood, it is avoided out of ignorance. Several valid reasons for avoiding probate exist, however. First, settlement of an estate through a trust is usually much less expensive than the probate process. Second, unlike a will, the terms of a trust are confidential and not a matter of public record. Therefore, estate settlement through a trust is appealing because it is private, involving only those people who are to receive benefits under the trust. Finally, trust settlements do not require the lengthy process of opening the estate, obtaining court authority, and gathering assets, all of which are essential to a court-supervised probate administration.

## Tax Savings

Trusts, whether living or testamentary, can save taxes. In the case of living trusts, some specialized trusts offer income tax advantages to the trustor. To obtain major tax savings, an irrevocable form of trust is almost always involved. Great caution should be used in attempting to achieve immediate tax savings, because tax laws may change that could defeat the trust's original purpose.

If the trust continues at death, other forms of tax savings may be available, such as savings of federal estate and state inheritance taxes. When someone dies, the assets of many estates are subject to federal estate taxes and usually some form of state inheritance tax. The complexity and intricacies of federal estate tax law and its interrelationship with the various state inheritance tax laws will not be covered here. However, usually the tax savings offered by a testamentary trust are substantial and should not be taken lightly.

Remember, though, that the primary purpose for establishing a testamentary trust should not be tax savings. Often estate planners are so concerned about minimizing taxes that they lose sight of the personal objectives of the client. The human needs of the client's family and the client's desire to fulfill obligations of love and affection should, in most cases, be taken into consideration before the concern over lowering taxes.

## Family Protection

Protection of the family is a broad topic. The desirable goal is to keep the family intact by preserving the family home, relieving the survivors of responsibilities connected with investments and other property, and supplying the income needed to maintain the family's normal standard of living. This situation occurs when the head of the household was either the sole supplier or major contributor of family income and support. When the family fortune remains intact and is administered for the benefit of the entire family, there is more financial leverage than if the wealth were distributed to individual family members.

Family protection also includes providing for children's special needs. Leaving property in a testamentary trust for children eliminates the need to appoint a guardian. The testamentary trust also allows the family assets to be retained in trust for the children's benefit for whatever length of time the testator prefers. Most testamentary trusts provide that the children will receive assets when they reach age 25, 30, or 35. Guardianships, however, must terminate when the child attains legal age, which in most states is age 18. By using a testamentary trust, the assets may be withheld in the trust and distributed when the children are more financially mature.

Many families now consist of parents with children from previous marriages living together as one family unit. In such situations, a testamentary trust is an excellent way to provide for the surviving spouse and the family unit, while ultimately being able to funnel the assets of the deceased spouse to his or her own children.

Testamentary trusts are also an ideal way to provide lifelong care for beneficiaries with special problems, such as children who are physically or mentally handicapped. Individuals who abuse alcohol or drugs or who are financially irresponsible may be protected from their destructive tendencies by placing property in a testamentary trust. These trusts are usually structured to provide for their basic needs and for emergency funds.

### Separate Estate

Finally, a trust may be established to hold a separate estate. Professional and business people may want to create a trust to differentiate their personal assets from their professional or business assets. A separate estate is also sometimes necessary to avoid a conflict of interest. The most notable example of this would be elected officials who create a **blind trust** to continue as long as they remain in office. In this trust, the property is invested and managed without the trustor's knowledge. The officials are, therefore, able to enjoy the benefits of their property but cannot be accused of conflicts of interest arising from the property ownership because they have no idea what specific property—such as stocks and bonds—are included in the trust.

### DURATION OF A PERSONAL TRUST

Whether discussing living trusts or testamentary trusts, the question arises about the length of the trust. The question can be considered in two ways: how long *may* a trust continue and how long *should* it continue?

How long may a trust continue is a legal question based on statutory limits. The ordinary limit is determined by what is known as the **rule against perpetuities.** This rule of common law voids any estate or interest in property that will not take effect or vest within the span of a given life or lives existing when the estate was created, plus 21 years and the period of gestation. In many states, this rule has been modified by statute.

The rule against perpetuities is handed down from English common law. Historically, a trust held in perpetuity was considered to be against public policy because eventually the trust could generate sufficient wealth to rival the wealth of the kingdom. Until comparatively modern times, English law held that even charitable trusts could not be held in perpetuity. In the United States, charitable perpetual trusts have always been recognized as in the public interest and are exempt from the rule against perpetuities.

In drafting trust agreements, care must be taken to ensure that the agreement does not violate the rule against perpeptuities. If at the time a trust becomes irrevocable it is impossible to determine whether the rule against perpetuities will be violated, the trust may be voided at that point. This would, of course, completely defeat the trustor's intention.

How long should a trust continue is an entirely different question. The answer depends on the facts in each individual situation. A trust established for family protection would typically last for the life of the surviving spouse and until all of the children have reached a financially responsible age. A trust established to protect an incompetent would last for the life of that person. Basically, a trust should last long enough to accomplish the objective for which it was created, but not so long that it violates the rule against perpetuities.

## POWERS OF THE TRUSTEE

To ensure the efficient and economical administration of a trust account, the trustee's powers should be clearly stated in the trust agreement. A failure to include the appropriate powers to carry out the intent of the trust may cause uncertainty and delay, impair investment performance, and prevent the trustee from acting in the best interests of the beneficiaries. Many states have a comprehensive statute listing the powers of trustees, which are often extensive enough for the trustee to administer the trust successfully. In those states, many lawyers simply refer to these statutory powers rather than list them in the trust agreement. In other states, these statutes are quite restrictive and specific powers must be granted to the trustee in the trust agreement to meet the statutory requirments. Several of the more important powers are discussed next.

### Powers to Manage Investments

Three powers that apply to trust investments are extremely important. These are the powers to retain original investments, to purchase additional investments, and to sell. Trust agreements should specifically state the trustor's or testator's investment objectives.

When serving as trustee, bank trust departments generally prefer as few limitations on their investment authority as possible. Many clients, however, want to retain control over their investments. As the investment climate changes constantly—often overnight—placing investment restrictions on the trustee may work against the trust beneficiaries' best interests, possibly resulting in client dissatisfaction. However, if the trustor wants to provide guidelines or limitations on the trustee's investment authority, they should be explicitly stated in the trust agreement. In such cases, the bank may want to include a provision in the trust agreement relieving it of responsibility and liability for following the investment directions of the trustor.

## Powers to Manage Property

Another important set of express powers includes those pertaining to the management of property contained in the trust, such as the power to lease property, to establish reserves, and to borrow. These powers are particularly important when real property constitutes all or part of the trust assets.

The power to lease trust property and to extend such leases beyond the trust period is important so that the trustee's options in negotiating favorable rents are not limited. The power to establish reserves is also important, because keeping up property requires available funds. Real property may need nothing but routine maintenance for several years and then suddenly require a major capital investment to fix the roof. If so, appropriate reserves need to be available to repair the roof and meet other contingencies. Another essential is the power to borrow, which offers liquidity to the trust estate. With such power, the trustee can opt to borrow needed funds, rather than being forced to raise the money by selling securities or other assets, which may be disadvantageous at times.

## Powers to Administer the Estate

Powers dealing with the trustee's bookkeeping, accounting, and safekeeping responsibilities are also extremely important. These include the power to hold the securities within the trust estate in the name of the nominee rather than in the specific name of the individual trust. This increases the bookkeeping convenience of the trustee, making prompt sales and deliveries possible as well as timely crediting of dividends and interest. Holding securities in the nominee's name also protects the confidentiality of the fiduciary relationship because the specific name of the trust is not used for security registration. Other powers—to vote securities by proxy, to lodge assets with an outside depository, to allocate or apportion stock dividends equitably among income and principal beneficiaries, to distribute from the trust estate in cash or in property—all significantly add to the profitable and productive administration of the trust estate.

### Powers Dealing with Services' Billing

A provision pertaining to fees for services administered by the trust department is a necessary power. Older trust agreements may have defined the basis on which the fee was to be computed. This may have been appropriate when prices were stable and the costs of doing business were static. However, most agreements that contain such a provision are highly unprofitable during inflationary times. Modern trust instruments generally have a provision authorizing the trustee to charge a reasonable fee for services rendered.

### Powers to Change Locations

A power to move the location of the trust becomes helpful when one bank is asked to accept a trust that another bank administers. This power to move the "situs," or place, of the trust usually includes a provision that releases the new trustee from liability for the acts of the first trustee.

### Powers to Resign

Finally, an important power granted to the trustee is the power to resign. A bank trust department will find it much easier to withdraw from an undesirable trusteeship if the trust contains such a specific power.

### PROVISIONS OF THE TRUST

Of the provisions in a trust instrument, two of the most important are the dispositive provisions and the spendthrift provision. Other provisions are fairly standard.

### Dispositive Provisions

The **dispositive provisions** generally relate to the disposition of income earned by the trust estate and the eventual distribution of the trust assets or principal. The income is generally payable to or for the benefit of the trustor or to a beneficiary in some form of regular installment. All of the income does not have to be paid out, however. Part of or even the entire income of the trust estate may be accumulated for future distribution.

The dispositive provisions are the core of the trust agreement and establish the agreement's individuality. In fulfilling the purpose of the trust through the dispositive provisions, the trustor is limited only in that the trust may not be immoral, illegal, contrary to certain public policies, or violate the rule against perpetuities. Otherwise, only the trustor's imagination and objectives set the boundaries.

When the primary motive of the trustor in creating the trust is the welfare of the immediate beneficiaries, the trustee is usually given the authority to distribute, at its discretion, the principal of the estate if the income is not enough to meet the beneficiaries' needs. This authority is commonly referred to as "the right to invade." If, however, the trustor's primary motive is to hold the trust estate intact for ultimate beneficiaries, discretionary power over principal disbursements may be much more limited in regard to the immediate beneficiaries.

When the trust ends, the dispositive provisions should define in unmistakable terms who will receive the trust assets. Contingent beneficiaries should also be named or appropriately identified to ensure that no part of the trust is without an ultimate beneficiary.

## Spendthrift Provision

Another important provision of the trust instrument is the **spendthrift provision,** which is inserted to protect the assets against the improvidence of a trust beneficiary. Any trust with a spendthrift provision in it is referred to as a spendthrift trust. The provision makes certain that the beneficiary's interest in the income and principal of the trust estate will not be wasted by the beneficiary or reached by his or her creditors through legal process. For example, if a beneficiary assigns his or her share of the trust assets to secure a loan, this assignment is not binding on the trustee if the beneficiary defaults on the loan. Some states have expressed statutory provisions governing the creation of spendthrift trusts. In no state, however, can a trustor include a spendthrift provision in his or her favor. As creator of a trust, an individual could not transfer all of his or her assets to it and then retreat behind a spendthrift provision to avoid current creditors.

## PERSONAL TRUST ADMINISTRATION

No discussion of trusts would be complete without examining the actual administration of trusts. Whether they are trusts under will, trusts under agreement, insurance trusts, or trusts by order of the court, the trustee has two kinds of service of equal importance to perform—those that are business related and those of a personal nature. The creator of a trust expects the trustee to exercise good business management and to act as a counselor to the beneficiaries.

## Business Considerations

The business side of the administration of personal trusts includes the following:

- establishing the account and keeping accurate records

- managing the assets

- complying with the trust terms

- closing the account

### *Establishing the Account*

Once the purpose for the trust has been identified and a suitable agreement prepared, the next step is to set up the account. The trust officer should first review the document for clarity and technical correctness, making sure that all assets being deposited to the trust are in proper form for transferral to the account. Practically all trust institutions have a sophisticated computerized form of trust accounting. If so, it is the trust officer's job to see that the proper computer records are created to administer the estate. It is also the trust officer's responsibility to notify the bank departments that will be immediately affected by the assets of the trust account. This is particularly true when the assets are real estate or a highly volatile securities portfolio. In addition, the trust officer should establish centralized files to keep all trust documents, correspondence, and memos, and ensure that they are easily accessible.

### *Managing the Assets*

Management of the trust property begins with the analysis included in the previous step. The trust officer must identify the assets and immediately take steps to see that they are secure. Securing personal property usually entails placing it in the trust institution's vault. With real property, a physical inspection may be necessary to make certain it is secure. The property should then be expeditiously transferred to the name of the trustee or its nominee registration.

Once the property is properly identified, secured, and transferred to the trust department, it is ready for management. The trust officer should examine the investment powers outlined in the trust agreement, the purpose for which the trust was established, and the needs of the beneficiaries. This comprehensive approach provides the trust officer with the best understanding of how to manage the trust property appropriately.

In the past, trust departments were fairly conservative in their management of trust property, attempting to standardize the property management of all trust accounts. Recently, a more tailored approach that attempts to match the needs of each trust account with the best investment alternatives available has become common.

Managing the property also includes collecting income from the investments. For securities such as stocks and bonds, the process involves a timely collection of the dividends and interest the securities accrue. For real estate, the trustee should endeavor to negotiate and collect favorable leases and rents.

A periodic review is essential to sound property management. The nature of the trust property and the needs of the beneficiaries determine how frequently the review should be conducted. An active trust account may need a monthly or even weekly review. On the other hand, it may be acceptable to review less active trust accounts on a quarterly or semiannual basis. A regulation of the Comptroller of the Currency requires that all trust accounts be reviewed at least once each calendar year or within 15 months of its previous review.

### Complying with Terms of the Trust

Complying with the terms of the trust is the heart of administrative responsibility. It is essential that the trust officer know the specific instructions in the trust agreement and act with the needs of the beneficiaries in mind. Some trust agreements may be precise and direct payment of a specified dollar amount on a regular basis to the beneficiary. Sometimes the trustee is given discretion in how much income is distributed and to which of several beneficiaries. This is known as a **sprinkling trust.** Other instruments may instead direct the payment of the entire net income, regardless of the amount earned. Since the income produced by the trust account may be greatly affected by adjustments to the investments, the trustee actually has considerable control over the income beneficiaries receive. This is why the needs of the beneficiary are an important consideration in administering a trust.

Thought also must be given to the eventual beneficiaries of the principal of the trust estate. The income beneficiary needs not be, and frequently is not, the individual who will eventually receive the principal trust assets. The beneficiary of the principal, who will ultimately receive the trust assets, is also known as the **remainderman.** As this individual has no current interest in the trust, he or she would like to see the trust assets grow so that more money will eventually be available for distribution. This objective of growth, however, is at odds with the objective of producing income for the benefit of the current beneficiary. As a rule, assets that generate large amounts of income have little growth associated with them. Conversely, assets with significant growth potential seldom produce significant current income. Consequently, the trustee must walk a delicate line between the interests of the income beneficiary who desires to maximize current income and the interests of the remainderman who would like to see the trust estate grow. Usually, but not always, the interests of the current income beneficiary are considered first. Situations may develop, however, when the interests of the two should be more balanced, sometimes even favoring the benefit of the principal beneficiary. Again, analyzing the needs of the beneficiaries and the original intent for which the trust was created should offer some clues as to the best way of solving this dilemma.

Trust agreements have either liberal or restrictive standards for invading the trust principal. Thus the trust officer must be guided by the terms of the trust agreement when deciding whether to distribute the principal. Careful drafting is required for the discretionary provisions because some words have established, legal connotations. Language such as "the trustee may distribute principal for the beneficiary's education, health, maintenance, and support" are fairly routine within trust agreements. Legal dictionaries and case law have provided an ascertainable standard for such language. Those drafting the document are occasionally careless, however, and sometimes include such words as "happiness." Some courts have held that the word happiness is tantamount to a power of withdrawal because whatever makes the beneficiary happy constitutes an appropriate disbursement from the trust account. Exercising discretion over principal distributions from the trust estate is undoubtedly one of the heaviest burdens professional trustees bear.

### Closing the Account

One last consideration of the business side of administering a trust account is knowing how to properly close the account. To do so, the trustee has three duties to the beneficiaries: identifying, locating, and accounting to them. The trustee then distributes the trust assets in accordance with the trust terms. In a well-drawn trust instrument, closing the account is a routine matter because there will be no doubt about the time of termination and who the beneficiaries are. Occasionally, however, either because of poor drafting of the trust agreement or because of unfortunate events leading to the premature death of the last beneficiary, the trustee must determine who the principal beneficiaries are when the trust is closed. This can be an onerous task, particularly if the trust instrument specifically provided for the distribution to heirs-at-law or those who would normally inherit the property in the event of no named beneficiary. Some suggest that, if no named beneficiaries survive to take distribution of the trust, a favorite charity of the trustor should be named to receive the trust assets.

## Personal Considerations

The business end of trust administration may often seem easy and straightforward in comparison to the personal demands, which often require that the trust officer act with understanding and compassion. Every letter or phone call from a trustor or beneficiary requires the trust officer to wear a different hat of empathy. It is not uncommon to deal with the concerns of a client with a $1 million account, and 5 minutes later take a call from a client with a $50,000 account and living expenses far above the means of the trust.

### Understanding the Wishes of the Trustor and Beneficiaries

To properly administer a trust, there must be an understanding of its terms and the reason for establishing it. Discovering the underlying reason for creating a trust is best done by personally knowing and understanding the trustor. Accomplished trust officers are skilled at engaging in casual conversation with trustors to draw out their innermost wishes about the trust account and the eventual beneficiaries. These conversations are often jotted down as memos and placed in trust files for future reference. When the time comes that the trustor or testator is no longer available to explain the intent of the trust, the memos prove invaluable in making decisions personally affecting the trust's beneficiaries.

Trust officers also should be personally familiar with the beneficiaries. There is no standard or model beneficiary; beneficiaries defy categorization. The needs of one beneficiary cannot be compared to the needs of beneficiaries in similar accounts because each individual is different. Personal contact with the beneficiaries is important to fulfilling the intent of each trust account and is undoubtedly the most intriguing and rewarding aspect of the trust officer's job.

### Financial, Emotional, and Educational Counseling

Every contact with a client demands knowledge of a different subject, or at least how to find it. Some areas that a trust officer is expected to know include the stock market; estate and inheritance tax; trust law; real estate, including apartments, homes, commercial property, leases, insurance, ranches, and farms; life insurance; international and commercial banking; the local, national, and international economy; money markets; estate planning; business entities, including sole proprietorships, general and limited partnerships, and corporations; current events; business law; and accounting practices.

While a trust officer is not expected to be superman—or superwoman—a broad educational background is desirable. On top of that, good human relations skills are critical. The trust officer must be capable of dealing with the family and personal problems that arise. With the loss of the major wage earner, many families find their income sharply reduced and must rely on the trust officer's experience in planning a new household budget so the family can live within its income. Trust officers are often faced with counseling beneficiaries of different trusts to match their living requirements to the financial capability of the trust. Members of a family with a trust producing income of $50,000 a year obviously have different alternatives available than a family with a trust producing only $10,000 of annual income. Expenditures that are reasonable in the former situation may be extravagant in the latter. The trust officer must resist the temptation to apply his or her own standard of living to the situation and, instead, review each case on the merits of the trust resources and the needs of the family.

Educational plans must often be developed for young beneficiaries and on occasion altered midstream. Expensive schools and colleges that may have been planned while the parent was alive, may be entirely unaffordable after the parent's unexpected death. In such instances, the family must be counseled to make plans that provide an education for the children within the family's means. Trust officers are also called to counsel minor beneficiaries in choosing a vocation. Frequently, the trust officer is the only person qualified to stand in place of a deceased parent and must counsel a minor beneficiary as he or she believes the parent would have counseled the child.

Trust officers should be cautious in volunteering unsolicited personal advice or service. Yet, because family problems do arise and there is an element of control over the family's means of support, the trust officer is often looked to for personal advice and assistance.

## GUARDIANSHIPS

A **guardianship**, called a conservatorship in some states, is a court-appointed arrangement for the financial protection of the estate of an incapacitated person. Because state statutes vary markedly in their definition of guardianship and conservatorship, confusion abounds in the use of these terms. In this text, guardianship is used. However, trust officers should be familiar with the terminology that is appropriate to his or her state.

The term "guardianship of the estate" is sometimes used to distinguish the guardian's role as protector of property from "guardianship of the person," in which the main focus is the individual's physical protection and well-being. Usually, bank trust departments prefer to accept only appointments as guardians of the estate.

Guardianships are established for individuals who are considered legally incapacitated and who

- own property not otherwise protected

- have business affairs that are jeopardized by their incapacity

- need funds for support or education, and protection is necessary to provide those funds

- require funds for support or for support of their dependents

The most common instances of legal incapacity are minors and adults who are incapacitated by medical causes or senility. Other forms of adult incapacity include mental illness, addiction to drugs or alcohol, confinement, detention by a foreign power, or disappearance.

### Voluntary Versus Involuntary Guardianship

A guardianship may be either voluntary or involuntary. When the process is voluntary, a person concerned about his or her own incapacity may petition the court to establish a guardianship. In this instance, no hearing is necessary, and the court will appoint the guardian requested in the petition.

Several terms may be used to describe an individual subject to a guardianship account, but "protected person" is most common. In some states, the title to the guardianship property passes to the guardian, which, in effect, results in a court-appointed trust relationship. In other states, the title to the property remains with the protected person, but is subject to the guardianship proceeding. This parallels a court-appointed agency. In either case, administration is the same.

Most state statutes require the appointment of a guardian for incapacitated persons. If no one comes forward to become a guardian, the statute indicates an order of preference among prospective guardians. In all states, a trust institution by its charter or by statute is authorized to act as a guardian. The trust institution is appointed guardian by the court and is generally subject to continuing supervision by the court.

When individuals, such as a relative or family friend, have been appointed as guardians, their inexperience and mismanagement frequently have resulted in a loss of some or all of the guardianship property. Thus there is a growing tendency in many jurisdictions for the courts to appoint trust institutions to serve as guardians. The courts have found trust institutions to be experienced and reliable in performing their legal guardianship duties.

### Establishing a Guardianship

To establish a guardianship, an interested person—a relative, a dependent, or even a creditor—of the incapacitated person must petition the court to appoint a guardian. The protected person and other interested persons are notified of the guardianship hearing, which is held to determine if the guardianship is really necessary. Usually, such hearings are uneventful and the guardian is subsequently appointed. Once the court has determined the necessity of a guardianship, an order is entered and a document, the **letter of guardianship,** is issued. This document is the guardian's authority to act on behalf of the protected person.

### Duties of a Guardian

A guardian's role is an interesting hybrid that combines the duties of a personal representative and those of a trustee. In many respects, the duties of a guardianship are like those of trust administration, a topic that was covered earlier in this chapter. The guardian's first responsibility is to gather the assets of the protected person. Ownership of property is transferred to the name of the guardian or the guardian's nominee. An inventory of the guardianship property should be filed with the court, usually not more than 60 or 90 days from the date of the guardian's appointment.

*Managing the property.* After gathering the property, the next responsibility is to manage the property in the best interests of the protected person. The guardian is responsible not only for the care, safeguarding, and conserving of the property, but also for making it reasonably productive and profitable. Guardians are usually conservative in their investment approach because the court exercises strict supervision over the investments. There are two overriding concerns to the investment philosophy of a guardian. The first is to meet the needs of the protected person. The second objective is to conserve the assets subject to the guardianship. The guardian should follow the most conservative investment path that will accomplish these two objectives.

*Making an accounting.* The next major responsibility of the guardian is to make an accounting periodically to the court and provide copies to the court's list of interested parties. In most states, accountings are required annually, usually within 30 days from the anniversary date of the guardian's appointment. If the guardianship is terminating, the accounting is referred to as the **final accounting.**

The accounting process is the means by which the court supervises the performance of the guardian, and interested persons are informed of the condition of the guardianship estate. The accounting usually follows a prescribed form. First, the property available at the beginning of the accounting period is itemized. All receipts to the property are listed, followed by a list of all disbursements made to or for the benefit of the protected person. Any capital changes to the assets of the guardianship are noted, and a complete summary of the assets that remain at the end of the accounting period is provided. These figures are usually accompanied by a narrative discussion that briefly explains the routine matters of the accounting and may deal in more detail with some intricate matter such as involved sales or exchange of assets. Also any litigation entered into on behalf of the protected person is included in the narrative.

*Terminating and distributing the property.* The guardian's final responsibility is to terminate the guardianship and distribute the property at the appropriate time. Generally, two events terminate a guardianship.

In the event that the protected person dies, the guardianship immediately terminates and the assets are distributed to the personal representative of the estate of the deceased protected person.

The other event that terminates a guardianship occurs when the incapacity affecting the protected person is resolved. If the guardianship was based on the ward's lack of legal age, it will terminate when the ward reaches the age of majority—18 in most states. As long as no other forms of legal incapacity exist, the guardianship is terminated and distributed to the ward regardless of his or her financial responsibility at the time. This factor is often cited as a major reason for couples with children to have a will in which a guardian of the person is nominated and a testamentary trust established for the children's protection.

If the ward had suffered an incapacitating stroke and then made a medical recovery, this incapacity has been resolved. Other examples include an alcoholic who has become rehabilitated or a prisoner who has been freed after serving his or her sentence. A voluntary guardianship may be terminated the same way it was set up—by the protected person petitioning the court to terminate.

## SUMMARY

The subject of this chapter is personal trusts and guardianships. A trust is essentially a business and personal relationship through which one party assumes ownership of property and a separate party enjoys the benefits of that property.

There are several kinds of trusts: active, passive, and standby trusts; revocable and irrevocable trusts; and living and testamentary trusts. With an active trust, the trustee is required to perform some duty; with a passive trust, the trustee serves only as a titleholder. A standby trust falls between the two—the trustee has no responsibility in the management of the property until some event occurs such as the trustor dies or is incapacitated. Revocable and irrevocable trusts are, as their names suggest, trusts in which the trustor has reserved the power in the former, or given up the power in the latter, to revoke the account at any time. The majority of trusts administered by trust departments are either living or testamentary trusts. A living trust is created by a contract between a living individual and an individual trustee or trust institution. A testamentary trust is created by a provision in a decedent's will.

Regardless of the type of trust, however, almost all have five basic elements: a trustor, a trustee, a beneficiary, property, and a trust agreement. Most trusts are created to provide the trustor and beneficiaries with professional property management and investment service, alleviate concern over future incapacity, avoid probate, obtain tax savings, provide financial protection for family members, or hold property as a separate estate.

To properly set up and administer a trust estate, the trust officer must first determine the duration of the trust. How long a trust *may* continue is limited by the rule against perpetuities, which varies from state to state but typically encompasses the lifetimes of the individuals involved plus 21 years and the gestation period. How long a trust *should* continue is governed by the type of trust and the reason it was established. Another important consideration is the powers of the trustee, which, if not obtained directly from state statute, should be clearly granted in the trust agreement. Without the power to manage investments, manage property, administer the estate, assess fees for services, change locations, and resign, the bank may be impeded in acting in the best interests of all concerned. The dispositive and spendthrift provisions are other important components of a trust agreement. The dispositive provisions relate to the disposition of income earned by the trust estate and the eventual distribution of trust assets or principal. Spendthrift provisions guard against the improper use of trust assets by a beneficiary.

The professional administration of a personal trust requires the trust officer to master both business and personal aspects. On the business side, the administration of personal accounts includes establishing the account, managing the property, complying with the trust terms, and recordkeeping. The personal aspects of trust administration may include establishing a rapport with the trustor or the beneficiaries and, on occasion, financial, emotional, or educational counseling.

The chapter concluded with an examination of guardianships. A guardianship is a court-appointed arrangement to protect the estate of an individual who is incapacitated or not of legal age. A guardian's role is a combination of the roles of trustee and personal representative. In a guardianship, property must be managed in the best interests of the protected person. An annual accounting must be made, and the guardianship must be ended and the property distributed at the appropriate time. Death, coming of age, and medical recovery are common reasons for a guardianship to end. In the case of a voluntary guardianship, the protected person may petition the court to end the arrangement.

### QUESTIONS FOR REVIEW

1.  What are some of the basic differences between a trust and an agency relationship?

2. Define the terms trustee, trustor, and beneficiary. In a trust agreement, can a person be named as both a trustor and a beneficiary? Why?

3. What would you recommend to a client who wishes to avoid his or her estate going through probate? What arguments could you offer to a young, single professional who is not entirely convinced about the need to create a living trust?

4. What is the rule against perpetuities? Should all trusts be created for the maximum period of time allowed by the rule against perpetuities? Why?

5. Why is it generally in the trustor's best interest if there are few limitations imposed on the bank's (acting as trustee) powers to manage investments and property?

6. What provision might be inserted into a trust agreement if the beneficiary is predisposed toward excessive gambling?

7. What is entailed in establishing and managing trust property? Is the process computerized in any way at your bank?

8. Briefly explain the duties of a guardian. What events automatically terminate an involuntary guardianship?

9. Why should young adults with minor children have a will?

*7* Estate Settlement

## INTRODUCTION

This chapter examines yet another type of personal fiduciary service that banks provide, that of settling an estate following the death of a client. We will first consider the principal ways estates are settled under probate and introduce several important terms regarding estate settlement. Next, the chapter discusses how estates are settled with and without a will and the implications of both for the beneficiaries. Finally, each of the major steps in estate settlement—from opening the estate to paying claims, settling taxes, and distributing the assets—is examined.

## THE BANK'S ROLE IN PROBATE

In estate settlement, the modern and preferred legal term applied to the bank's role is **personal representative.** As personal representative, the bank acts in the capacity of an **executor,** a personal representative named in a will to settle the estate, or as an **administrator,** a personal representative appointed by a court to settle the estate of a person who died intestate or whose will did not name an executor who was able to serve. In some states the traditional term executor or administrator is still used in place of personal representative.

In settling an estate, the bank goes through a series of legal steps, from the admission of the will to the court to the final distribution of the assets to the estate beneficiaries. This process of transferring assets from the decedent's name to the names of his or her heirs and beneficiaries is referred to in the United States as **probate,** which in a legal sense means proof. In other words, the court must have proof that the will, if any, is valid and that the estate is in order (with all taxes and claims settled) before the heirs and beneficiaries receive any of the estate property.

Ways of settling estates that do not involve probate are not considered in this chapter. Such estates will be settled outside of the probate courts when all of an individual's assets are held in a form of joint ownership that conveys survivorship rights, such as a joint tenancy or tenancy by the entirety. As the surviving party is entitled to full ownership of the property involved, there are no assets to probate. Probate is also avoided when an individual dies with a trust that provides for control of all assets in the trust for the benefit of specific individuals other than the beneficiaries of the trustor's estate. In such a trust, ownership is in the name of the trust and not the individual, who thus avoids the need for probate.

Should probate be avoided? There is no definitive answer. Several factors are involved, including an individual's desire for control over his or her assets throughout life. Probate normally will be avoided if the estate is small, and the estate can be settled without a court proceeding under a state's Small Estates Act.

Banks are ideally suited to serve in the capacity as personal representative of an estate. Trust departments are staffed with experts to handle the complex administrative and legal issues that often arise. Trust departments are objective—not taking sides when there are differences of opinion among beneficiaries. Trust departments can commit the time and resources to see that all tasks are accomplished within legal time constraints. And trust departments are reliable.

As an example of the role a bank and its trust officers play in the probate process, let's consider the following case.

### Customer Profile: A Probated Will

Bill Harley, a highly successful insurance executive, suddenly died of a heart attack at age 57, leaving his wife, Ann, and their twin daughters, Kim and Karen, aged 17. With the girls about to start on their college careers, Ann had recently received her real estate broker's license and works for a local firm in their small town. Bill's sudden death has left the family quite bewildered and apprehensive about the future. The family attorney, Jim Willis, has arranged for the family to meet in his office to discuss the will and to meet the trust officer, Terry Trowbridge, from their bank. The bank has been nominated personal representative or executor and has asked Jim to represent it, as he had drawn up the original will.

At the meeting in the attorney's office, Terry advises the family that Bill Harley had prudently kept his original will with the bank and that it was signed and witnessed. He had delivered the will to Jim, who filed it with the local probate court.

After these introductory remarks, Jim, Terry, and the family go over the will. The attorney advises them that almost the entire estate will be distributed to the bank as testamentary trustee for the benefit of the family, except for two $10,000 cash bequests to the daughters. Terry warns Ann and the girls that he does not yet know the size and nature of the estate assets, but that probate and the settlement of the estate should take 8 to 12 months, and several important legal requirements must be met before the court will allow distribution to the testamentary trust.

First, the will must be entered into probate and the bank appointed as personal representative. Then the personal representative has to prepare and file an inventory of assets with the court; notify the heirs and beneficiaries; publish public notices of Bill's death for the benefit of creditors; pay all taxes, justifiable claims, and administrative expenses; and make a final, formal accounting to the court. When these steps have been completed, Kim and Karen—provided that they are 18 years old—will receive their specific cash bequests and the estate will be distributed to the testamentary trust established in the will.

Terry promises to keep Ann informed throughout the estate settlement and be available to answer any questions or help with any difficulties that might arise. Ann has already had some difficulty because the state Department of Revenue placed a freeze on the joint savings account that she and Bill had. The bank has been unable to release the money she needs to pay the girls' tuition for the fall semester. Upon hearing this news, Terry calls the state revenue department and has them release the savings account and all other accounts so that Ann can use them. Since the bank will be acting as personal representative in settling the estate, the revenue department can release the account right away on the strength of the bank's reliability. As the meeting draws to a close, Terry asks Ann and Jim to help him find Bill's records to prepare a detailed inventory of assets.

The Harley family's situation and its needs are typical. As the example showed, Terry Trowbridge, the trust officer, has begun to help the Harley family get through the estate settlement period as quickly, painlessly, and economically as possible.

## TESTATE SUCCESSION: THE WILL

When a deceased person (typically referred to in legal circles as the decedent) has made and left a valid will, he or she is considered to have died **testate;** if there is no will, he or she died intestate. A will is defined as a legally enforceable declaration, usually in writing, of the wishes of the testator (the person making the will) about matters to be attended to after his or her death, particularly in regard to the disposition of property. A will is revocable or amendable by a **codicil,** a legal amendment, until the testator's death.

Although some states recognize oral as well as handwritten wills, to ensure that any will is valid in any state, a client is well advised to have a will in writing and properly witnessed under the supervision of an attorney. It should be signed and attested to by two or three witnesses called **attesting witnesses.** Trust department officers and employees often act as attesting witnesses for their bank's clients.

## Testamentary Capacity

The person making the will should have **testamentary capacity**—that is, he or she should be 18 years of age or older and be of sound mind. State laws vary about what constitutes acceptable testamentary capacity, but in general, at the time a will is executed, a testator should be able to

- recall the nature and extent of his or her property

- know and remember the persons who would normally inherit the property

- understand the manner in which the will that is executed will distribute property among the beneficiaries

- understand the act that is being made and the implications of that act

The alleged lack of testamentary capacity and the exertion of undue influence on a testator are the most common grounds to contest a will by those who feel that the decedent unjustly forgot them. Some companies now offer prospective testators the unique service of recording their last will and testament on video tape to help refute any possible allegations of lack of testamentary capacity.

## The Contents of a Will

Exhibit 7.1 shows a typical will. A discussion of its various parts, paragraph by paragraph, follows.

*Introductory paragraph.* Language in the introductory paragraph of the will normally identifies the testator by name and states that previous wills are revoked. This revocation is redundant, however, since the execution of a new will automatically revokes any previous will. If a person is executing a new will, unless otherwise advised by his or her attorney, that person should destroy

EXHIBIT 7.1   Sample Will

## LAST WILL AND TESTAMENT
## OF MARY JOHNSON

I, MARY JOHNSON, of Portland, County of Multnomah, State of Oregon, do hereby make, publish, and declare this to be my Last Will and Testament, and revoke all Wills and Codicils heretofore made by me.

### I

I direct my personal representative to pay from my estate all my just debts and expenses of my last illness and funeral and final interment and the expenses of administration of my estate.

### II

I direct my personal representative to pay from my estate all inheritance, estate, transfer, and succession taxes which become payable by reason of my death and authorize it to contest or compromise any claims for such taxes. I further direct that all such taxes shall be paid without apportionment thereof and without withholding or collecting any part thereof from any beneficiary under my Will or under any life insurance of mine which may be subject to such tax or from the surviving owner of any property owned jointly with me, it being my intention that all such taxes shall be paid from my estate as an expense of administration.

### III

I declare that I am a widow; my husband, EDWARD JOHNSON, having died October 12, 1957. I have no children or lineal descendants.

### IV

I give and bequeath to my niece, SALLY JOHNSON, if she survives me the following:

1. My diamond ring with gold setting
2. My black fur seal coat
3. $10,000 in cash

### V

I give, devise, and bequeath all of the rest, residue, and remainder of my estate to my brother, JOHN JONES.

Page 1—LAST WILL AND TESTAMENT of MARY JOHNSON

EXHIBIT 7.1 continued

Should my said brother predecease me, then I leave all of my said residuary estate to my nieces and nephews, to be divided among them equally per capita and not per stirpes.* Should any of said nieces and nephews predecease me, his or her share shall not descend to his or her heirs but shall be divided among my nieces and nephews who do survive me.

VI

I nominate and appoint the XYZ BANK OF OREGON, a national banking association, as personal representative of this my Last Will and Testament. My personal representative shall have full power without requirement of any order of court to continue, operate, discontinue, or wind up any business, partnership, or other contract or transaction in which I may be interested at the time of my death; to borrow money as occasion may require; to compromise, settle, or waive any claim due to or by my estate, and to sell for cash or on credit at public or private sale, assign, transfer, convey, lease, or mortgage any real or personal property belonging to my estate, without petition to, or license or leave of court, and without issuance of notice or citation and without reporting to any court or securing from any court any order authorizing or confirming any such sale, or other disposition.

IN WITNESS WHEREOF I have hereunto set my hand to this, my Last Will and Testament, this 14th day of January, 1967.

/s/ MARY JOHNSON

The foregoing instrument was, on the date it bears, signed, published, and declared by MARY JOHNSON to be her Last Will and Testament in our presence who at her request and in her presence and in the presence of each other, all being present at the same time have hereunto subscribed our names as witnesses.

/s/ RICHARD PETERSON
Residing at: 1234 "A" Avenue
Portland, Oregon 97201

/s/ GERRY SMITH
Residing at: 5678 "B" Avenue
Portland, Oregon 97201

Page 2—LAST WILL AND TESTAMENT of MARY JOHNSON

*stirpes—essentially, position in the family

---

previous wills to avoid confusion. This opening paragraph also usually affirms that the testator is of sound mind. As the individual is presumed to have testamentary capacity, this statement is unnecessary, but traditional.

*Section I.* This section contains a charge to the personal representative to pay debts. This, too, is unnecessary since state probate laws usually require that debts be paid. In some states, a personal representative may only pay a set amount toward funeral expenses unless directed otherwise in the will.

*Section II*. In section II, the discussion of payment of estate and inheritance taxes is particularly important because language in this paragraph states that those taxes will not be apportioned among the recipients of the taxed property. This will has what is often referred to as a tax clause, which means that all estate and inheritance taxes are paid from the residue of the estate. The individual parties receiving property—whether joint property or property subject to the will—do not pay the taxes. The absence of this clause would have required, for example, Terry Trowbridge to withhold the proportioned amount of taxes from Kim and Karen Harley's specific cash bequests. Thus they would not have received their full $10,000 each. The tax clause is often overlooked by attorneys and, if the testator did not intend the beneficiaries to pay estate taxes, the results can cause unnecessary unhappiness when the final distribution is made.

*Section III*. This section makes it clear that the testator, Mary Johnson, is a widow with no children or grandchildren.

*Section IV*. In section IV, a typical specific bequest of various items of miscellaneous personal property is made to Sally Johnson, who also receives a general cash bequest of $10,000. If a testator has definite ideas regarding the disposition of his or her furniture, furnishings, and equipment, that disposition is best made known in the will, item by item. Considerable grief and family strife arise from disputes over tangible property in estate settlements. The sentimental value that family and close friends place on these items, in addition to the intrinsic value, can cause emotional trauma. The will is the appropriate place to thoroughly define the disposition of these items.

*Section V*. Language in section V disposes of the residuary estate—the estate remaining after all claims, administrative expenses, taxes, and specific cash bequests have been deducted. Mrs. Johnson's brother, John Jones, is the recipient of the estate that is left after the bills are paid and the other beneficiaries have inherited their specific bequests. The residuary estate, the tangible bequest, and the cash bequest were made to specific individuals. In some cases, however, it may be preferable for the testator to make specific or residuary bequests to a trustee for the benefit of one or more of the distributees. For example, rather than leaving the entire residuary estate to a spendthrift son, it could be left to the bank trust department as trustee for the benefit of that son. The will would then create a testamentary trust that would require additional language to incorporate the trustee's duties and powers.

*Section VI*. This section of the will defines the personal representative's powers. In many states, this is not necessary since state probate laws delineate the powers of the personal representative. Normally, in the final section the personal representative—the executor—is appointed.

## Probate Requirements

When the testator dies and the will is admitted to probate, the attesting witnesses traditionally were required to sign affidavits affirming the proper execution of the will. This requirement sometimes caused considerable delay in initiating probate proceedings if the attesting witnesses could not be found. Modern probate procedures in some states allow the attesting witnesses to sign an affidavit when the will is drawn stating that the will has been properly executed. However, other states only require an affidavit if the will is challenged.

Further delay in settling the estate may result if the original will cannot be found at the decedent's death. The original will, with signatures of the testator and the witnesses, is important because it has to be filed with the court. Without the original will, substantial red tape hampers getting a copy accepted by the court.

If a bank trust department is named as personal representative, the best place to keep the original will is in the bank's vault. Most bank trust departments have facilities for safeguarding wills, and readily do so at no charge. They will also provide the testator with a receipt for that document. Bank safe deposit boxes are also good storage places. However, at the death of the testator, they may be frozen by the state. Having the will filed with the trust department is preferable so that the trust officers can quickly arrange to have it presented to probate court, as in the Bill Harley situation.

Before concluding this discussion of wills, it is important to note that a testator should have an attorney—not a bank trust department—draw up his or her will. Most state bar associations would deem it "practicing law" if a bank were to draw up a will or trust agreement. In the Harley case it should be noted that Jim Willis was asked to represent the bank as personal representative. He did so not only because he was the family attorney, but because he drew up Bill Harley's will. Bank trust departments often engage the services of the attorney who drew the will. The testator is assumed to have had that intention by asking the attorney to arrange the estate plan.

## INTESTATE SUCCESSION: WITHOUT A WILL

When someone dies intestate, there is no will. In such cases, the state in which the decedent is domiciled at his or her death then proceeds to apply the intestate succession law of the state's probate code. When a person's property passes under that law, the disposition of those assets often differs from what the decedent would have wanted. For instance, in many states if Bill Harley had died intestate, one-half of his estate would have been distributed to his wife, and one-quarter of his estate would have been distributed to each of his daughters. This would have presented some serious problems to Ann Harley, because she would have had only half of Bill's estate available to her directly. The remaining half would be administered under a court-supervised guardianship (or conservatorship), as both Kim and Karen are minors. Such a conservatorship would mandate distribution when the child reaches the age of majority, which is age 18 in most states.

Trust officers should review the intestate succession section of their state's probate law to determine how property is passed to those who survive the decedent. Generally, the right to receive property from a decedent under intestate succession depends on whether there is a surviving spouse or heir. An heir is a person directly related by blood, such as a natural child, parent, brother, sister, or in many states, legally adopted child. A person dying intestate and without any surviving spouse or heir will have his or her property **escheat** (revert) to the state of residence. Considering these possible outcomes of dying intestate, the importance of having a will is apparent.

Having a will is especially important for young couples with children. A will can indicate one's choice of guardian for the children and can establish a trust for their benefit.

## STEPS IN ESTATE SETTLEMENT

Let's now turn to the estate settlement process. The major steps include

- opening the estate
- collecting and appraising the assets for inventory
- developing a budget and paying claims
- settling all income, inheritance, and estate taxes
- making a final accounting to the court
- distributing the assets

### Opening the Estate

In opening an estate, several steps are taken. First, a review of the decedent's property is made. Then the original will is secured and a personal representative is appointed. When these tasks are complete, notices are sent to heirs, legatees, and interested persons.

#### *Reviewing the Decedent's Property*

Whether the decedent died testate or intestate, the estate is subject to state probate laws and will be administered through the county probate court having jurisdiction. As noted previously, property passes without probate if it is held jointly with right of survivorship or is in trust at the time the decedent dies, at which time the terms of the trust determine the disposition. Therefore, the initial step in opening an estate is to review what is owned in the decedent's sole name.

In the Harley case, if Bill had died and his assets were owned jointly with right of survivorship with Ann, his will would have had no effect. Bill and Ann did maintain a joint savings account that became immediately available to Ann for the family expenses during probate. As the bank was nominated personal representative, Terry Trowbridge was able to release the funds in the account from the freeze imposed by the state revenue department. Since the bank is responsible for paying income and inheritance taxes, the revenue department is assured that whatever is owed will be paid.

### Securing the Original Will

The second step in opening an estate is securing the will. Without an original will, it is considerably more difficult to admit the will to probate. Jim Willis, Bill Harley's attorney, was wise in depositing the will with the bank so that it could be presented promptly to the probate court.

### Appointment of a Personal Representative

With the original will available, Jim Willis can prepare the formal petition for appointment of the personal representative. This petition provides the probate court with basic information concerning the decedent, including name and address, Social Security number, the probable value of the estate, the names of heirs and legatees, the name of the attorney representing the estate, and the name of the personal representative nominated in the will. Then the attorney presents the petition, the will, and the affidavit of attesting witnesses to the court, requesting that the personal representative be appointed and that a certificate of authority to settle the estate be issued to the representative. This certificate is referred to as a **letter testamentary.**

### Notice to Heirs and Legatees

In most states, probate laws require that a formal notice be sent to all of the decedent's heirs and legatees, or distributees. This requirement serves to protect any heirs not in close proximity to the decedent from improper omission when the property in the will is disbursed. A **legatee** is a person who is actually named or remembered in the decedent's will, in contrast with heirs who are blood relatives or next-of-kin. The personal representative can use this occasion to mail a copy of the decedent's will or, if the legatee is to receive only a specific bequest, to quote that section of the will in the covering letter. Once

EXHIBIT 7.2   Sample Notice to Interested Persons

**Estate of MARY JOHNSON aka MARIE JOHNSON**
**NOTICE TO INTERESTED PERSONS**
**No. E-000**

Notice: The Circuit Court of the State of Oregon for the County of Multnomah, has appointed the undersigned personal representative of the Estate of MARY JOHNSON, aka MARIE JOHNSON, deceased. All persons having claims against said estate are required to present the same, with proper vouchers to the personal representative at 111 Main Street, Anytown, USA within four months from the date of first publication of this notice as stated below, or they may be barred. All persons whose rights may be affected by this proceeding may obtain additional information from the records of the court, the personal representative or the attorney for the personal representative.

Dated and first published August 4, 1988.

The National Bank, Attn. Jim Adams, Personal Representative, 111 Main Street, Anytown, USA.

Attorney for the Personal Representative: Joseph Smith, P.O. Box 121, Anytown, USA.

(Aug. 4, 11, 18, 1988)

---

the notice is sent, an affidavit of mailing that notice is filed with the probate court.

### Notice to Interested Persons

This notice, sometimes called the notice to creditors, is published in the local newspaper in the jurisdiction where the decedent died. The notice formally advises those with claims against the decedent's estate to present their claims within the expiration date stated in the notice. Normally, the expiration date is 4 to 6 months after publication of the first notice. A sample notice is presented as exhibit 7.2.

Once the will has been admitted to probate, the personal representative appointed, and the appropriate notices made, the personal representative can then proceed with the trust department's work of settling the estate.

## The Inventory: Collecting and Appraising Assets

In the process of settling an estate, the personal representative must meet several important deadlines. The first of these requires that the personal representative file an inventory with the probate court. In most states, this deadline must be satisfied within 60 days of the personal representative's appointment. The personal representative must meticulously and thoroughly gather all assets the decedent owned. Each asset is then entered in the personal representative's books and listed at its exact date-of-death value—as if the decedent had actually cashed in all the assets on that date. For instance, if a decedent owned a real estate contract, the value of that contract would be the same as if he or she had been paid the principal value of that contract plus accrued interest to the date of death. Similarly, the value of the decedent's stocks would be the market value on the date of death plus the accrued dividends to which he or she was entitled, but had not yet received.

In marshaling the assets of a recently deceased person, the personal representative must make a thorough search of the individual's safe deposit boxes and personal records. A discussion with the people who knew the decedent's business affairs is also imperative. Using the Bill Harley case as an example, Terry Trowbridge would make arrangements with Jim Willis and Ann Harley to inventory Bill's safe deposit box. He would also obtain as much information as possible for Jim Willis about Bill's assets and ask for Ann's help in searching the business records to make certain that all assets were discovered and properly inventoried. Although Terry Trowbridge's bank has the facilities for valuing the stocks and bonds, Terry might find that he would need to hire an appraiser to determine the value of the family's miscellaneous personal property, such as jewelry and automobiles. In addition, Terry would arrange for an appraisal of the insurance agency that Bill and his partner, Fred Tibbits, owned.

Once a personal representative has identified and valued all the assets subject to probate, the formal inventory can be prepared. A sample of a completed inventory filed with a probate court is shown in exhibit 7.3. Again, note that exact valuations were made for all assets to the date of Mary Johnson's death.

When appointed, the personal representative assumes responsibility for the security of all assets in the estate. Therefore, he or she must move immediately to identify the assets and store them as quickly as possible to ensure that they are adequately safeguarded and insured. Such items as jewelry, for instance, should be secured in the bank's vault. Real estate must be properly insured against fire and liability. If the bank trust department fails to insure a residence adequately, the bank will have to pay for any loss incurred if the property were destroyed by fire.

## Budget and Policy Considerations

Once the assets in the estate have been identified and recorded on the trust department's books, the trust officer is able to determine how much cash is necessary to settle the estate. The officer also has to make a policy decision

EXHIBIT 7.3  Sample Inventory

**THE NATIONAL BANK OF ANYTOWN**
**PERSONAL REPRESENTATIVE OF THE ESTATE OF**
**MARY JOHNSON**—Deceased
**(trust account number)**

INVENTORY

**Cash:**

Checking Account No. 050-0073-013,
The National Bank

| | | | |
|---|---|---|---|
| Balance: | $1,889.99 | | |
| Less outstanding checks: | $1,293.08 | $ | 596.91 |

Savings Account No. 9-107121-7,

| | | | |
|---|---|---|---|
| The Savings and Loan Association | | $ | 58.97 |
| | Accrued interest | $ | .20 |

**Bonds:**

$800 United Airlines 4¼%
Subordinated Debenture, dtd.
3/21/66, due 7/1/92, Ctf. No. X10
@ $500, and Nos. C10924/5/6 @
$100 each, all reg. n/o Mary

| | | | |
|---|---|---|---|
| Johnson (@ $47.75) | | $ | 382.00 |
| | Accrued interest | $ | 8.03 |

**Stocks:**

2 Shs. AT&T Company $4.00
Convertible Preferred Shares,
Ctf. No. 01X, reg. n/o Mary

| | | | |
|---|---|---|---|
| Johnson (@ $50.6875) | | $ | 101.38 |
| | Accrued dividend | $ | 2.00 |

36 Shs. AT&T Company, Capital
Stock, Par $33⅓, Ctf. No. 001X @
8 Shs. No. X100 @ 10 Shs., and
No. 1X0X @ 18 Shs., all reg. n/o

| | | | |
|---|---|---|---|
| Mary Johnson (@ $46.0625) | | $ | 1,658.25 |
| | Accrued dividend | $ | 30.60 |

**Real Estate Contract:**

$20,000 contract between Mary
Johnson as seller and William Jones
as purchaser, dtd. 7/12/72, payable
$155/mo., including 8% int., on 12th
each month, covering property
described as follows:

EXHIBIT 7.3 continued

Lot 8, Block 7, Any Addition to
Anyplace, Anytown, USA.
Balance of $14,320 with
interest paid to 2/16/84          $14,320.00

Accrued interest    $    65.28

**Real Estate:**
Interest in residence located at 6825
   S.W. Highway, Anytown, USA,
   legally described as:

     Lots 6 and 7, Block 3, View
     Addition, in the City of X,
     County of Y, State of Z.

Full value of Parcel $70,000          $70,000.00

**Miscellaneous Personal Property:**
1979 Cadillac Coup de Ville
   automobile, serial no. 01256.          $ 8,421.00

Miscellaneous household furniture,
   furnishings, and equipment located
   in decedent's residence.          $ 4,201.00

TOTAL      $99,845.62

---

about which, if any, assets should be sold to raise the necessary amount of cash. To do these tasks effectively, the trust officer should prepare a formal estimate of cash requirements while preparing the estate inventory.

It is important to remember, however, that, during the course of settling the estate, the personal representative's only duty is to safeguard the assets subject to probate until they can be passed to the distributees. In most states, the personal representative has the additional power to sell assets to pay claims, taxes, and administrative expenses. No provision exists, though, to allow the personal representative to invest in any additional assets during the probate period (except in risk-free instruments—like U.S. Treasury obligations—as approved by that state's probate law).

If the estate is sizable and liquid (that is, with considerable cash assets), the personal representative should pay as soon as they are presented all legitimate claims, expenses of the last illness and the funeral, and any initial administrative expenses.

Because the rules regarding payment of claims differ among states, all trust officers should become familiar with their state laws. Typically, if a claim is submitted to a personal representative and not acted on within 60 days, it is allowed automatically. Thus, a personal representative must move quickly to pay or deny the claims.

Normally, the large expenses of a typical estate are the estate and inheritance taxes, cash bequests, and the compensation of the personal representative and the attorney for the estate. The typical budget shown in exhibit 7.4 presents all costs in administering the estate and indicates when those expenses will probably occur.

The Office of the Comptroller of the Currency requires that bank trust departments under its regulatory jurisdiction make a formal review of the assets contained in each new estate within 60 days of the bank's appointment as personal representative. The budgeting process helps the bank's trust officer to review the cash needs of the estate with the trust management committee and any plans for raising cash if the estate is not liquid. The process is advantageous to the client because the committee members formally examine the account and can challenge the proposed decisions.

Occasionally, the estate may be insolvent—that is, the claims may exceed the value of the estate. In this instance, the state's probate laws specify the priority for paying claims, administrative expenses, and, perhaps, support to the family.

Most state probate laws normally permit family allowances to ensure that the immediate family is not left destitute during probate. The surviving spouse or minor children usually submit a petition to the court outlining their own assets and needs for support. If support is granted, the probate court allows it only for the amount of time authorized by local probate law.

## Settling All Tax Obligations

After it has been determined how much cash is necessary to settle the estate and which, if any, assets should be sold to pay claims, the next step is to settle all tax obligations—income taxes and estate and inheritance taxes.

### Income Taxes

Returning to the Harley case, one of Terry Trowbridge's duties will be to file a final income tax return if the Harleys had been filing jointly. After that filing, the estate will file income tax returns as a separate tax entity, reporting the income earned during the probate period.

The taxes levied during probate are referred to as **fiduciary income taxes** and the rules that apply to them are unique and complex. An adequately staffed

EXHIBIT 7.4   Sample Estate Budget

## ESTATE BUDGET

Estate of ___Joseph Smith_____ , deceased   No. (trust account number)

| | |
|---|---|
| Cash legacies | $ ___41,400___ |
| Estimated unpaid claims, loans, etc. | ___6,000___ |
| Estimated executor's fee | ___7,400___ |
| Estimated attorney's fee | ___8,200___ |
| Family allowance—_____ months | ___0___ |
| Estimated federal estate tax | ___38,000___ |
| Estimated Oregon inheritance tax | ___24,080___ |
| Estimated federal income tax to date of death | ___1,100___ |
| Estimated Oregon income tax to date of death | ___500___ |
| Estimated federal income tax during probate | ___2,000___ |
| Estimated Oregon income tax during probate | ___600___ |
| Estimated real estate taxes | ___700___ |
| Misc. costs of administration (publications, appraiser's fees, filing fees, etc.) | ___350___ |
| Other cash requirements (describe) | ___0___ |
| Total estimated cash requirements | $ ___130,330___ |
| Cash on hand | $ ___123,750___ |
| Estimated income—_12_ months (check testamentary trust terms for distribution to income beneficiaries) | $ ___15,000___ |
| Total estimated available cash | $ ___138,750___ |
| Balance to be raised | $ ___0___ |

Approximate dates cash will be needed

| | | | |
|---|---|---|---|
| ___Immediately___ | , 1988 | $ | ___7,950___ |
| ___Nov. 15___ | , 1988 | $ | ___65,380___ |
| ___Jan. 15___ | , 1989 | $ | ___15,600___ |
| ___Feb. 1___ | , 1989 | $ | ___41,400___ |
| _____ | , 19 | $ | _____ |
| _____ | , 19 | $ | _____ |
| | TOTAL | $ | ___130,330___ |

Remarks: (Use reverse side tumble sheet.)

Date ___August 3___ , __1988__.          Prepared by ___Trust Officer_____

897T   8/68

trust department usually has experts in fiduciary taxation that can save money in the estate settlement process. These tax experts immediately begin postmortem tax planning to ensure that the estate and its beneficiaries pay the least amount of income tax. The Internal Revenue Service (IRS) and perhaps the state Department of Revenue perform an audit of the last 3 years' income tax returns before they allow the personal representative to make a final distribution of the assets.

*Estate and Inheritance Taxes*

The major delay involved in settling an estate is the filing and release of estate and inheritance taxes. Federal estate taxes are due 9 months after the date of death, and most state inheritance taxes are also payable at that time. The **estate tax** is a federal tax on the transfer of property from a deceased person to another individual. An **inheritance tax** is a state tax usually levied on the recipient of the property.

With both taxes, the size of the estate is the major factor in determining the amount owed. After 1987, the credit on property transfers is $192,800, which means that the gross taxable amount has to be at least $600,000 before a federal estate tax return has to be filed or tax paid. At the state level, note that some states no longer have an inheritance tax.

To expedite the estate settlement process, the personal representative should, if possible, file and pay any estate and inheritance taxes before the 9 months allowed. If a large amount of estate and inheritance tax is due, however, it might be better to wait until the due date to pay, so that no interest income is lost. In most states, the state inheritance tax release arrives considerably sooner than the federal estate tax release. Once the federal estate tax, state inheritance tax, and income taxes are filed, the personal representative can begin the process of closing the estate, retaining only a small reserve for any income, inheritance, or estate tax contingencies.

## Final Accounting

A final accounting to the court is the next step in the closing process. The personal representative submits to the court an account of all receipts and disbursements made during the probate period. After the filing, the final accounting is mailed to the beneficiaries who are given a specified period of time to object to it. If no objections are made within this period, the probate court approves the accounting. The final accounting cannot be filed, however, unless the notice to interested persons has expired, the state income tax clearance (where required) has been received, and the state inheritance release has been filed. If the estate is large or complex and administration has taken more than one year, there may be a need to file an annual accounting on the anniversary date of the court appointment.

### Distribution of Assets

When the court has approved the final accounting, the court issues an order, often called the **decree of distribution,** directing the personal representative to distribute the assets. If the assets cannot be equally divided according to the terms of the residual dispository provisions of the will, the personal representative may have to prepare a distribution schedule (see exhibit 7.5). This is often necessary since some distributees sharing the residue of the estate may desire certain items as part of their share. Residual beneficiaries must provide the personal representative with written approval of any disproportionate distribution. They should also be advised that such distributions may have some income tax consequences.

The personal representative is responsible for delivering the assets to the respective residual beneficiary and for properly transferring ownership. For instance, stock and bond certificates should be reregistered in the name of the respective beneficiary, and real estate contracts should be formally assigned from the estate to the beneficiary. The trust officer obtains receipts for the distributions.

When the distribution is complete, the personal representative presents those receipts and a supplemental final accounting to the court, requesting that the estate be closed and that the personal representative be discharged. When the probate court finds the supplemental final accounting and the receipts from all beneficiaries in order, the court issues an order of discharge.

The distribution process described here may differ in some states, and the trust officer should learn the particulars of his or her state's laws regarding this practice. For example, some states have enacted legislation allowing probate under nonintervention powers. Although still under the jurisdiction of the probate court, the process can be much less formal and without intervention of the court once an order of solvency has been entered.

### Personal Services to Beneficiaries

As has been mentioned throughout this text, it is essential that a trust officer bear in mind the personal needs of the people being served. This is especially true during an estate settlement. As personal representative, a trust officer's responsibilities extend beyond merely ensuring that the decedent's estate is in accordance with legal requirements. When a tragedy strikes, as in the case of Bill Harley's death, the trust officer must be empathetic and patient with the family. Little things, like Terry Trowbridge's immediate call to release the joint

EXHIBIT 7.5   Sample Distribution Schedule

## **LAWRENCE RYAN**—Deceased
## **(trust account number)**

### DISTRIBUTION SCHEDULE

Assets on hand as of Order of Distribution,
dated April 18, 1988:

| | |
|---|---:|
| Cash (5/31/88) | $ 8,269.78 |
| 14 shares General Motors Corp. | 916.00 |
| 417 shares Massachusetts Investors Trust | 3,970.00 |
| 144 shares Portland General Electric Co. | 2,690.93 |
| 150 shares Public Service Company of Indiana | 4,087.00 |
| 101 shares Wellington Fund, Inc. | 896.00 |
| Mortgage—principal plus interest | 21,001.63 |
| Note plus interest | 13,313.13 |
| Savings certificate Oregon Mutual Savings Bank | 9,016.90 |
| Savings certificate Pacific First Federal | |
|    Savings and Loan Association | 5,000.00 |
| Total available for distribution | $69,161.37 |

Distribution:

⅓—Margaret

| | | |
|---|---:|---:|
| Note plus interest | $13,313.13 | |
| Savings certificate Pacific First Federal | 5,000.00 | |
| Cash | 4,740.66 | |
| | | $23,053.79 |

⅓—Robert

| | | |
|---|---:|---:|
| One-half mortgage | 10,500.82 | |
| Savings deposit certificate—Oregon Mutual | | |
|    Savings Bank | 9,016.90 | |
| 45 shares Portland General Electric stock | 840.92 | |
| Cash | 2,695.15 | |
| | | $23,053.79 |

⅓—Peter

| | | |
|---|---:|---:|
| One-half mortgage | 10,500.81 | |
| 99 shares Portland General Electric stock | 1,850.01 | |
| 14 shares General Motors Corp. | 916.00 | |
| 417 shares Massachusetts Investors Trust | 3,970.00 | |
| 150 shares Public Service Co. of Indiana | 4,087.00 | |
| 101 shares Wellington Fund, Inc. | 896.00 | |
| Cash | 833.97 | |
| | | $23,053.79 |
| | | $69,161.37 |

savings account, tend to cement good relations during the entire settlement process. A trust officer is often heavily relied on for personal advice and guidance—for example, to assist in selling personal belongings or to help settle family, financial, and business matters. At other times, a trust officer may be called upon simply to lend an ear to a grieving family member. An appreciation of both the business and personal demands of the trust business is the key to being successful at it.

## SUMMARY

In settling estates, a trust department officer acts in the capacity of executor, a personal representative named in the will, or as administrator, a personal representative appointed by the court. In settling a will, the personal representative must go through a series of steps, beginning with the admission of the will to the court through the final distribution of the assets to the beneficiaries. The process of distributing assets from the decedent's name to the name of his or her heirs is referred to as probate.

Without exception, it is preferable for individuals to leave a will, to die testate, than to neglect to leave a will and die intestate. Under intestate succession law, the disposition of assets may be contrary to the decedent's wishes—for example, all property may revert to the state in the event there is no surviving spouse or heirs.

A will is a legally enforceable declaration of the wishes of the testator regarding matters to be attended to after death. In making a will, the person should exhibit testamentary capacity—that is, a clear understanding of what is being willed to whom and the implications involved. All wills should contain certain information, such as the identity of the testator, an authorization to pay all debts and taxes, a disposition of the estate, and a definition of the personal representative's powers.

The normal procedures in an estate settlement begin with a review of the decedent's property, a securing of the original will, and the appointment of a personal representative. As personal representative, a trust officer's responsibilities include giving notice to heirs, beneficiaries, and interested persons; collecting and appraising assets; drawing up a budget and perhaps selling some assets to meet any outstanding debt; settling all tax obligations (income taxes and inheritance and estate taxes); making a final accounting to the probate court; and finally, distributing the assets to the beneficiaries. Throughout this process, the trust officer should bear in mind that there is a personal, as well as a business, dimension to the proceedings.

## QUESTIONS FOR REVIEW

1. Explain the distinction between dying testate and dying intestate. Give some examples of why it is preferable to avoid an intestate succession.

2. What factors would a court consider in deciding whether a person was of sound mind when he or she made a will?

3. Define residuary estate. What would you recommend to a client who is anxious to control an heir's spending of assets left to him or her in the client's will?

4. Explain the relative advantages and disadvantages of securing a will under a mattress, in a bank vault, in a safe deposit box.

5. Briefly describe the step-by-step process of settling an estate.

6. Identify some of the major expenses typically connected with the settlement of an estate.

SECTION *3* Corporate and
Institutional Services

"The paramount duty of a prudent trustee is that of loyalty
to the trust beneficiaries. The trustee must administer the
trust solely in the best interests of the beneficiaries and
may not place himself in a position where the
performance of any of his duties can be affected by his
personal interests."

—Roy M. Adams and Carter Howard
*partners, Schiff Hardin & Waite*

## INTRODUCTION

The needs of institutions for trust services are not all that different from the needs of people who buy personal trust services. Chapter 4 pointed out that personal trust services meet at least three basic human needs: security, peace of mind, and control. Institutions seek basically the same values when appointing a bank trust department to administer their trust assets or perform services in connection with their debt and equity issues.

An institutional client is interested in preserving its assets, just as a father is, for example, when he establishes a trust for his children. In the case of an institution, an overriding concern is maintaining the value of the assets, even making the value grow. A charitable foundation may want to exist indefinitely, making its assets available from time to time for a specific charitable purpose. The bank trust department's job as trustee is to provide security to the trust assets so that the foundation's purpose is realized. The trust department is responsible for preserving and enhancing trust assets, and ultimately providing security to the original vision of the foundation.

Peace of mind is also a goal of institutional clients. For instance, a company that appoints a bank trust department to perform stock transfer services is seeking a reliable agent that will perform these specialized duties and leave the company free to pursue its business. The company—say a biotechnology firm—does not have the resources to keep its own stock ownership records or register and reregister stock certificates. It does not want to worry about those tasks and so appoints an expert to perform them. A reliable transfer agent gives the company peace of mind.

Finally, institutional clients seek control over their assets. A good example of the need for control is a company that sponsors an employee pension plan. The pension plan is responsible for paying out enormous sums of money to the participants when they become disabled or retire. The amount of money is much more than was contributed by the company or the participants. Therefore, the amount paid into the plan must be invested to make it grow. A bank, when serving as a fiduciary for an employee pension plan, is responsible for making the money in the plan grow so that the participants can eventually collect the amount of pension benefits to which they are entitled. The company's management specifies its funding policy for the pension plan, including investment objectives, cash flow information, and future projections of contributions and benefits payments. Then it is the fiduciary's job to invest the assets according to management's goals.

In summary, institutional clients of bank trust departments—companies, states and municipalities, charities, and other institutions—all look to their agents and fiduciaries to perform services that give them security, peace of mind, and control of their assets. Most institutions have neither the expertise nor the staff and resources to perform their own services. Moreover, federal laws require the appointment of a trustee in certain situations, such as to administer a corporate bond indenture or an employee benefit plan. Institutional services are a vital and diverse area of the trust department's business.

Before elaborating on the needs of the various parties in an institutional trust arrangement, it will be useful to look briefly at the history of corporate trusts and agencies. The historical view gives an understanding of why bank trust departments engage in fiduciary and agency services.

## HISTORY OF CORPORATE TRUSTS
## AND AGENCIES

It is 150 years ago and a major lumber and trading company needs funds to pay off some of its debt and expand its operations into the booming American frontier. Carried along by a mixture of greed and optimism, a company employee issues unauthorized or fraudulent stock certificates to public investors and promises a windfall. When the investors slowly realize that their certificates are worthless and news of the scandal spreads, a serious erosion of investor confidence ensues. Other young companies find themselves unable to raise capital at a time when the U.S. economy offers seemingly endless opportunities.

To restore investor confidence, companies begin to appoint trust companies as stock transfer agents, which, as intermediaries between the issuers and the investors, can prevent the overissuance of stock, the issuance of fraudulent certificates, and other abuses. One of the first companies to accept these agency duties in 1836 is the Pennsylvania Company for Insurance on Lives and Granting

Annuities. Shortly after, the Girard Trust Company, the New York Guarantee and Indemnity Company, and the Beaver Meadow Railroad and Case Company begin performing corporate agency and fiduciary services for American companies.

Now it is 1869, and the New York Stock Exchange issues a rule that all shares of active stock listed on the exchange must be registered at an agency appointed by the exchange. This action gives considerable impetus to the practice of appointing agents to handle many of the important tasks associated with stock issuance.

The next 100-plus years witness a number of significant landmarks in the history of corporate trust services:

*1874.* The first separate trust department is formed in a financial institution, the Boston Safe Deposit and Trust Company.

*1897.* The Trust Division is formed in the national association for banks, the American Bankers Association.

*Early 1900s.* Many states become active in regulating securities transactions by passing so-called blue-sky laws, which are designed to stem the issuance of fraudulent securities that were popularly called "pieces of the blue sky."

*1913.* National banks are empowered by the Federal Reserve Act to serve as agents for corporate issuers of securities.

*1933.* Commercial banks are barred from underwriting and distributing securities, other than the general obligations of municipalities, under the Glass-Steagall Act.

*1939.* Corporate bond issuers are required to appoint independent trustees to protect the interests of bondholders under the Trust Indenture Act.

*1975.* Transfer agents are brought under the SEC's regulatory reach by the Securities Act Amendments, which amended the Securities Exchange Act of 1934.

*1988.* Historic legislation is debated in Congress to repeal the Glass-Steagall Act and give banks full securities powers beyond the agency and fiduciary services they have traditionally provided. Other legislation is introduced to modernize the Trust Indenture Act to the needs of contemporary institutional trust practice without undermining its purposes.

These and related developments over the past 150 years have culminated today in a formidable system of regulation that protects both investors and issuers of securities from fraud, dishonesty, self-dealing, and conflicts of interest. Although many of the laws are being updated and refined, and others are being either expanded or scaled back, there is general agreement that a system of regulation is necessary to the smooth functioning of the trust and securities businesses.

Although the history of corporate trust and agency services is perhaps the most colorful, other types of institutional accounts also have an interesting history. For example, fiduciaries for employee pension plans became subject to certain standards under the Employee Retirement Income Security Act of 1974 after broad public concern was voiced over the future viability of the Social Security system and the needs of individuals to have a more secure means of saving for retirement.

Community trusts, charitable foundations, and other trust arrangements for charitable, educational, and similar purposes became prevalent in the early 1900s when wealthy Americans, made rich by the prospering industry in the United States, began to feel a need to return some of their fortunes to society. The first community trust—the Cleveland Foundation founded in 1914—was funded by gifts and bequests from the citizens of Cleveland for the benefit of members of the community.

Each type of fiduciary and agency function mentioned in this section arose from a desire by people and institutions to put their money to work, either to raise more money or to benefit people in some way. Bank trust departments play a pivotal role in this human endeavor.

## AN OVERVIEW OF FIDUCIARY
## AND AGENCY FUNCTIONS

A bank trust department can serve in either a fiduciary or an agency capacity for corporate and institutional trust accounts, including employee benefit plans, charities and institutions such as hospitals and colleges, and corporations that issue stocks and bonds. The enterprise a trust department undertakes determines whether its primary function is to provide services for the entity that appoints it or to protect the interests of investors or beneficiaries.

These, briefly, are the kinds of fiduciary services a bank can perform.

*Bond trustee.* Appointed to administer corporate bond issues, bond trustees are responsible mainly for protecting the interests of the bondholders. Their other duties may include administrative and transfer functions.

*Trustee for an employee benefit plan.* The Employment Income Security Act of 1974 requires the appointment of a trustee to protect the interests of participants in an employee benefit plan. The trustee may also perform investment management, recordkeeping, and other administrative functions.

*Trustee for charitable and institutional trusts.* Managing and holding cash and other assets, collecting income, paying out money, and preparing reports are among the duties of a trustee for charitable and institutional trusts.

As these brief job descriptions show, a trustee can perform fiduciary and agency duties simultaneously. Its primary responsibility, though, is to preserve and protect the interests of investors, in the case of a bond trustee; the participants, in the case of an employee benefit plan; and beneficiaries, in the case of a charitable or institutional trust.

A bank can also act solely in an agency capacity for corporate trust accounts. In these cases, its primary customer is the company that appoints it. However, an agent for a corporate issuer of securities also serves the needs of the company's investors. The following types of corporate agencies are the most common.

*Paying agent.* A paying agent for corporate and municipal bonds pays interest periodically to investors and repays the principal amount upon maturity of the bond issue. A paying agent for equity securities pays out declared dividends to shareholders.

*Transfer agent.* When they issue securities, corporations require the services of a transfer agent to issue stock certificates, cancel and reissue certificates when the securities are bought and sold, and maintain ownership records.

*Bond registrar.* This agent performs transfer functions for registered bond issues.

*Stock registrar.* The primary responsibility of a stock registrar is to prevent the overissuance of stock by keeping records of the total authorized shares of outstanding stock and the number of shares canceled and reissued daily. Registrar functions may be performed by the transfer agent, whose duties are closely related.

*Special purpose agents.* Banks trust departments also perform a number of special agency functions when circumstances warrant. For example, a subscription agent may be appointed by a company to handle stockholders' subscription rights, which give certain stockholders the first opportunity to buy the company's new stock issues. An exchange agent's services may be required when new securities are issued to replace old issues, such as when companies merge or recapitalize. A conversion agent handles the exchange of one class of securities for another when, for example, stockholders exercise their rights on convertible stocks or bonds. Redemption agents handle preferred stock and bond calls. These and other special agency functions are handled by banks and trust companies.

Each of these fiduciary and agency functions will be discussed in more detail in upcoming chapters.

## SERVING DIVERSE CUSTOMERS' NEEDS

A bank serving corporate trust clients has different constituents, depending on the tasks it is appointed to perform. For example, a company that appoints a bank trustee to administer its employee benefit plan cannot expect the trustee to put the company's needs uppermost. Instead, the trustee's first duty is to protect the interests of the employees who participate in the plan. As such, the trust department works for the participants, not the plan's sponsor.

The needs of the corporate trust marketplace, therefore, are defined by the function the bank performs. A bank's service orientation depends on whether it is acting as an agent or a fiduciary, as well as the type of trust arrangement for which it is responsible. Furthermore, the trust department is capable of serving in many different capacities on behalf of corporate trust customers or in the interests of investors and beneficiaries. This chapter will try to delineate the needs of the trust department's many constituents and how a bank meets those needs.

## Meeting the Needs of Corporate Securities Issuers

Companies have sometimes processed their own stock transfers and kept shareholder records. On certain occasions in history, though, this practice has given rise to fraud and an attendant loss of investor confidence. A few companies continue to undertake their own stock transfer functions, with varying results. It is most common, however, for companies to appoint transfer agents to handle administrative and processing tasks.

The reason that companies seek experienced agents to handle stock and bond issuance relates primarily to the number and complexity of the administrative and processing tasks. An agent has the appropriate expertise, staff, and systems to handle those tasks, unlike the securities issuer itself.

An agent also specializes in the applicable laws and regulations that must be followed with respect to the securities issuance. For example, the Shareholder Communications Act of 1985 established standards for communications between the registrants (issuers of stock) and the beneficial owners (entities or individuals who actually own the shares, although they may not hold them in their own names). The Securities and Exchange Commission's (SEC) rules implementing the Shareholder Communications Act set forth specific procedures that must be followed for distributing proxy materials, annual reports, and other materials to the beneficial owners of the securities, even when the securities are actually held by a bank or depository as the nominee.

Compliance with the SEC's rules is more certain if an agent handles the processing and distribution activities, rather than the issuer itself. Why? Agents who specialize in the services they offer to securities issuers are usually in a better position to stay abreast of laws and regulations affecting the securities marketplace, and they typically have the in-house expertise required to establish and maintain compliance.

In summary, although companies are not prohibited from performing their own agency services for stock issues, they generally appoint third-party agents who have the automated systems, depository access, expert staff, and other resources to handle these complicated functions with ease. Transfer agents and the other special agents offer convenience, reliability, and professionalism, or peace of mind, to their corporate clientele.

## Meeting the Needs of Issuers of Debt

The Trust Indenture Act of 1939 requires corporate entities that issue bonds to appoint a trustee to monitor the indenture governing the debt issue and safeguard the rights of bondholders. The Trust Indenture Act applies only to corporate bond indentures, but its principles are widely accepted and form the basis for municipal bond indentures as well. Trustees serve in a fiduciary capacity for state and municipal bond issues, and as with corporate bonds, their primary duty is to protect the interests of bondholders. As this book goes to press, Congress is considering a revision of the Trust Indenture Act, to modernize its provisions but maintain the basic purpose of protecting the rights of bondholders.

Bond trustees may also serve in an agency capacity for the corporate and municipal issuers of bonds, keeping ownership records, monitoring the payment of interest and principal to bondholders, administering accounts, and performing other administrative and recordkeeping functions. Again, these services afford the issuers of debt securities convenience and reliability, as well as the assurance that federal and state laws are being adhered to. Thus the risk of conflicts of interest or other irregularities are minimized.

## Meeting the Needs of Investors

The investors in securities also benefit from corporate agency and trust services. In fact, investors' interests are the primary consideration of bond trustees, who are required by law to protect the rights of bondholders even to the extent of representing them in legal action if the issuer defaults on payments of bond interest or principal.

Bank trust departments serving in an agency or fiduciary capacity for a stock or bond issue are the primary contact the investors have with their investment. By providing accurate, prompt, legally correct, and courteous services to investors, the trust department sets the foundation for good relations between issuers and their holders. The issuing entity, of course, benefits too when its investors are satisfied with the transfer, payment, and other services they receive.

Relationship banking is as important to corporate clients and their investors as it is to personal trusts and agencies. Investors benefit from the convenience, accuracy, and reliability afforded them through the services of professional corporate agents and fiduciaries.

## Meeting the Needs of Beneficiaries

Participants in employee benefit plans and the beneficiaries of charitable and institutional trusts rely on trust fiduciaries for a range of services that meets their needs. For example, the trustee of an employee pension plan, charged by law to act solely in the interests of the participants and the beneficiaries of the plan, has a number of duties with respect to the plan trust, including managing the assets of the trust and paying benefits and expenses. The participants and beneficiaries of the pension plan benefit greatly when these functions are handled with skill and care because as trust assets grow, so does their share in those assets. More importantly, however, risk of loss is minimized with professional fiduciary services, assuring that pension plan participants and their beneficiaries receive the full retirement benefits to which they are entitled.

Other ways that bank trust departments directly serve the needs of corporate trust beneficiaries is through expert management of profit-sharing plans, thrift or savings plans, and employee stock ownership plans. Individual participants in well-managed employee benefit plans have a personal financial interest in the way plan assets are invested and managed. By providing accurate, reliable, and responsible investment management services, a bank trust department protects and enhances the financial situation of all the plan's participants.

The beneficiaries of institutional and charitable trusts also rely heavily on the bank trust department that manages the trust. Their activities are funded out of the assets of the trust, and their continued ability to function and perform community and charitable services depends on the expertise and skill of the trustee. By investing trust assets and performing the many fiduciary and agency services connected with administration of such a trust, the beneficiaries—charities, colleges, hospitals, community organizations, and public and private foundations—are free to carry on their work to benefit all members of a community. In a very real sense, the skills of a bank trust department acting as trustee for a charity or institution benefit society at large by making possible a myriad of activities in the arts, education, medicine, community support services, and welfare.

## SUMMARY

The values received by institutional clients of bank trust departments are essentially the same as those provided to individuals with personal trust accounts: security, peace of mind, and control. By providing expert fiduciary and agency services to companies and institutions, bank trust departments relieve their clients of the day-to-day tasks associated with account administration and, in addition, preserve, protect, and enhance those assets so they can be productive.

The history of institutional trust and agency services illuminates the needs they serve. Whether in response to abuses, laws, or economic pressures—or simply because of convenience and common sense—a whole range of services to institutions and companies has evolved. Bank trust departments perform these services in a timely, reliable, accurate, and professional manner, giving their clients the assistance they require, the expertise they seek, and the protection they deserve.

In providing the services of a fiduciary or agent, the bank trust department also serves the needs of the other parties to the account, such as individual investors, participants, and beneficiaries. In fact, a bond trustee or employee benefit plan fiduciary is bound by law to protect the interests of the bondholders, participants, and beneficiaries, respectively.

Unlike a trustee or fiduciary, an agent for a corporate issuer of stock is not charged directly with protecting investors. Nevertheless, when an agent performs its job accurately, on time, and in a courteous manner, the investors benefit. They are not only assured that the company's records accurately reflect their ownership position, but they also receive their dividends in the right amount, correctly addressed, and on time.

Special purpose agents perform a number of tasks of critical interest to investors, such as processing bond calls, distributing shareholder materials, and making notification of tender offers. Satisfied investors encourage good relations between companies and their shareholders, and a proficient corporate trust department has a critical role in the development and maintenance of company-investor relations.

All the responsibilities and tasks mentioned in this chapter will be the subject of more detailed discussion in the chapters that follow.

## QUESTIONS FOR REVIEW

1. Individual customers who buy personal trust services seek security, peace of mind, and control. Explain how those values relate to the needs of a company or institution that appoints a bank trust department to perform fiduciary or agency services.

2. Why do most companies appoint agents to perform the processing and administrative tasks connected

with a public issuance of stock? What has history shown to be the danger of a company performing its own transfer and other agency services?

3.  What is the thrust of the Trust Indenture Act? How does it apply to municipal bond issues?

4.  To whom is a corporate bond trustee most directly responsible? Is a bond trustee ever put in a position of being legally opposed to the corporation that appoints it?

5.  Name some of the benefits a bank trust department serving as corporate agent provides to a company that issues stock. Similarly, what benefits do investors receive from an agent's services?

6.  What is a common, basic goal of a charitable or institutional trust, and how does a bank trust department help meet that goal?

7.  In what way does a bank trust department acting as a fiduciary for an employee benefit plan benefit the participants in the plan? To whom is the fiduciary directly responsible?

8.  Besides preserving the assets of a trust account, what does a trustee or fiduciary try to accomplish so that the trust assets continue to fulfill the needs of those whom the trust is intended to benefit? In whose interests are these efforts made?

*9* Employee Benefit Trusts

## INTRODUCTION

There are several good reasons for a company to establish a benefit plan for its workers—for example, to attract and retain employees and to save on taxes. Social Security alone is often insufficient to meet the income needs of retirees. Consequently, farsighted employees look for an employer that offers some form of supplemental retirement income or assists its workers in saving toward that goal. Employers that offer an employee benefit plan can better recruit employees and retain the ones they have. Tax savings are also realized because the amount of money an employer contributes to a plan is subtracted from its taxable income. Furthermore, the income earned by the assets held in the trust is tax exempt.

For these and other reasons, employee benefit trusts are popular with companies and constitute a fast growing area of bank trust services. This chapter begins with an introduction to the terminology and advantages of employee benefit trusts. Next, we will look at the different kinds of trusts, including pension plans, profit-sharing plans, thrift or savings plan trusts, and employee stock ownership plans. Following this, we will consider the specifics of creating and administering trusts. As trustee of an employee benefit plan, a bank's duties encompass such steps as managing assets, paying benefits, and compiling and submitting reports and other communications. The chapter ends with a brief look at the future prospects for employee benefit trusts.

## BASICS OF EMPLOYEE BENEFIT TRUSTS

In a general sense, employee benefit trusts are a kind of trust account used for setting money aside to take care of employees' future financial needs. The money to fund the plan is contributed either by the employer or by both the employer and the employees. The employer that sets up the plan is often referred to as the **sponsor;** the employees who take part in a plan are referred to as **participants.**

Before becoming participants in an employee benefit plan, employees may have to meet certain qualifications to determine their eligibility. Most often, eligibility is based on length of employment, age, and job status (for example, whether a full-time employee). Upon becoming a participant in the benefit plan, the employee is subject to the **vesting** rules of the plan. These rules determine how much of a nonforfeitable share (a **vested interest**) the employee has in the plan. Many employee benefit plans have a gradual vesting schedule in which an employee's vested interest grows over time. For example, under the Tax Reform Act of 1986, pension plans must be set up so that plan participants are 100 percent vested after 5 years of service or 20 percent vested after 3 years of service plus 20 percent more for each year following until they are 100 percent vested after 7 years. If an employee should leave the company before the 5-year or 3-year mark, he or she may not be entitled to participate in the plan. Employee benefit plans can be a powerful inducement for employees to remain with the same company for at least the period of time it takes to become vested.

## TAX ADVANTAGES OF
## EMPLOYEE BENEFIT TRUSTS

Much of the popularity of employee benefit trusts lies with their tax-exempt status. To qualify for tax-exempt status, plans must meet certain standards set forth by the Internal Revenue Service—for example, avoiding discrimination in eligibility, contributions, or benefits in favor of employees who are officers, shareholders, supervisors, or highly paid personnel. Some of the tax advantages offered by employee benefit trusts follow:

- Employer contributions are deductible for the year in which they are made. The employer obtains a current deduction, even though employees receive their benefits much later. Thus the company is able to accumulate funds for its employees and experience current tax advantages.

- All earnings and gains on the funds are completely exempt from state and federal income taxes. Therefore, the monies compound tax free and increase at a far greater rate than they would if they were subject to tax.

- Employees are taxed only on benefits actually made available. If an employee receives a lump sum on retirement, the balance may be eligible for additional tax relief through a special 5-year average provision for this situation.

- If the company's contributions to the plan are paid to the employee's beneficiary after his or her death as a life annuity, they may not be subject to the federal estate tax.

## TYPES OF EMPLOYEE BENEFIT TRUSTS

There are many kinds of trusts to meet the retirement and savings needs of those in the workplace. Employee benefit trusts can range in size from a few thousand dollars to hundreds of millions of dollars, and they can be established by public or private entities. The most common benefit trusts for employees are pension plan trusts, profit-sharing trusts, thrift or savings plan trusts, 401(k) trusts, and employee stock ownership trusts. These trusts will be considered in this section.

The self-employed, although precluded from participating in employer-sponsored plans, can set up Individual Retirement Accounts (IRAs) and 401(k) plans. Other types of employee benefit trusts not included in this introduction to employee benefit trust services are those that are established for health and welfare, supplemental employment benefits, vacations, and apprentice training.

### Pension Plans

Perhaps the most common type of employee benefit trust is the **pension plan.** Under most pension plans, an employee receives a reduced salary at retirement, which continues for his or her lifetime. For example, after working 25 years with the same company, an employee may upon retirement be entitled to receive 50 percent of his or her final salary as measured in any of a number of ways. One commonly used formula determines the final salary by taking an average of the yearly salaries over the five years immediately preceding retirement. Another alternative—referred to as an **integrated retirement plan**— calculates the total retirement benefit by combining the funds received from the plan and Social Security. Using the same example, the pension benefit of an integrated retirement plan would be 50 percent of the final salary less some portion of the amount supplied by Social Security. No more than one-half of the amount supplied by Social Security can be offset, however.

## Pension Plan Funding

There are many ways in which pension plans are funded. Pension plans may be contributory—that is, employees contribute to the fund—or they may be noncontributory, without employee contributions. The level of employer contributions depends in large part on how the plan is set up. With a **defined-contribution plan,** the employer pays a certain amount into the plan on behalf of each participant for each period. Since only the amount of the contribution is known, the eventual amount to be received by each participant depends on the return realized on the money invested in the pension plan. This type of pension plan is common with union-management pensions. As part of the union contract, the company agrees to contribute a specific sum of money for each participant into the pension plan. Under the Taft-Hartley Law, such pensions are run by a joint union-management board of trustees who determine employee benefits and either invest or supervise the investment of funds.

An alternative to the defined-contribution plan is the **defined-benefit plan** in which a predetermined benefit is to be paid to participants at retirement, usually a portion of compensation. To provide a preset retirement benefit, contribution levels are based on such factors as investment results and actuarial determinations of age, compensation, and years of service. For instance, if investment earnings fall short, the company must make larger contributions. Or, if the typical employee retires at age 56 and lives to be 74, the employer contribution will be larger than it would be for an employer with a work force that retires, on average, at age 65 and lives to be 72.

Some pension trust agreements require the trustor to purchase an annuity contract from an insurance company for the employee immediately on enrollment of the employee or just before his or her retirement. Since the 1950s, however, another type of trust arrangement has become popular—the **fully trusteed plan.** The fully trusteed plan became prevalent because of collective bargaining, favorable tax laws, and most importantly, the desire by plan sponsors to have more control and flexibility over their expenses. In a fully trusteed plan, the corporation contributes cash and securities to a trustee to be invested and administered. As each participating employee reaches retirement age or becomes disabled, the trustee begins paying him or her an annuity out of the trust estate.

Under the fully trusteed plan, the trustee may have full investment responsibility, have just an advisory role, or act only on the corporation's or some other party's (such as the sponsor's or investment manager's) instructions. Contributions to the trust fund are based on periodic calculations of an independent actuary retained by the corporation to appraise the future liabilities of the fund.

Many pension funds offer the employee an alternative that provides annuity payments for an individual's spouse or other dependent after the employee's death. When an employee chooses this alternative, the regular annuity that the employee alone would receive is reduced to compensate for the provision that benefits will be paid for the duration of two lives rather than one.

## Profit-Sharing Trusts

A corporation can also set up a trust to share profits with its employees. Under a **profit-sharing trust,** a specific amount or percentage of its net profits is placed in a trust for future distribution among its employees in accordance with the terms of the plan. The amount set aside is tax deductible to the company, and the employer's contributions and investment earnings do not become a tax liability to the participants until they withdraw their money. As with a pension trust, an employee has a strong incentive to remain with the company and, by sharing in the company's profits, also has the financial inducement to do a good job.

### *Differences Between Pension and Profit-Sharing Plans*

The terms of a profit-sharing trust instrument are similar in many respects to those of a pension trust. Requirements concerning the eligibility of the participants, however, tend to be more flexible than those governing pension plans. Profit-sharing plans are subject to applicable provisions of the Internal Revenue Code and Employee Retirement Income Security Act. Other basic differences between pension trusts and profit-sharing trusts follow:

- With a pension trust, contributions are determined based on what is needed to provide a predetermined amount of retirement income or benefit or a predetermined percentage of the employee's salary. In a profit-sharing trust, contributions are based on the company's earnings, and a certain amount of benefits is not promised to the participants. The amount of profit-sharing benefits depends on the value of the fund when an employee's interest is withdrawn.

- Pension plan benefits usually are payable only at retirement, death, or disability, and then only if the employee is already vested. On the other hand, cash disbursements from an employee's account in a profit-sharing plan can be made at specific times during employment or during a layoff, discharge, or resignation. (However, the Tax Reform Act of 1986 imposes an additional 10 percent income tax on any amount withdrawn before age 59½, unless it is rolled over to an IRA. This may change not only the behavior, but the plan design as well.)

- Profit-sharing benefits are usually made in a lump-sum payment. In other words, the participant receives the benefit all at once, not in monthly payments like a pension. Profit-sharing benefits are also usually allocated in proportion to annual compensation, and not on the basis of other factors, such as age and years of service.

- An employee can usually become fully vested in a profit-sharing plan more rapidly than in a pension plan. (This may change, however, when the 5-year vesting requirement mandated by the Tax Reform Act of 1986 is implemented.)

- Employees do not contribute under most profit-sharing plans but do contribute under some pension plans.

- The earnings from a profit-sharing trust account usually go to plan participants. The employer's contribution is not changed by the earnings from the investments, only by the profits of the company. If the investments are managed well, each participant's interest in the plan is worth more money. Furthermore, if an employee leaves the company before becoming fully vested, the amount he or she forfeits remains in the plan and is usually shared by everyone left in the plan. With a pension trust, increased investment earnings or forfeited benefits usually lower the employer's contribution to the plan.

### Thrift or Savings Plan Trusts

Another variation of an employee benefit plan is the **thrift** or **savings plan trust.** Such plans offer retirement benefits based on the employee's savings and company contributions. Under a thrift or savings plan, the employee chooses the amount he or she contributes up to a specified maximum (for example, 6 percent of the employee's salary), with the company matching a portion or all of that amount—typically, from 25 percent to 100 percent of the amount the employee allocates. Thus employees are rewarded for saving.

Thrift or savings plans are generally more liberal than pension plans. They allow vesting earlier, sometimes permit withdrawal of employee contributions, and make all benefits available at the employee's death. They are similar to pension and profit-sharing plans in that the employer's contribution is tax deductible to the company, the earnings by the plan are tax exempt, and the employee does not pay taxes on the amount contributed by the company until he or she withdraws the money from the plan.

### 401(k) Plan Trusts

A 401(k) plan can be set up as a profit-sharing, thrift, or savings plan trust. The difference is that contributions by employees to 401(k) plans are made *before* taxes, whereas those to profit-sharing, thrift, or savings plans are made *after* taxes.

### Employee Stock Ownership Plans

**Employee stock ownership plans** (ESOPs) allow employees to buy shares of the company with a tax-deductible contribution from the employer. Contributions may be in company stock or cash, or may be made by borrowing on the employer's credit to invest in qualified employer securities. Under an ESOP, the employer's contribution goes into an employee's account for the purchase of stock—an arrangement that benefits both the employer and the employee. It is good for the company because more money is made available to finance its growth, and like other plans, it provides an incentive for an employee to remain with the employer. Employees benefit because, as stockholders, they receive dividends and, with the employer's contribution, can purchase shares of the company they work for.

### ESTABLISHING AN EMPLOYEE BENEFIT TRUST

Before turning to the responsibilities of a trust department in administering an employee benefit plan—either as trustee or agent—let's first look at how a plan is established. Basically, corporations must take several steps in setting up an employee benefit trust. The following is a typical procedure.

*Step 1: The plan.* The corporation's management, often with the help of a consultant on employee benefit plans, designs the plan best suited to its needs and those of its employees. The plan provides the details of the arrangement—eligibility, benefits, retirement age, administration, vesting, and so forth. A plan for a profit-sharing arrangement includes a formula for calculating the share of profits that will be set aside, invested, and managed until retirement benefits are paid. When a pension plan is involved, a plan formula determines the amount of pension benefits that employees receive on retirement.

*Step 2: The trustee.* The corporation's management selects a trustee. The trustee may be an individual, a group of individuals, or a bank with an established trust department. Most choose a bank and its trust department.

*Step 3: The trust.* The corporation's attorney usually draws up the trust agreement, often working with the trustee's suggested form of agreement. The trustee or its attorney always approves the instrument from the legal perspective before the trust agreement is signed and made final. Provisions of the trust agreement should encompass the trustee's receipt of the property the company is transferring, the trustee's investment duties, payment of funds and the committee or group authorized to make payments, and the way that the trustee must account to the corporation and its designated committee or board. The trust instrument also should cover the trustee's removal or resignation, power of amendment, and the terms under which the trust may be terminated.

*Step 4: Employee acceptance forms.* If the employees will be contributing to the plan, an employee acceptance form is needed. By signing the form, the employee accepts the terms of the plan and agrees to contribute, usually by authorizing deductions from his or her salary.

*Step 5: Board and stockholder approval.* The corporation presents the plan to its board of directors for adoption. Before that, however, many corporations now submit their plan to the stockholders for approval, although this may not be legally required.

*Step 6: Disclosure.* The plan is submitted to the IRS for exemption ruling as a qualified plan. The initial disclosure documents, such as the summary description of the plan, are prepared for employees and the appropriate government agencies.

## ADMINISTERING EMPLOYEE BENEFIT ACCOUNTS

A trust department can serve as either trustee or agent for an employee benefit plan. If named as trustee for a plan, the trust department bears fiduciary responsibility to the employees who participate in the plan. As such, the trust department works for the participants—not the plan's sponsor—and is obligated to protect the interests of the participants.

As trustee, the trust department may also manage the assets in the employee benefit trust account. The trust department's investment officer decides which investments (like stocks and bonds) to buy or sell. Ordinarily, the trustee holds the assets and collects dividends and interest earned by the account. It may also be responsible for paying out benefits to the participants and preparing reports on the employee benefit trust account. These reports show all of the assets held and the transactions posted to the account. Other reports showing the vested interest are sent to plan participants, and reports required by the government are compiled and sent to the appropriate agency. A detailed discussion of these functions follows later in this chapter.

Sometimes the trust department acts only as agent for the plan. An officer of the company or some other responsible person is appointed by the company to be the trustee, while the trust department serves as investment manager, adviser, or custodian. As an investment manager or adviser, the trust department manages the assets or gives advice to the trustee on what investments to make. As custodian, which the trust department can do concurrently, it holds assets, collects income, and processes transactions requested by the trustee or investment manager.

## Regulatory Considerations

Unlike individual trusts, which are regulated by states, employee benefit trusts are strictly governed by federal regulation, primarily the Internal Revenue Code and the Employee Retirement Income Security Act of 1974 (ERISA). To ensure compliance with these and other regulations, banks must report to a host of federal agencies, among them the Departments of Labor and Treasury, the Pension Benefit Guaranty Corporation, the Federal Reserve Board, the Federal Deposit Insurance Corporation, and the Office of the Comptroller of the Currency. Failure to comply with ERISA provisions and applicable regulations may constitute a violation of civil and criminal law.

As mentioned previously, employee benefit plans must meet Internal Revenue Code qualifications to qualify for tax-exempt status. The regulatory reach of ERISA extends to practically all aspects of employee benefit trust administration. ERISA's primary emphasis is on protecting and benefiting pension plan participants, which it does through directives that are quite definitive in some respects, but general in others, such as the management of pension fund assets. The key ERISA requirements of trustees will be discussed in the following sections of this chapter. But regardless of the task, the trustee of an employee benefit plan has fiduciary responsibility and must act solely in the interests of the plan participants.

## Organizational Structure

Ideally, lines of authority within the trust department should be clearly drawn between those responsible for investments and those responsible for administration. The organizational structure should be simple and should offer maximum communication among its members. The structure should enable corporate customers to reach the appropriate individual with authority, who can respond promptly and expertly.

When possible, separate support groups should be established for specific administrative areas, such as accounting, recordkeeping, benefit payments, and investment performance. Each support group should have clearly defined management and decision-making responsibility.

In addition to support group heads, the staff administering an employee benefit account might include the following professional positions.

*The division or unit head.* This individual makes and directs policy, solves problems, and reports directly to the head of the trust department.

*The administrator.* As the account manager and coordinator of all services relating to the account, the administrator implements policy. He or she becomes the focal point for the customer and for bank personnel and reports directly to the unit head.

*Legal reviewer.* This person ensures that the employee benefit plan is administered according to the provisions of the trust agreement. He or she coordinates the advice of counsel and reports directly to the unit head.

*Operations officer.* He or she staffs and maintains administrative support services and reports directly to the unit head. The chiefs of the specialized administrative groups—for example, the heads of accounting, cash control, and benefit payments—report directly to the operations officer.

A key individual is the administrator who has complete control over every aspect of the day-to-day operations of the account, except for investing the trust funds. The administrator is responsible for establishing and maintaining all records. He or she authorizes the type and frequency of accountings and special reports, transactions and asset statements, security advices, and benefit procedures. The administrator obtains information and documentation from the customer and makes certain that the investment officer is aware of pertinent information relating to the account. No changes in the procedure established for the account may be made without the administrator's consent.

As soon as there is an indication that the bank will be appointed as trustee, the administrator should have the opportunity to review the proposed plan and the publications prepared for the employees to ensure that the plan's provisions are consistent and compatible with the bank's administrative services, procedures, and capabilities.

## Asset Management

As trustee of an employee benefits account, most trust departments are called upon to receive, hold, invest, and reinvest the assets of the trust. This extremely critical function must be performed as prescribed by the retirement plan, the trust agreement, and in compliance with ERISA. It includes a determination of funding policy and the setting of investment goals and objectives.

## Funding Policy

ERISA requires that every employee benefit plan includes a procedure for establishing and effecting a funding policy that is consistent with the plan's objectives. Thus the fiduciary must determine the plan's short- and long-term financial needs. Much of this information is supplied by corporate management, and should include future projections of contributions and benefit payments. In response to ERISA, corporate customers have gone even further and furnished trustees with written statements of funding policy, including investment objectives, guidelines, and cash flow information. In some cases, there are even corporate prohibitions or percentage limitations on types, quality, and classes of securities. Most managements, however, furnish broad statements emphasizing the trustee's and investment managers' sole discretion over trust fund investments.

The trustee should consider several factors in determining the investment policy to be followed. The first is whether the plan is defined-benefit or defined-contribution. As mentioned earlier, in a defined-benefit plan, the amount to be received by a plan participant at retirement is defined in advance. The funding of the plan is based on the employer's contributions plus the return on the investments. Therefore, the greater the contribution supplied by the investments, the less financial commitment is needed from the employer. Conversely, poor investment results may result in a shortfall that will have to be made up by the employer. For a defined-contribution plan, the amount provided by the employer is defined, and the participant receives a proportional share of that amount. Thus investment results directly affect the level of retirement benefits that participants receive.

Another factor to consider is the maturity of the plan. The age distribution of the employees plays a large part in determining whether current funding levels will always be sufficient, and if not, how long it will be before benefits paid out exceed incoming contributions and investment earnings.

A third factor is funding methods and actuarial assumptions. Most companies use conservative accounting methods for arriving at funding levels. Actuarial assumptions—including such variables as the expected growth of salaries; the anticipated growth of employees in the group; the expected rate of return on trust assets; and the projected rate of mortality, disability, and employee turnover—all affect the amount of annual contribution the employer must make to provide the needed funding.

Because the rate of return on the assets of an employee benefit plan can greatly affect both the amount of contribution required by an employer and the amount of benefits received by plan participants, a trustee has an obligation to manage trust assets profitably, yet cautiously. To this end, certain constraints are imposed on trustees by ERISA and other regulations. Some of the most important follow.

*Prudent-man rule.* A trustee of an employee benefit trust must abide by the prudent-man rule of investment responsibility requiring the trustee to manage investments prudently, intelligently, and with due regard for the safety of the investment. (You may want to refer back to chapter 2 for Justice Putnam's remarks in the landmark case *Harvard College v. Amory* of 1830.) While not definitive in nature, the prudent-man concept implies that trustees must meet a high standard of investment management. At the very least, prudence dictates that the trustee understands the market and takes careful steps to protect and preserve the assets.

*Asset diversification.* ERISA regulations require that pension assets be diversified to reduce the risk of substantial financial loss. In diversifying assets, a trustee should consider the plan's objectives, its assets, general financial conditions, the benefits and risks of various kinds of investments, distribution by location and by industry, and maturity dates. Although, in theory, spreading investments by locality, type of securities, and type of industry minimizes heavy losses, in practice, significant losses can still result by a slump in the entire securities market, for example.

Corporations frequently appoint several investment managers for a single plan, which helps increase the amount of diversification in the trust portfolio. One manager may be assigned to invest only in bonds, while another invests only in stocks. However, both are required to adhere to the diversification and prudent-man standards in choosing investments for the trust.

*Prohibited transactions.* The manager of the assets of employee benefit plans is prohibited from participating in certain transactions—namely those in which a relationship may exist between the pension fund assets and the fiduciary's own account. For example, a bank may be charged with conflict of interest if it loans money to itself as trustee and secures the loan with trust assets. This policy barrier between the trust department and the rest of the bank is sometimes referred to as the Chinese Wall, which is designed to comply with Glass-Steagall Act provisions mandating the separation of investment and commercial banking activities. In fact, this separation has been strictly defined to include trust department use of any material inside information that may come into the possession of other bank departments in making investment decisions. Violations of this prohibition on self-dealing—whether in actually making investments or merely tapping inside information—have been the basis for large damage awards granted by courts over the last decade.

In formulating an investment strategy, the trustee of an employee benefit trust should consider all the variables affecting the objective of the pension portfolio. Obviously, asset diversification, the prudent-man rule, and the Chinese Wall dictate to some extent what investments can and should be made. For instance, as a way of complying with the prudent-man rule, most pension fund investments concentrate on short-term instruments, bonds, and stocks.

Besides these legal and regulatory constraints, other factors considered in an investment strategy are return objectives, risk, liquidity, and tax considerations.

*Return.* The type of employee benefit plan has some bearing on return objectives. In a defined-benefit plan, the actuarial assumptions determine the minimum interest return that must be earned from the invested funds. Any return below that level will cause the company to increase its contribution and, conversely, any return higher than that necessary will reduce the amount contributed by the company. During periods of high interest rates, the investment manager should have little problem with exceeding the actuarial assumption rates with fixed-income investments.

The return objectives for defined-contribution plans may be entirely different, however, as the amount to be received by plan participants is determined by the return on the pension investments. Therefore, investment strategy could emphasize long-term return through a growth-oriented portfolio.

*Risk.* Risk is directly tied to return. That is, when deciding how to maximize the return on assets, the investment manager must take into account the risk of loss as well as the opportunity for gain. The degree of acceptable risk may vary depending on the type of pension plan being managed. For example, with a defined-benefit plan, the risk of not achieving the actuarial assumption rate must be carefully weighed because otherwise the company's contribution would need to be increased. This, is turn, would affect the company's liquidity and net earnings. For a defined-contribution plan, a relatively higher level of risk may be acceptable in the hopes of realizing a correspondingly higher return that would benefit the plan participants.

Other factors to be considered are the company's capital structure and the plan's maturity. A risky company—for example, one that is in a cyclical industry or is highly leveraged—may warrant a conservative approach to its pension assets. Or if a plan is paying more out in benefits than is being received in contributions, a low-risk posture should be taken.

*Liquidity.* Most employee benefit plans are financially sound—contributions and investment income exceed benefits paid out, and liquidity is not generally a problem. An investment strategy can therefore weigh the relative merits of the investment return on short-term assets versus long-term assets. If liquidity is questionable, a pension portfolio of short-term funds would be desirable.

*Tax considerations.* As noted earlier, there are no tax obligations with IRS-qualified employee benefit plans until benefits are withdrawn by participants. Investment gains and income are not taxed to the trust. In maximizing the return on assets, investment managers therefore do not have to take into account the tax implications of an investment decision. Consequently, municipal bonds or other tax-free instruments and real estate tax shelters are not appropriate pension fund investments.

## Paying Benefits

Under the terms of a typical trust agreement, the trustee is authorized by the plan's administrative committee to pay monies from the trust fund to members, retired members, and their beneficiaries. The trust instrument specifies the need for proper evidence of appointment of administrative committee members and individuals authorized to act on the committee's behalf in issuing instructions to the trustee, including specimens of their signatures.

The administrator must ensure that the appropriate documentation is available to identify those individuals authorized to issue payment-of-benefits instructions. Their signatures must be established as bona fide. No responsibility is more essential to the proper exercise of fiduciary responsibility, although the task is routine. Those responsible for processing payment instructions must check the authority of every instruction received. Any discrepancies should be brought immediately to the attention of the trust administrator and dealt with promptly.

Checks representing periodic or recurring payments and single or lump-sum payments are usually issued by trustees directly to participants in the plan and their beneficiaries. Often, benefit payment checks are issued exclusively by administrative committees of the corporation. Then the trustee only has the responsibility to supply monies on time in accordance with the committee's properly authorized instructions.

In addition, the trust administrator may consider providing the following services to the corporate administrative committee:

- When the account is first established, the administrator might prepare a manual describing in detail the procedures for initiating, superseding, and terminating payments.

- The administrator might supply the committee with employee forms and advise it on the information

required of each potential payee. The administrator
should not have the responsibility for calculating
individual benefit payments; this is the committee's
responsibility.

- As payments are completed, the administrator might
  provide detailed listings to the committee.

- The trust administrator should not give tax advice,
  but when responsible for making the benefit
  payments, the administrator should furnish
  appropriate tax information statements indicating
  total amount paid and any federal and state taxes
  withheld.

## Reports and Communication with Clients

In addition to the reporting and disclosure requirements of ERISA, the trustee
must provide the client with accurate and complete reports at regular intervals.
Employee benefit plan trust agreements typically include a provision that the
trustee must keep detailed accounts of all investment receipts, disbursements,
and other transactions. Usually within 3 months of the close of the trust year, the
trustee must file a detailed report of all activity during the report period. These
annual reports, supplemental reports, and asset valuation reports constitute the
bulk of the trustee's written communication with the client.

### The Annual Report

This important communication between the trustee and the client contains a
comprehensive statement of assets held, with book and market values stated
cumulatively for each investment. It includes detailed schedules of contributions, other receipts, income collected, benefit payments, other distributions,
sales, redemptions, collections, acquisitions, and administrative expenses.

### Supplemental Reports

Trustees usually supplement the annual report, perhaps as often as monthly,
with statements of cash and noncash security transactions and statements of
assets held. The trustee provides supplemental information on property that
was acquired or disposed of during any given period, usually at least quarterly.

### Asset Valuation Reports

For thrift and profit-sharing plans, the trustee must prepare complete reports
on the value of the assets in the account at specific dates. These reports must be

accurate and timely because they are crucial to properly maintaining the account records of individual participants and to distributing benefits on time.

### *Other Communications*

The primary contacts between the bank trust department and the customer should be the administrator and the investment officer assigned to the account. These officers must be alert to the client's changing requirements and make every effort to meet the customer's needs. The administrator should also be watchful that the trust agreement is amended when necessary. For example, changes in the trust instrument would be required to provide expanded coverage if the corporation were involved in a merger or acquisition.

Trust agreements may also be changed to accommodate new types of investments, possibly in highly specialized investment markets. The bank officers should work together to present investment suggestions and prepare the background information and administrative support that will enable the corporate client to make the best decisions for their employees' benefit plan.

Maintaining good relations with the client is a crucial aspect of the trust officer's job. Such a position requires individuals with good interpersonal skills, as well as expertise in investments and administration. The overriding objective is to offer the client a quality product that will result in profit for the trust beneficiaries and the bank. The trust department's reputation for obtaining good investment performance, while providing high-level account administration, is strengthened with each satisfied client.

## TRENDS IN EMPLOYEE BENEFIT TRUSTS

For bank trust departments, employee benefit trust accounts promise to continue as a major source of banking business. One reason is the growing recognition that Social Security is no longer sufficient as a sole means of retirement income. Recognizing this, Congress is considering several bills to encourage employers to establish private retirement plans. One means of doing this, contained in the language of many legislative proposals, is to expand the use of **Simplified Employee Pension** plans (SEPs). SEPs are, like Individual Retirement Accounts, extremely easy to set up and are designed to serve the needs of the self-employed and the small business owner.

Congress is also acting to make it easier for employees to obtain pension benefits and to take those benefits with them when they transfer from one job to another. For example, it was once common for an employee to have to work 10 years to become vested in a company pension plan. However, the Tax Reform Act of 1986 changed this for most retirement plans. Under the act, companies have until 1989 to adopt accelerated vesting schedules. One option available to employers is to guarantee workers full benefits after 5 years; another is to use a graded vesting that grants workers 20 percent of their benefits after 3 years, increasing to 100 percent after 7 years. Regardless of the schedule chosen, it is certain to radically revise the scope and nature of employee benefit plans. Currently, only about 2 percent of companies offer their employees vesting pay after 5 years of service.

Another trend is the right of **pension portability**—that is, the right of employees to take their vested pension benefits along with them as they transfer from one job to another. Pension portability has become a popular issue with Congress, in part because today's work force is prone to switch jobs and wants to accrue retirement benefits regardless of how much time was spent at any one job. In the past, if an employee worked 9 years at one job and then moved on to another and worked 9 more years before retiring, there was a strong likelihood that he or she would not be vested under either company's retirement plan and would not have a private pension to look forward to. If Congress has its way, for vesting purposes, the employee would carry those 9 years of employment with the previous employer over to the new job.

The legislative initiatives pushing pension portability and quicker vesting schedules follow such past congressional actions as the Retirement Equity Act of 1984, which extended the time employees are allowed to leave their jobs and, if later rehired by their company, to regain previously vested benefits. Taken together, it is apparent that the number of employees covered by private benefit plans will grow astronomically in the future. This trend will have major implications for trust services—both in the number of plans and in the design and funding of those plans.

## SUMMARY

Employee benefit trusts are types of trust accounts used to set money aside for employees' future financial needs. Before participating in an employee benefit plan, employees may have to meet certain qualifications, such as length of employment, age, and job status, to determine their eligibility. However, to become vested in an employee benefit plan, an employee must remain with the company for a predetermined length of time. Such plans are beneficial to employers wishing to recruit and retain employees.

Employee benefit trusts also offer tax advantages. Employer contributions are tax deductible and all earnings and gains accumulating in the trusts are exempt from state and federal income taxes. Benefits paid to employees are taxed only when made available.

There are several types of employee benefit trusts, including pension plans, profit-sharing plans, thrift or savings plan trusts, 401(k) plans, and employee stock ownership plans. Pension plans may be defined-contribution or defined-benefit—an important distinction for a trustee in deciding how to manage trust assets.

A trust department can serve as either trustee or agent for an employee benefit plan. As trustee, the trust department bears fiduciary responsibility to the employees who participate in the plan. Ordinarily, the trustee's functions include holding the trust assets, collecting dividends and interest earned by the account, paying out benefits to the participants, and preparing reports on the account.

The trust department may also manage the assets and decide which investments to buy or sell. In this role, the trustee must abide by the prudent-man rule, ensure adequate asset diversification, and maintain a barrier (a so-called Chinese Wall) between pension fund assets and the fiduciary's own account. Keeping in mind these regulatory restrictions, a trustee must consider return objectives, risk, liquidity, and taxes when drafting an appropriate investment strategy.

Employee benefit trusts promise to continue as a major source of banking business. Recent legislative actions have made it easier for employee benefit plans to be established, and Congress is looking at ways to help employees become vested in pension plans and to take their vested benefits with them as they move from one job to another.

## QUESTIONS FOR REVIEW

1. What advantages could you cite to an employer weighing whether to establish an employee benefit trust?

2. What are some of the factors considered in determining an employer's contribution for a defined-contribution plan? For a defined-benefit plan? How would a fall in stock market prices affect an employer's contribution to a defined-contribution plan and to a defined-benefit plan heavily invested in the market?

3. Give three examples of how pension and profit-sharing plans differ.

4. What benefits does an employee stock ownership plan offer to an employer?

5. What provisions are usually found in an agreement establishing an employee benefit trust?

6. Define the prudent-man rule. Give some examples of how trust assets might be invested in violation of this rule. What is the Chinese Wall and what implications does it have for trust asset management?

7. What steps are involved in paying employee benefits to a recently retired pension participant?

8. What reports are typically prepared by a trustee to provide a client with a complete and accurate accounting of an employee benefit trust?

CHAPTER *10* Corporate Trusts
and Agencies

### INTRODUCTION

The corporate trust business differs from the investment recordkeeping and discretionary functions that form the backbone of traditional trust services to individuals, charities, and employee benefit accounts. In the corporate trust business, bank trust departments assist corporations in issuing securities, acting as either trustee or agent depending on the type of securities issued and the responsibilities assumed.

To introduce this complex subject, the chapter begins by considering how corporations raise capital by issuing securities and the bank trust department's role in that process. This discussion includes an overview of the various types of corporate debt securities, such as first mortgage bonds, debentures, equipment trust certificates, revenue bond issues, and convertible issues. We will then look at the principal document used to establish a corporate trust—namely, the trust indenture. A description of the corporate trustee's role, responsibilities, and duties, and a review of applicable regulations concludes the discussion of corporate trusts.

Bank trust departments also provide corporate agency services, acting in such capacities as registrar, paying agent, transfer agent, and exchange agent. The chapter closes with the many agency services banks offer in relation to corporate bonds and equity securities.

### BASICS OF CORPORATE TRUSTS AND AGENCIES

For most corporations, the primary source of capital is money supplied by stockholders, who hold certificates of stock as evidence of their ownership rights in the corporation. Capital supplied by stockholders is often referred to as **equity capital.** When the equity capital supplied by stockholders is insufficient to meet all of a corporation's financing requirements, as is almost always the case, the corporation resorts to borrowing to raise the necessary capital. Capital supplied by a corporation's creditors is often referred to as **debt capital.** Depending on the nature and size of the company, there are various sources of debt capital. Loans from commercial banks are the largest source of financing and are available to businesses of all sizes. For example, provided that standards of creditworthiness are met, both the family operated clothing retailer and the large department store chain can take out a short-term bank loan to finance the purchase of inventory. However, large corporations and state and local entities have access to another source of debt capital often unavailable to businesses of more modest size. If a corporation needs a large amount of money that it will not be able to pay back for several years, it often borrows from the general public or institutional investors by issuing bonds or other debt securities.

Before the mid-1800s, corporations issued their own stocks and bonds. However, in an effort to raise as much capital as possible, many companies overissued stock or engaged in other fraudulent practices. The end result was an erosion of investor confidence, which seriously damaged the ability of all companies to procure necessary financing. To restore credibility, some corporations began to appoint trust companies as trustees of their debt issues.

Banks therefore play a crucial role in helping corporations raise money from the public. In issuing bonds, stock, and other securities, corporations require operational and information services to meet their responsibilities to their stockholders and owners of debt instruments. These services offered by banks to the corporate customer are commonly referred to as corporate trusts and corporate agencies.

## APPLICABLE LEGISLATION

Any study of the role and responsibilities of a corporate trustee should be prefaced with a basic understanding of the key federal statutes governing the issuance of securities. The economic health of the United States is closely tied to the ability of businesses to raise capital. If abuses occur, such as the overissuance of stock or a misrepresentation of the financial strength of the issuing corporation, the confidence and trust of securities investors are shaken. Both corporations and trust institutions suffer as a result.

The Great Depression is the most somber reminder of the consequences when the nation's credit mechanisms break down. Following the collapse of the stock market in 1929, Congress passed a series of major acts to protect American investors from any repeat of the tragedy. These acts imposed new regulations on top of the so-called **blue-sky laws,** which represented efforts by states to control securities fraud but, in practice, had given free rein to the business community. The legislation of the 1930s did not apply to all securities. It exempted, for example, securities of public authorities, securities issues not exceeding $1 million, securities that are privately placed, and securities issued by charities. Most bond issues, especially those handled by banks not in major money centers, meet at least one exemption. Nonetheless, all publicly offered corporate security issues of $1 million or greater are subject to regulation, and it is essential that all trust officers have at least a basic comprehension of the major post-Depression acts that govern long-term corporate finance.

### The Securities Act of 1933

One of the first legislative efforts by Congress to halt deceitful securities practices was the Securities Act of 1933, sometimes referred to as the "truth in securities" act. Its intent was to safeguard the public from misrepresented and fraudulent securities issues by establishing a full disclosure filing process that requires all new securities to be fully and clearly described in the offering literature and sales presentation.

Prior to a securities offering, the **obligor** must file a detailed registration statement with the Securities and Exchange Commission (SEC) declaring its intent to issue the securities, and provide data on the issue and the corporation. The statement and the offering literature and sales presentation may then be investigated by the SEC for false or misleading content. Certain issues are exempt from the registration requirements, including short-term commercial paper, government obligations, and securities issued by banks and trust companies (but not bank holding companies). Violations of the registration requirements or any fraudulent disclosures may result in severe legal penalties.

### The Securities Exchange Act of 1934

The Securities Exchange Act of 1934 created the SEC, a five-member board appointed by the president with the advice and consent of the Senate. The SEC is an active regulator of the securities industry. It monitors the activities of corporate issuers of securities, especially when a merger or acquisition is involved. The Securities Exchange Act also granted powers to the Federal Reserve Board to establish regulations for the extension of credit for the purchase and holding of securities. Referred to as margin requirements, they apply to both banks and brokers.

### The Glass-Steagall Act

As part of the Banking Act of 1933, the Glass-Steagall Act was prompted by the government's desire to restore public confidence in banks following the collapse of financial markets during the Great Depression. A key provision of the act paved the way for the separation of the commercial and investment banking functions, with the result that commercial banks were prohibited from selling securities and investment banks were forbidden to accept deposits. Under the Competitive Equality Banking Act of 1987, commercial banks are no longer prohibited from engaging in certain securities activities following the March 1, 1988, lifting of a moratorium imposed on the act.

## The Trust Indenture Act of 1939

The Trust Indenture Act of 1939 represents the federal government's first effort to regulate corporate trust indentures. The act states, "Every bond or other debt security which is offered to the public by use of mails or the channels of interstate commerce must be issued under an indenture which has been qualified by the Commission." In other words, the act requires that trust indentures and the accompanying registration statement be submitted to the SEC for approval. For the indenture to be qualified and the registration statement to become effective, the following requirements must be met:

- A nonaffiliated trustee must be appointed to safeguard the interests of the bondholders.

- Specific responsibilities of the trustee and the corporation must be stated. For the trustee, this includes representing the bondholders in case of default, making payments of interest and capital, and submitting reports to creditors on the condition of the issue and on its pledged security. The corporation is responsible for providing the trustee with financial data.

- Minimum standards of responsibility and accountability should be outlined for trustees, and inserting provisions that would absolve the trustee of considerable responsibility is prohibited.

- Any conflict of interest between the corporation and the trustee and between the underwriters of the issue and the trustee must be eliminated.

- The trustee must file a statement of eligibility and qualification.

## The Uniform Commercial Code

Unlike the above federal legislation, the Uniform Commercial Code has been adopted in various forms by all states, except for Louisiana. The Uniform Commercial Code governs commercial credit transactions of all types, including securities transactions. Article 8 of the code makes all investment securities negotiable—that is, transferrable; places administrative responsibility on the trustee or other fiduciary; and defines the responsibilities of the trustee, registrar, and the transfer agent. Article 9 establishes uniform rules for security transactions involving personal property.

## CORPORATE TRUSTS

As mentioned earlier, the long-term financing needs of corporations are often met by borrowing from the public. When this borrowing is through the issuance of a bond or other debt security, the Trust Indenture Act of 1939 requires that an independent trustee be appointed to protect the interests of the bondholders. A bank trust department frequently serves in this capacity—acting as an intermediary between the borrower (the corporation) and the lenders (the general public and institutions) for the life of the debt obligation. As such, the bank represents both parties. The trustee's fees are paid by the issuer of the security, but if problems arise in regard to the loan—for example, if a corporation is slow in meeting its obligation or defaults entirely on the debt—then the trustee acts as a representative of the borrowers.

It is important to note here that a trust department's services differ from those of an investment banker, who might purchase or underwrite the corporation's securities and try to find buyers for them. As mentioned earlier, under the Glass-Steagall Act, commercial banks are prohibited from such activities. As corporate trustee, the bank manually certifies or authenticates the bonds to show that they have been issued under a particular agreement. It is the corporation (often referred to as obligor) that issues the bonds and delivers them to the lenders.

When a corporation borrows from the investing public—perhaps from thousands of individual lenders—it can not realistically enter into a separate mortgage or loan agreement with each one. Thus the corporation executes an agreement—an indenture—with a bank trust department and the bank acts as trustee for all lenders. The indenture creates the trust and establishes the terms and conditions for borrowing—including restrictions on the activities of the corporation while the indenture securities are outstanding; remedies available in the event of default; and the rights, duties, and obligations of the corporation, the security holders, and the trustee.

## Types of Corporate Bonds

Bonds issued under a trust indenture may be either **secured,** payment of the obligation is guaranteed by the pledge of collateral, or **unsecured,** when the obligation is not backed by collateral. There are several kinds of secured and unsecured corporate debt securities, including first mortgage bonds, debentures, equipment trust bonds, revenue bond issues, and convertible bonds.

### First Mortgage Bonds

A popular form of long-term, secured debt is the **first mortgage bond.** A first mortgage bond is secured by a mortgage on land, buildings, or equipment. The mortgage is held by the trust institution, which will act as trustee, and is not subordinate to any other claim.

### Debentures

Unsecured bonds are usually referred to as **debentures.** A debenture is only backed by the general credit of the issuer, and is not secured by specific assets of the corporation. Generally, the maturity of a debenture is shorter than for a bond.

### Equipment Trust Bonds

With **equipment trust bonds,** the corporation uses its equipment as collateral for the loan. For example, railroad, airline, or trucking companies may back their issues with locomotives, planes, or trucks. For the duration of the loan, the trustee legally owns the equipment and leases it to the corporation. Proceeds from the sale of the equipment trust bonds are used to purchase the equipment. The rental from the lease, which is usually for 8 to 15 years, pays all the interest and principal on the bonds. When the lease is fulfilled, the equipment belongs to the corporation.

Although the bonds are executed by the trustee, they carry a written guarantee that the company will pay the bondholder directly. Administering the equipment trust is usually not difficult. However, should the corporation default, the trustee's role becomes challenging.

### Revenue Bond Issues

Many banks derive a considerable share of their business in appointments as trustee for special purpose **revenue bonds** issued by states, municipalities, or public and quasi-public authorities. Typically, these public bodies issue revenue bonds to finance the construction of bridges, turnpikes, waterworks, sewage treatment plants, and other public facilities. Industrial revenue authority commissions, established to promote industry in a particular area, issue industrial revenue bonds. Revenue bond issues are considered a type of municipal bond.

Revenue bonds are secured primarily by the income to be generated by the facilities once they are built. The trustee may also have title to real property, such as land or buildings, and is named as mortgagee on all insurance policies for the benefit and additional security of the bondholders. With this type of indenture, the bank's primary responsibility during the construction phase is to receive, hold, and invest the proceeds of the bond issue in a separate construction account until they are paid out for the construction costs. At the completion of the project, the trustee receives and disburses revenues that the project produces according to the trust indenture's terms.

### Convertible Bonds

A **convertible bond** gives the holder the right to exchange it for some other type of security, usually the common or preferred stock of the issuing corporation.

## The Corporate Trust Indenture

Under the Trust Indenture Act of 1939, every debt security that is sold interstate must be issued under an indenture approved by the SEC. An indenture is a contract underlying a securities issue. Signed by the issuing corporation and by the trustee acting for the investors, an indenture sets the rights and responsibilities of the corporation, the trustee, and investors and details the terms of the security issue.

Although an indenture essentially is a contract that enables corporations and public authorities to borrow money from an individual or institution, there is confusion about its nature. Most courts now agree that the indenture does not create a trust relationship in the usual sense—that is, an arrangement in which someone transfers legal title to property to the trustee that manages the property for beneficiaries named in the trust. Some judges have held, however, that the trustee has the full extent of fiduciary responsibility. Nevertheless, a trust created by a corporate bond indenture differs from the general concept of trust. Three of the most important differences are the following:

- Under a corporate trust indenture, the trustee does not take possession of the property or have a right to possession until a default occurs.

- The beneficiaries under a corporate trust indenture often are not known to the trustee and change frequently, since investors often trade bonds.

- A corporate trustee has fiduciary responsibilities to both the bondholders and the issuer. In the more traditional trust, the trustee has a responsibility to act only in the interest of the beneficiaries.

Typically, a **corporate trust indenture** includes introduction clauses, conveyances or granting clauses, and sections detailing the conditions under which bonds may be issued. Although indentures have many similarities in form and substance, no two indentures are exactly alike.

The indenture should specify every agreement the corporation makes to induce the public to lend to it. In the indenture, the corporation must pledge its full "faith and credit" to carry out the terms of the agreement. The most important term is the corporation's promise to repay the money borrowed and interest on the loan periodically.

### The Role and Duties of a Corporate Trustee

When approached to serve as trustee of a corporate bond account, a bank trust department should first determine whether the potential trust represents an acceptable source of business. The experience and reputation of the corporation are considered along with an examination of whether there is a potential conflict of interest and a careful review of the indenture. As trustee, the responsibilities include authenticating and delivering securities, closing the transaction, and administering the trust. A look at each of these responsibilities follows.

#### Determining Acceptability

In determining whether a potential trust is acceptable to its bank, trust department representatives should first examine the corporation that will be the obligor. In evaluating the prospects of success, the experience and reputation of the corporation's management are key factors, particularly if the trust indenture is a new undertaking. Although the trustee does not in any sense guarantee the bonds issued under a trust indenture, the participation of a responsible trust institution inevitably influences the investing public. Therefore, the bank must be satisfied that its appointment as trustee is not motivated by the obligor's desire to make speculative securities seem more salable because a well-known trustee is involved. A bank can seriously injure its reputation if it becomes associated with securities that are speculative in nature and may eventually be defaulted upon.

Once the company's experience and reputation have been verified, the trust department should examine the lending relationship that the commercial side of the bank has with the corporation. For example, conflict-of-interest charges could arise if an obligor defaults on an unsecured bonds issue—leaving the bondholders without payment—but recently had paid on a commercial loan with the same bank. Thus the bank trust department may decide to avoid even the appearance of conflict of interest by refusing to serve as trustee for a bond issue when a commercial loan is outstanding.

### Reviewing the Indenture

If a decision is made to proceed with the corporate trust, the next step is to review the indenture prepared by the attorneys of the obligor. Representatives of the bank trust department should carefully analyze the proposed agreement, paying particular attention to provisions that give the trustee authority to act. The trustee's attorney should determine that the indenture is legally correct, while the trust officers must make certain that all provisions are clear and realistic and can be carried out efficiently.

Because the trustee is, by implication, responsible to the bondholders for everything in the indenture, it should also review those terms of the trust indenture that are primarily issues for negotiation between the corporation and the bond purchasers. A careful review paves the way for the smooth administration of the trust, which is a corporate trustee's primary responsibility.

### Authenticating and Delivering Securities

In no phase of its duties is the trustee confronted with greater responsibility than in its role of authenticating and delivering bonds. When it authenticates bonds, the trustee is declaring publicly that the bonds, often amounting to millions of dollars, have been issued under the terms of the given debenture. The terms are technical and often require considerable experience and skill to interpret. A trustee cannot be too careful in matters involving the authentication and delivery of bonds.

Except for private placements, in which the obligor sells securities directly to the lender, most corporate debt securities are sold through underwriting syndicates—a group of investment bankers who sell securities to the public. The obligor and the manager of the underwriting syndicate develop a purchase agreement that includes the date and time the syndicate manager will instruct the trustee about registration and the denomination of each certificate. The purchase agreement also identifies the date, time, and place that the trustee must make the securities available to the syndicate manager to examine and package into separate deliveries for each member of the underwriting syndicate. As most syndicates' head cashiers are in New York City, the examining and packaging process frequently occurs there.

Given the volatility of the security markets, and the key role that interest rates play in determining the success of the venture for the underwriter, the trustee is under pressure to authenticate and deliver the securities rapidly. Industry practice gives the trustee about 2 business days from the time blank debt certificates are received from the bank note company that printed them and registration instructions are obtained to the time when the trustee must have the securities available in New York for inspection.

Since thousands of certificates may have to be registered and manually authenticated by signature, the utmost coordination and efficiency are required. If the trustee cannot fulfill these obligations on time and the transaction is delayed, the trustee could be liable for a substantial sum.

### Closing

The final step in issuing and selling corporate bond issues involves delivering the securities to a syndicate manager's representative who pays the obligor for the securities. The purchase agreement frequently requires that these two exchanges take place in different cities. Usually, representatives of the obligor, the underwriting syndicate, and the trustee meet before the closing (called the preclosing) to review and approve the closing documents. At the closing, each party to the transaction receives a complete set of closing documents for its files. When all parties are satisfied that the package of closing documents is complete and accurate, the obligor authorizes the trustee to deliver the securities to the underwriter. If two cities are involved, a representative of the trustee will telephone the correspondent New York bank, which had examined and packaged the securities, and authorize their release to a representative of the underwriter. Simultaneously, the obligor acknowledges receipt of payment for the securities. The closing is then completed; however, the trustee's work in establishing and administering the trust is just beginning.

### Administering the Trust

In carrying out its primary responsibility to administer the provisions of the indenture, the trustee performs three principal functions:

- If the issue is secured, the trustee takes title to the collateral—usually a mortgage on real property—and ensures that it will be appropriately maintained.

- In administering the contract, the trustee makes certain that indenture provisions are met, including examining reports from the corporation and consulting engineers, accountants, and other professionals.

- If the obligor defaults, the trustee has the responsibility of enforcing the applicable provisions of the contract and representing the bondholders in the event of legal action.

For the same bond issue, a corporate trust department can also act as registrar and paying agent (more on these functions in a moment). These multiple jobs must be handled separately, however, to assure that none of the responsibilities are compromised.

## CORPORATE AGENCIES

In addition to serving as trustee for corporate bond accounts, a bank trust department also performs agency services—that is, services that are distinct from the fiduciary powers implied when acting as trustee. As a corporate agent, the bank is responsible for doing only what the owner of the assets instructs it to do. For example, a trust department can be employed to keep stock ownership records, collect and distribute dividends and interest payments, and exchange one kind of stock or bond for another.

Agency services relating to corporate bonds are discussed first, followed by a detailed look at agency services relating to equity securities—also known as common stock.

### Corporate Bond Issues

As well as administering the indenture as the contract between the borrower and the lender, the corporate trustee must make certain that agency services are provided for the bonds from the time they are issued until the time they are retired or redeemed. In some cases, the bank designated as trustee may also be appointed principal agent. Often, however, one bank serves as trustee, protecting the security of the indenture and administering its provisions, while another bank serves as principal agent, providing the associated agency services.

Since the country's principal financial center is New York, some purchasers of securities prefer to have facilities in that city to provide agency services for corporate bond issues. New York banks and brokers hold millions of bonds. If a large number of bonds are bought in New York, then mailing expenses are considerably reduced. Consequently, many indentures require the obligor to designate an office or agent in New York City where demands or notices may be served and where the indenture securities may be presented for payment, registration, exchange, and so on.

When a bank outside New York City is named trustee, usually the bank is also named as principal agent, with a New York bank—frequently, a correspondent of the trustee—named as coagent. The New York bank may perform all requisite agency functions, including that of the authenticating agent for the trustee—

that is, signing the securities to be issued on registration of transfer, exchange, or partial redemption. Occasionally, a coagent is also named in other cities in addition to New York. In that case, the trustee must closely coordinate the activities of all the agents. A principal agent should exercise appropriate control over other agents that report and account to it.

### Bond Registrar

A bank trust department acting as an agent for the registration and transfer of bonds is called a **bond registrar.** This agency records changes in the ownership of bonds from the bearer to a designated owner, from one designated owner to another, and from a designated owner to the bearer.

A bond registrar keeps complete ownership records for registered bonds, rather than merely making and recording the transfer as a transfer agent for stock sometimes does. In addition, the bond registrar usually must maintain a record of the certificate numbers of all outstanding bearer bonds in preparation for a bond call. The number of registered bondholders of any issue is usually small compared with the potentially enormous number of stockholders of one corporation. Thus the accounting records for registered bonds are far less extensive than those for stock.

The number of registered bondholders is increasing substantially because the issuing organizations favor registration and because many bank trust departments prefer to register bonds held in trust accounts. Trust departments prefer registration as it eliminates clipping and collecting interest coupons, which is necessary when a bond is not registered.

### Paying Agencies

Although corporations sometimes make bond interest and principal payments themselves, more typically they engage the services of a **paying agent.** The trustee for a bond issue is often appointed paying agent as well. If so, the functions are quite distinct and should be handled separately. Bank trust departments also act as paying agents for the interest or principal on bonds issued by states, counties, towns, school districts, and other government units, and the revenue bonds of public authorities. Banks cannot handle obligations of the federal government, as that task is performed by Federal Reserve banks.

Organizations issuing securities sometimes find that their obligations are accepted more readily if interest and principal payments can be made by a copaying agent in a major money center. For example, a public authority in Virginia might find more acceptance for its bonds in New England if a well-known New York bank were the copaying agent.

The paying agent's primary responsibility is to make principal and interest payments to bondholders when due. Most bonds pay interest every 6 months, with the rate and timing set in advance. The bonds also mature on a certain date, at which time the paying agent pays the bondholder the face amount. The paying agent is also responsible for paying the principal amount of any bonds that are called prior to maturity (no interest is payable after the call date).

When and how payments are made depend on the type of bond. A **registered bond** has the owner's name on it. Because the bond ownership is identified, the paying agent makes interest payments directly to the bondholder, whose name it keeps on record. A **bearer bond** does not have the owner's name imprinted on it, nor does the trust department have any record of bondholders. Consequently, interest payments are made only when a bearer bondholder clips coupons from the bond certificate and presents them to the paying agent. Upon verifying the authenticity of the coupons, the paying agent makes a check out to the person who presented the coupon. When the bond (registered or bearer) eventually matures or is called, the bondholder presents the certificate and, in return, receives a check from the paying agent for the face amount of the bond. If called before maturity, any premium set forth in the indenture is also paid.

Before making interest or principal payments, the paying agent should determine whether the issuer has sufficient funds available in collected form. After payment, the agent cancels the bonds or coupons and either destroys or delivers them to the issuer. The paying agent must submit all registered bonds that are paid to the bond registrar, who removes them from the registration records. If no assignment is involved, the agent must certify that the registered owner was paid.

Because paying agents deal with large amounts of money and high volumes of certificates and coupons, all payments must be made promptly and without error. Any mistakes are likely to be costly. Although counterfeits are rare, the agent must constantly be on guard against them. Stop-payment orders should also be watched for—including orders involving coupons from unredeemed, previously called bonds on which interest is no longer being paid.

## Corporate Equity Securities

As mentioned earlier, corporations also raise capital by issuing equity securities, or common stock. When agency services are needed involving common stocks, corporations often turn to bank trust departments. Corporations could undertake most of these agency services, but trust departments are usually better equipped to provide detailed recordkeeping services, particularly given the high volume of work entailed in stockholder accounting. In deciding whether to accept an appointment as an agent for equity securities, a trust institution should follow the same guidelines as outlined in corporate trustee appointments.

The major types of agencies that bank trust departments perform for their corporate clients can be broadly classified as transfer agencies, registration agencies, paying agencies, and exchange agencies.

### Transfer Agencies

When acting as a **transfer agent,** a bank trust department has the substantial responsibility of transferring stocks so that the corporation suffers no losses and is not liable for damages. This requires the agent to act with the same care that it would exercise if it were the corporation. Transferring stock entails issuing the stock certificate and recording the change in ownership. In addition, the bank trust department often keeps the stock ownership records. Alternatively, another agent or even the issuing corporation itself may perform the stock recordkeeping.

If acting as principal transfer agent, a bank trust department not only transfers the stock of its corporate customer, but also maintains all shareholder records. These records include the names, addresses, and tax identification numbers of all shareholders; the certificate numbers and dates of issuance to each shareholder; and the number of shares represented on each certificate issued, along with the total holdings of each shareholder. The principal transfer agent may also disburse dividend checks, prepare lists of stock owners, take geographical or other surveys, and send out financial information to shareholders, including **proxies**—papers that evidence authority to vote. When a bank serves as a cotransfer agent, its responsibility is usually limited to effecting transfers from one owner to another and reporting the transfers to the principal transfer agent. A cotransfer agent does not maintain master shareholder records.

*Transferring original stock.* Before a corporation can issue stock, certain government and corporate requirements must be met. A trust institution should begin its duties as transfer agency only after the corporation's board of directors appoints the agent and presents papers showing the corporation's authority to issue stock.

Stock certificates generally must be signed by officers of the corporation and the transfer agent, as well as by an officer of the registrar, if there is one. The corporate officers' signatures on stock certificates are permitted to be in facsimile form. However, authorized officers of the transfer agent and the registrar must manually sign the certificates.

Most new certificates that a transfer agent issues are exchanged for certificates of shares already outstanding. When originally issued, stock may be based on money payments, on an exchange for property or other stock, or on services made to the corporation. The transfer agent should have evidence that the corporation has complied with all government regulations and that it has paid its taxes. In addition, the agent should determine that the corporation is not issuing more shares than the corporation's charter or articles of incorporation allow.

*Transferring stock already outstanding.* The problems and responsibilities involved in the transfer of stock already outstanding are quite different from those involved in an original issue. In transferring outstanding stock, the primary responsibility is to ensure that the registered holder has assigned his or her ownership of the stock to the new owner. The transfer agent must establish the identity of the individual transferring the stock and establish that person's right to transfer the stock.

If the transferor is an individual or a partnership, the identity of the person whose signature appears on the assignment is established by having a financial institution or a national stock exchange member guarantee the signature.

The right of a stockholder to transfer stock is not as easily established if the transferor is a corporation, one acting in a fiduciary capacity, or an agent. Even a witnessed and guaranteed signature of an individual signing as trustee, executor, attorney-in-fact, or the signature of some officers of a corporation may not be enough. The signature may be genuine, but the question remains about the individual's authority to make the assignment.

Although some laws protect the transfer agent in special situations, the agent must determine whether the signer has the power to bind the corporation. Is the alleged trustee or executor actually the trustee or executor, and has he or she the power to sell or otherwise transfer ownership? Does the attorney-in-fact have the right to act on behalf of the principal in such an important matter as the transfer of stock? The agent should obtain satisfactory answers to these questions before a stock transfer can be made safely. The transfer agent establishes the facts by obtaining authenticated documents from the corporation, a court, or from the person signing the transfer document.

*Additional duties.* Other duties involved in stock transfer agencies may include the following:

- providing custody and safeguarding unissued certificates

- destroying canceled certificates, if permitted

- providing replacement for lost certificates based on the corporation's authority and receipt of an indemnity bond with corporate surety

- ensuring that all shareholders inquiries are promptly and accurately answered within the SEC's requirement

- maintaining an adequate supply of unissued certificates

### Registration Agencies

A **stock registrar** makes certain the transfer agent does not issue more shares of stock than were authorized. To do this, the registrar keeps a record of how many shares of stock the transfer agent has issued, canceled, and reissued. Another function of the registrar is to prevent certificates being transferred when a stop-transfer order is in effect for a given security.

The registrar of a stock issue, like a transfer agent, receives an appointment from the corporation's board of directors. Since the registrar is not required to verify the propriety of the transfer or to maintain stockholder records, the duties are much simpler than those of a transfer agent.

Although the New York Stock Exchange once required that a registrar operate independently of both corporation and transfer agent, one trust department usually performs both functions today. When a bank trust department acts in both capacities, the roles should be independent of one another, with separate records kept.

### Paying Agencies

Bank trust departments also assume the duty of disbursing dividends—a type of paying agency. Because ownership records are used for this purpose, it is common for the transfer agent (who keeps the ownership records) to be appointed dividend paying agent as well. It is also a good arrangement for corporations, which given the vast numbers of public stockholders are usually disinclined to undertake the considerable chore of dispatching dividend checks promptly and maintaining accurate records.

Bank trust departments have developed procedures for performing efficiently and economically the major, periodic duties associated with paying agencies. Modern computer systems can calculate the dividend, print the check with the stockholder's address, insert the check and supplementary reports in an envelope, and apply metered postage.

Dividends are paid to stockholders in the form of cash, stock, or stock splits. After a dividend has been declared by the issuer, the paying agent determines who is entitled to receive the dividend and in what form. This determination is made based on the record date. Then the paying agent sends out checks in the case of cash dividends, or certificates in the case of stock dividends or stock splits.

Obviously, before disbursing dividends to stockholders, the paying agent must make certain that funds are available. Many agents make a practice of notifying their principals in advance that payments are due soon. This is especially true for municipal and other public obligations. The paying agent's task is made much easier if the funds are available in collected form no later than the date set for payment.

## Exchange Agencies

In an exchange agency, the trust department receives one or more kinds of securities and delivers other securities according to a previous arrangement. The principal types are agent for stock splits, agent for stock conversion, and agent for distribution of securities in a corporate reorganization. **Exchange agents** may also act as a depository for foreign securities.

*Agent for stock split.* When a corporation decides to split its stock, it increases the number of shares that the outstanding stock represents without actually selling any more stock. For instance, suppose that a corporation splits its stock on a three-for-one basis, each old share having a value of $45. After the split, each $45 share is converted to three shares worth $15 each. The outstanding stock has no greater intrinsic value than it had before the split, because no assets have been added.

Basically, an agency for a stock split is one of the simplest exchange agencies, but performing the duties involved frequently can be complicated. This type of exchange may require action from the entire body of stockholders.

The agent may handle requests for changes in registration, reports of previously unnoticed losses of certificates, and questions from individual stockholders about a range of problems. The volume of old certificates coming in and new certificates going out means that considerable care must be taken to avoid costly errors. Moreover, since the corporation's entire stock is involved, the dollar values exchanged may reach hundreds of millions or even billions.

Before a stock split, the agent must be certain that the notice sent to all stockholders states the exchange instructions clearly, and that the letter of transmittal is easily understood. The exchange agent must also arrange with the transfer agent for a mutually satisfactory and orderly procedure. Each lot of old stock certificates redeemed must be checked for the required endorsements, stop-payment orders, and payment of deferred taxes. Any special instructions concerning registration or delivery of new stock certificates would also fall to the exchange agent.

When the stock has no par value—no stated face value—or when its stated par value is reduced, a corporation may want to accomplish the split by simply mailing the additional shares. For instance, if the split is on a three-for-one basis, the transfer agent may be instructed to mail each stockholder a certificate for two additional shares of stock for each share registered in his or her name. The certificates held before the split remain outstanding.

*Agent for stock conversion.* Securities such as bonds and **preferred stock** are often issued with a provision that they may be converted, at the holder's option, into other securities—usually common stock of the corporation. (Preferred stock usually receives dividends before common stock and, if the corporation is liquidated, preferred stockholders are given preference to assets ahead of common stockholders. However, unlike common stock, preferred stock does not usually entail voting rights.) The conversion is usually handled by an exchange agent, which must develop a way to manage the actual conversion. The exchange agent may also have to solve problems of dividend adjustments and of fractional shares that result when the conversion price has changed—because of either a time lapse or a change in the common stock itself.

*Agent for distribution of securities in a corporate reorganization.* Bank trust departments also act as agents for the distribution of securities when

- a corporation is being reorganized and old securities must be exchanged for new ones

- a corporation merges or consolidates with another and its outstanding securities are exchanged for the other corporation's securities, or partly for cash and partly for securities

- a corporation wants to adjust its capital structure, for example, by exchanging high-dividend, preferred stock for stock yielding a lower dividend

- a company holding substantial ownership in one or more companies wants or is compelled to dispose of that ownership

*Depository for foreign securities.* When an exchange agent acts as the depository for foreign securities, American investors are offered a convenient way to invest in foreign securities, which are usually stock of major foreign corporations. A trust institution issues **American depository receipts** (ADRs) for a given foreign stock that will be deposited with it or with one of its branches or correspondent banks in the country where the stock is issued. These receipts are negotiable, registered, and are otherwise similar to ordinary stock certificates. The ADRs entitle holders to receive dividends on the foreign stock as the holder of record, after the depository's expenses and charges are deducted.

A holder may surrender his or her ADR to the agent, requesting that the deposited stock be delivered to him or her in this country or to a designated person in the foreign country. Generally, the individual handles such a transaction through a stockbroker. The broker has two ways to proceed: (1) he or she may find a buyer for the stock in the American market and transfer the ADR, not the stock, to the buyer; or (2) the individual may have the agent cancel the ADR and arrange the corresponding amount of stock to be sold abroad. The choice between the two procedures depends on which market offers the best net price.

## Other Corporate Agencies

Bank trust departments provide several other agency services, including the following.

*Agent for redemption of preferred stock.* This agency assists a corporation with its call of preferred stock. The agent verifies the corporation's instructions, sends notice to holders of the stock being called, receives the redemption money, and pays these funds against the surrender of the called stock.

*Subscription agent.* When a corporation wants to give its present stockholders the first opportunity to buy new securities it is issuing, it engages a subscription agent. The agent takes charge of the preparation and mailing of the warrants, splits the outstanding warrants into smaller denominations or groups them into large ones when the stockholders present them, transfers warrants from one registered stockholder to another, accepts payment for new securities, arranges for issuing and delivering the new securities to the subscribers, and accounts to the corporation for all funds paid to it.

*Warrant agent.* A **warrant** is a certificate that gives the holder a right to purchase shares of stock at a given price within a specific period. The basic difference between the warrant and subscription agency is that the certificates involved are likely to have been outstanding for several years. During this time, the holders exercise their options. The warrant agent countersigns the warrants when they are issued, splits and groups warrants, and accepts subscriptions if the warrants are exercised.

*Agent for securities purchase.* When a corporation decides to retire some of its securities—particularly common stock or bonds that cannot be called—holders may be invited to sell their securities. Corporations frequently engage a purchase agent to buy these securities. The agent publishes notices of the invitation to sell; receives, examines, and classifies the tender offers made by the stockholders; sends out notices of rejection or acceptance of tender offers; and arranges to split certificates if only some of the shares offered are accepted. The agent also returns shares tendered but not purchased, pays for shares that are purchased, maintains the necessary records, and makes appropriate reports to the corporation.

## SUMMARY

Corporate operations are financed by either equity or debt capital. Equity is usually held in the form of common stock, while sources of debt capital range from commercial loans to corporate bonds. In issuing bonds, stock, and other securities, corporations often require operational and information services to meet their responsibilities to their stockholders and owners of debt instruments. Banks often fill this need by supplying corporate trust and agency services.

Corporate trust activities are closely governed by federal and state regulations, including the Securities Act of 1933, the Glass-Steagall Act (part of the federal Banking Act of 1933), the Securities Exchange Act of 1934, the Trust Indenture Act of 1939, and Articles 8 and 9 of the Uniform Commercial Code. The Trust Indenture Act requires that trust indentures and the accompanying registration statement be submitted to the SEC for approval. An indenture creates the trust and establishes the terms and conditions for borrowing. Bonds issued under a trust indenture include first mortgage bonds, debentures, equipment trust bonds, revenue bonds, and convertible bonds.

A trust created by a corporate bond indenture differs from the general concept of a trust that has been considered in earlier chapters. For example, under a corporate bond trust, the trustee does not take possession of the property, the beneficiaries are unknown to the trustee, and the trustee has fiduciary responsibilities to the bondholders and the issuer.

Before agreeing to serve as trustee of a corporate bond account, a bank trust department must ascertain that the potential trust is acceptable. Then the indenture should be reviewed, the securities authenticated and delivered, and the closing documents reviewed and approved. Once the securities are sold, the corporate bond trustee must administer the trust, ensure that the trust indenture provisions are met and, in the event of default, represent the interests of the bondholders.

Bank trust departments also provide corporate agency services for both bonds and equity securities. As a bond registrar, the bank acts as an agent for the registration and transfer of bonds, and, as a bondpaying agent, the bank makes principal and interest payments to bondholders when due. Depending on whether the bonds are issued in bearer or registered form, the bank trust department may also have to deal with large volumes of coupons, as well as handling large numbers of bond certificates.

Agency services of common stock issues include transfer agencies (issuing stock, recording changes in ownership, and maintaining shareholder records), registration agencies (ensuring that the stock registrar issues the proper number of shares), paying agencies (disbursing dividend payments), and exchange agencies (replacing one kind of securities for another). A bank trust department may also act as agent for redemption of preferred stock, subscription agent, warrant agent, and agent for securities purchase.

## QUESTIONS FOR REVIEW

1. What is the difference between equity and debt? Referring to an annual report or income statement for a large corporation, how much of the corporation's equity is in the form of common stock, preferred stock, and retained earnings? Are there any other types of equity capital reported? What types of debt (liabilities) does the corporation report? What percentage is in the form of bonds or other long-term debt?

2. What act requires that all new securities be fully described in offering literature and sales presentations? What act separated the investment and commercial banking functions? What act stipulates that all trust indentures must be submitted to the SEC for approval?

3. For an indenture to meet with the SEC's approval, what are some of the requirements that must be met?

4. What is a debenture? What are the proceeds from the sale of revenue bonds typically used for?

5. What are some of the basic differences between a personal trust and a corporate trust?

6. Analyze the following statement: "An ideal arrangement is when a bank serves in the capacity of both corporate trustee and commercial lender to the same corporation. Then the bank can act quickly and call in its loans if it appears that the corporation may have difficulty making its bond payments."

7. What are the basic responsibilities of a bank trust department in administering a corporate bond trust?

8. What are the duties of a paying agent when handling registered bonds, bearer bonds, and stock?

CHAPTER  Charitable Trusts
and Agencies

## INTRODUCTION

Trust accounts can be established and held for charitable organizations. A charity is an entity that is set up for educational, religious, scientific, medical, or any other beneficent purpose, and includes such national organizations as the American Cancer Society and the Boy Scouts or Girl Scouts of America, and at the local level, the community volunteer fire department, Lions Club, or Parent Teacher Association. For a charity to be tax exempt, it must meet the qualifications mandated in the Internal Revenue Service Codes 501(c) or (d).

To further their work, charities usually receive gifts in the form of donations from people and businesses, who in return receive tax deductions that lower their taxable income. In addition, donations given by a decedent in his or her will are deducted from the total value of the estate before any estate or gift taxes are paid. Since tax-exempt charities cannot operate to gain a profit, they are defined as nonprofit organizations. As such, they are exempted from paying taxes on the income they receive from donations and interest earned on their passive investments. By structuring the tax code so that donations are tax deductible and nonprofit income is tax exempt, the government has created an environment in which charities can flourish. These tax inducements, combined with the altruistic character of the American people, has accounted for the growth of charities in this country and, consequently, of charitable trusts and trust services.

This chapter considers the types of charitable trusts that bank trust departments work with and the general and specialized agencies they provide. We will examine community trusts, public and private foundations, charitable remainder trusts, and institutional trusts as the major categories of charitable trusts.

# COMMUNITY FOUNDATIONS

A special kind of charitable trust account is the **community foundation,** which is set up by cities or towns for charitable purposes. The first community foundation, the Cleveland Foundation, was established in 1914. Since then, community foundations have been set up in many large American cities. The volume of property under administration in these trusts, as well as the annual additions to them and distributions from them for charitable, educational, and other public purposes, is growing rapidly.

A community foundation is established by leaders of the community to accept donations and make money available to those doing charitable work in the community. Donations—from cash gifts to assets such as stocks and bonds—are deposited in the trust, which may be held by a trust department or several trust departments acting as trustee. The income from the trust account is distributed among the designated recipients. Decisions regarding how the money will be allocated is typically made by a **distribution committee**—a group of people in the community who are usually appointed by a public official. Trust departments are usually not involved in decisions about the use of the community's trust income. Bank trust departments do, however, perform a number of other fiduciary duties, including investing, managing, and safeguarding the trust assets and collecting all income earned by the trust. The trustee also pays out the income to the distribution committee or agent and prepares reports detailing all transactions.

The characteristics of most community foundations

- provide for a wide range of services. The resolutions, trust agreements, declarations of trust, or corporate charters creating community foundations include every kind of charitable or public service. Usually the trust instrument lists every objective and also contains a general welfare clause to include purposes that may not have been considered when the document was written or that may have come into existence afterward. If separate foundations are transferred to the community foundation, the terms and beneficiaries of those trusts are, of course, honored.

- afford flexibility in how gifts are applied. Usually, a donor may specify how the gift should be used and the conditions for use. However, the gift is made with the understanding that if those wishes become impossible or even impracticable to carry out, the gift will be applied in a way that meets the general purposes of the community foundation.

- provide for impartial distribution of funds. The distribution of funds available to the beneficiaries is typically controlled by the distribution committee.

- provide for more efficient and economical administration of foundations. Some foundations—usually smaller, private ones—can be transferred to a community foundation, thus improving the distribution of funds.

In the early years of community foundations, only one trustee was involved. Today, however, the trend is toward multiple trusteeship. Trust institutions in a community often make joint or identical declarations of trust that recognize the same distribution committee.

Among the advantages of a community foundation are safety, equitable management of small and large gifts, and economy of administration—funds can be pooled for collective investment or placed in common trust funds. Community trusts enrich the lives of everyone in the community.

## PUBLIC AND PRIVATE
## CHARITABLE FOUNDATIONS

A **charitable foundation** may be either private or public. Private foundations are tax-exempt organizations established for a variety of charitable purposes. They have limited resource bases and must comply with strict Internal Revenue Service rules and regulations regarding reporting and minimum annual amounts paid to qualified recipients. Public foundations, on the other hand, receive their contributions from the general public, have less stringent reporting requirements, and no mandatory payout.

Charitable foundations are similar to community foundations in that their funds are received, invested, and paid out by a trustee, which also prepares periodic reports on the trust's activities. Disbursement decisions may be made by a distribution committee or by the trustee itself.

Unlike community foundations, however, charitable foundations are often created for special purposes and have some connection with the group for which the trust was established. Examples of public foundations created for special purposes are a regional church foundation established by a given denomination, a medical foundation sponsored by a state medical society, a Rotary foundation for educational loans set up by a local Rotary club, and a welfare foundation funded by a labor union for the benefit of its members' families. In addition, many individuals set up foundations during their lifetime or upon their death to further a particular cause—for example, a scholarship for worthy students or indigent elderly assistance. A charitable foundation has, therefore, a more specialized focus than a community foundation.

## CHARITABLE REMAINDER TRUSTS

**Charitable remainder trusts** have two purposes. First, they pay an income or annuity interest earned by the trust assets to the beneficiaries, who may be the **donor** (the person who set up the trust) or someone chosen by the donor, for example, a spouse or child. Second, such trusts provide that the trust assets (the "remainder") go to a charity or group of charities (often referred to as the remainderman) upon the death of the beneficiaries. For the donor to realize an immediate income tax deduction for this kind of charitable trust, it must be one of three kinds: charitable remainder annuity trust, charitable remainder uni-trust, or pooled income funds. The income tax deduction is computed using IRS actuarial tables to determine the remainder interest going to charity. The donor also avoids capital gains taxes on the sale of the donated property by the trustee. However, it is important to note that the trust is irrevocable and the trust agreement must be drafted very carefully to ensure the charitable deduction is realized.

This type of trust is very attractive to people who have low cost-based assets that are producing little or no income. By gifting such assets to a charitable remainder trust, they can increase their income, avoid taxation on the gain from the sale and reinvestment, and eventually help out their favorite charity.

As with the other trusts, the trust department, as trustee of a charitable remainder trust, can manage the assets, collect the income, and distribute payments to the beneficiaries. In addition, when the beneficiary dies, the trust department will distribute the assets to the charity or charities named by the donor or continue to hold the assets in trust for the benefit of the charity.

### Charitable Remainder Annuity Trusts

A **charitable remainder annuity trust** is one that individuals create either during their lifetime for themselves or others, or at death through their wills for the benefit of others. Charitable remainder annuity trusts pay the annuity beneficiary a set amount during his or her lifetime that cannot be less than 5 percent of the value of the property when the trust was established. The remainder interest—the property in trust—goes to the qualified charity at the annuitant's death. For example, if the donor gives $100,000 to an annuity trust and retains quarterly payments for life at the annual rate of 5 percent of the initial value, the trustee will pay the annuitant $5,000 per year. When the annuitant dies, the trustee distributes the property to the charity named in the trust.

### Charitable Remainder Unitrusts

This variation of the charitable remainder trust—the **unitrust**—provides that the lifetime beneficiary will receive a fixed percentage (not less than 5 percent) of the net fair market value of the trust as it is determined annually. Again, the remainder must be given to a qualified charity. For example, if the contribution to the trust is a house valued at $100,000 and the donor is to receive 5 percent of the asset's value for each year, the beneficiary receives $5,000 the first year, but $5,500 the following year when the trust assets are valued at $110,000.

### Pooled Income Funds

**Pooled income funds** provide a way for donors of smaller gifts to obtain an income interest during their lifetimes on their gifts, with the remainder interest given to charitable organizations. The charity's fund is, essentially, an investment fund for the contributions of many donors whose gifts would be difficult to administer individually. At the donor's death, the principal—the donor's proportionate share of the pooled funds—passes to the charity. Usually, the charity has a management agency relationship with a bank trust department to manage the funds.

### INSTITUTIONAL TRUSTS

Colleges, hospitals, and charitable organizations often establish an **institutional trust, foundation,** or **endowment fund** to receive the assets and cash donated to them. To be considered an institutional trust, it must be devoted exclusively to religious, charitable, scientific, literary, or educational purposes, and none of the trust's net earnings may go to private shareholders or individuals.

An individual benefactor may also create an institutional trust for the benefit of a public institution. An institution that is an absolute owner of an endowment, and not the trustee of its funds, may establish an institutional trust for its own benefit by transferring the endowment to a bank trust department to administer it according to the terms of the trust instrument. If an institution sets up a separate foundation, the trust terms usually direct the policy of how the income and principal may be disbursed. Often it establishes an investment committee of trustees to direct policy and review the investment performance of any money managers, such as banks.

The terms of an institutional trust are essentially the same as those of a personal trust and may be made inflexible or as fully flexible as those of a personal trust. The investment powers of the institutional trustee may or may not be limited, and the trustee may or may not be required to obtain approval from a committee or officer of the institution before making investment changes.

The trustee administers the property of the institutional trust in much the same way as a personal trust. When acting as trustee, the trust department manages assets, collects income, makes distributions, and prepares reports. If another party is the trustee, the trust department can still act as an agent of the trustee, perhaps buying and selling assets and otherwise serving as an investment manager. Some agencies for institutional trusts will be discussed later in this section.

The chief difference between an institutional and personal trust is that the trustee of an institutional trust is often required to work with specific representatives of the organization on many different issues. For example, the trustee would deal with the finance committee regarding investment changes, with the treasurer on income payments, and potentially with several officers of the organization when payments or deliveries of principal are involved.

The large endowments of well-known institutions usually have been accumulated over considerable time from a variety of sources and typically include outright gifts made during the donors' lifetimes, bequests under wills, and gifts in perpetual trusts. Such institutions receive unrestricted gifts of millions of dollars, which are given without conditions or limitations. An organization is free to use those funds in any way its governing body may choose, such as paying current expenses, constructing buildings, making improvements to existing buildings, or investing.

Establishing an institutional trust has three major advantages:

- An institutional trust relieves the organization's governing body of many business and investment responsibilities. Thus board members can devote energy to furthering the organization's goals. The organization is also free to select as board members men and women who are highly qualified to promote and serve the organization and its purposes, but who may be inexperienced in investing funds and in managing property.

- With an institutional trust, the duties and responsibilities connected with the proper investment of trust funds are clearly identified for the organization to help it manage property in a financially responsible way.

- An institutional trust encourages individual contributions to public institutions. People of means are more likely to make gifts to the endowments of institutions—particularly local and smaller ones—when they have assurance that the endowments are trusteed with a well-known and highly regarded bank trust department.

## INSTITUTIONAL AGENCIES

Bank trust departments also accept accounts as agents for endowments or as agents for an organization's financial secretary or treasurer. Since an organization that received gifts in trust cannot retrustee the property, it may create an agency to manage the trust property. A management agency for endowment property is adapted to the needs of the institutions holding the property in trust. As an agent for the financial secretary or treasurer of an organization, the bank trust department may perform only a few ministerial acts or have the extensive duties of a management agent. Examples of agency services follow.

*Cash-management agency.* This agency involves the temporary, efficient investment of all cash or cash equivalents. For example, if a foundation has cash scattered among banks and savings and loans, a bank trust department can consolidate the accounts and obtain the maximum return on short-term funds.

*Custodial agency.* These are the most basic services that a trust department offers and include safekeeping, recordkeeping, and accounting. These services relieve a foundation of the responsibility of managing securities, clipping coupons, and accounting for dividends.

*Management agency.* In addition to providing basic custodial services, this service offers a foundation investment management. With personnel experienced in trust and tax matters, trust departments are ideally suited to administer institutional trusts.

## MARKETING TO CHARITABLE ORGANIZATIONS

Large, well-established charitable organizations often manage their own endowment property and manage it well. Yet many colleges, universities, and small foundations need the services of a corporate fiduciary. Even the larger and more established charitable organizations are finding that only a well-staffed trust department offers the expertise to cope with investments, taxes, and government regulations.

Bank trust departments should therefore give serious consideration to actively soliciting the business of charitable and educational institutions. Trust departments that ignore this market may well miss excellent opportunities for increased business. This type of business allows the bank to fulfill its responsibilities to the community and to increase profits at the same time.

Having secured one or two large public foundation accounts, a bank trust department is in a position to demonstrate a high level of service and investment management performance that will, in turn, yield additional business. Usually, the most important and influential citizens of the community are asked to participate on the board of directors or as members of the finance committee of various public foundations. If a trust department does an excellent job for one foundation, the word spreads to other foundation boards on which they serve. Through its dealings with charitable trusts, a bank trust department may even attract the personal trust business of board members and others associated with the charitable organizations.

## SUMMARY

Bank trust departments offer trustee and agency services to charitable organizations. Charities receive most of their money in the form of tax-deductible donations from individuals and businesses. Since charities are defined as nonprofit organizations, they do not pay taxes on the income they receive from donations nor the interest income they earn on their investments. Charities frequently hold much of their assets in trust accounts. Those working for a charity are thus freed from such responsibilities as making investment decisions and managing property—tasks that they may be ill-suited for—and can concentrate instead on furthering the goals of their charity.

The community foundation is established by local leaders to accept donations and make money available to the community. Decisions regarding how the money will be allocated are typically made by a distribution committee, with the trust department handling such duties as investing, managing and safeguarding trust assets, collecting all income earned by the trust, and preparing transaction reports.

Charitable foundations, which may be public or private, are usually created for a special purpose and have some connection with the group for which the trust was established. For example, a medical foundation may be set up by a state medical society to perform charitable work within the state. A charitable foundation has a specialized focus and is different from a community foundation, which is created for the benefit of all community members.

Charitable remainder trusts accomplish two objectives: they pay an income or annuity to trust beneficiaries during their lifetimes and, upon their death, the trust assets are turned over to a designated charity or charities. The donor—the person who set up the trust—realizes a tax deduction and avoids capital gains tax on the sale of the donated property. Two variations of this type of trust are the charitable remainder annuity trust and the charitable remainder unitrust. A charitable remainder annuity trust pays the annuity beneficiaries a set amount over the course of their lifetimes, which cannot be less than 5 percent of the value of the property when the trust was established. Charitable remainder unitrusts provide that the beneficiaries will not receive less than 5 percent of the net fair market value of the trust, which is determined annually. In both cases, the trust assets remaining at the time of the beneficiary's death—the remainder—is donated to the appropriate charity or charities.

Pooled income funds provide a way for donors of small gifts to obtain an income interest during their lifetimes on their gifts, with the remainder interest given to charitable organizations.

Colleges, hospitals, and charitable organizations, and in some cases, individuals, may set up trusts for the benefit of an institution. The trustee administers the property of the institutional trust in much the same way as a personal trust—managing assets, collecting income, distributing payments, and preparing reports. The institution is free to use trust funds in any way it chooses, such as paying current expenses, constructing buildings, and making improvements to existing buildings. In addition to acting as trustee, bank trust departments also offer agency services—cash management, custodial, and investment management are three examples.

### QUESTIONS FOR REVIEW

1. Give some examples of charitable organizations that serve in your community. What reasons could you offer to convince these organizations that it would be in their interests to establish a trust account at your bank?

2. What is the basic difference between a community foundation and a public or private foundation?

3. What kind of trust account might you recommend to a client who wanted to provide for his beneficiaries over their lifetimes and then donate his estate to charity?

4. What are the duties of a trustee of an institutional trust? Is the trustee typically responsible for deciding how trust funds are to be spent?

5. Name three institutional agencies offered by a bank trust department.

6. Why should bank trust departments give serious consideration to soliciting the business of charitable organizations?

SECTION 4 Trust Department
Operations

"Our responsibility for the safe, responsible handling of
customer funds is never going to change. Commitments
to the traditional strengths and values of safety and
soundness will be with us however the financial services
business evolves. However, managing the business is no
longer a job which consists of the old, conservative,
cradle-to-grave, go with the flow, open the vault at
9:30 a.m. and lock it up at 3:30 p.m. type of job—that
mindset is gone forever."

—Richard J. Flamson III, *chairman and CEO,*
*Security Pacific National Bank*

CHAPTER *12* Organizational Structures
and Strategies

## INTRODUCTION

The preceding chapters covered the responsibilities of trust officers in providing trust and agency services for personal, employee benefit, corporate, and charitable accounts. A trust department is, however, composed of more than just its account officers. A board of directors, one or more committees, and executive officers oversee and administer the department.

Support personnel handle tasks such as income collection, tax and expense payment, securities processing, investment research, report preparation and mailing, dividend payments and reinvestment, vault control, recordkeeping, systems management, accounting, and auditing. Depending on the size and nature of the trust department, an account officer may handle many of these duties. But regardless of who performs these functions, everyone in a bank trust department is legally held to the highest standards. More importantly, a trust department is responsible for the money and assets of its clients, some of whom are the bank's biggest customers and all of whom are invaluable.

This chapter looks at some of the ways a trust department is organized, managed, and operated so that it can accomplish these diverse tasks while fulfilling its responsibilities to its customers. Then we will consider some of the strategies banks are employing to prosper in what has become a very competitive trust services environment.

## ORGANIZATIONAL STRUCTURES OF
## A BANK TRUST DEPARTMENT

How a bank trust department is organized depends on many variables such as size, the type of customer it serves, and the kinds of accounts it handles. A small community bank may emphasize personal agencies, trusts, and guardianships, while a large, money-center bank might concentrate on providing trust and agency services for corporations, institutions, and employee pension plans. Nonetheless, all trust departments share a common purpose and exhibit many of the same functions and organizational characteristics. Exhibit 12.1 shows a traditional trust department organized along the lines of functional responsibility—in this example, business development, trust administration, investment, and support services. Overseeing and managing these operations are the board of directors, trust committee, trust audit committee, and bank executives.

## Oversight and Management

The scope and complexity of a trust department's activities require that it be monitored and managed at several levels. The bank's board of directors, committees, and executives work together to see that the fiduciary and other responsibilities of the trust department are handled properly.

### Board of Directors

At the top of any trust department (as with every division of a bank) sits the board of directors. The board of directors is chosen by the bank's owners—whether one person or thousands of shareholders—to set overall operational policy and supervise the senior managers and officers of the bank. The board has responsibility for all matters related to the bank's exercise of fiduciary powers emanating from Regulation 9 of the Comptroller of the Currency. Regulation 9 includes statutory regulations for national banks and is generally accepted by many state banking regulatory agencies. The regulation also makes it clear that, although the administration of fiduciary powers may be assigned, the responsibilities cannot be delegated.

### Committees

To fulfill its trust oversight responsibilities, the board appoints one or more committees made up of some board members and several top officers of the trust department and the bank. Almost all banks have a trust committee whose job it is to review trust department policy, general operating performance, regulatory compliance, and profitability. Further, the trust committee exercises fiduciary discretion in making decisions reserved to it by the bank's bylaws and advises trust management on unusual or complex situations when requested.

Many banks also have a trust audit committee, which oversees the audit department. The audit department operates autonomously; its auditors answer to the board of directors or to the trust audit committee and not to the managers of the trust department. The audit department is responsible for ensuring that the bank's trust activities comply with bank policies and federal and state

EXHIBIT 12.1  Trust Department Organization (by traditional functions)

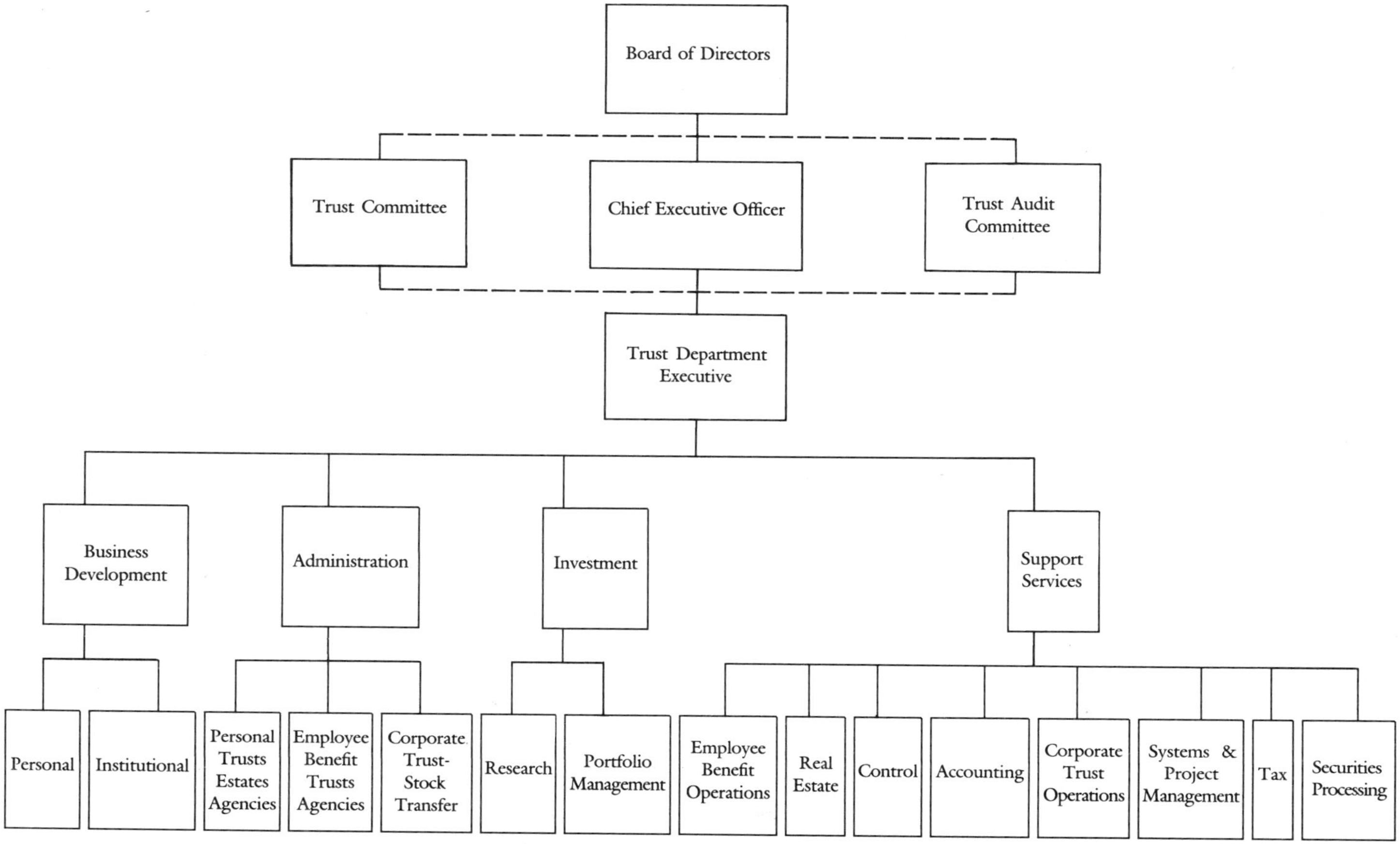

regulations. To a large extent, the quality of the trust department can be attributed to the efficiency and strictness of its auditors.

Although not shown in the organizational chart (exhibit 12.1), many banks appoint additional committees that typically fall under the trust committee and are given the task of overseeing specific trust activities. One such group is the trust investment committee, which watches over the investments that are managed by the trust department. The committee sets guidelines for investing in securities and other assets, and at least once a year, it looks at all the investments in each account.

Another common committee is the trust administrative committee. This group sets rules on how accounts are handled, and may also decide how to spend money from trust accounts for beneficiaries. For example, if a will or trust agreement is ambiguous about whether money is to be allocated for doctor's bills, college tuition, or a new car, a trust administrative committee may have the ultimate say on what expenses are proper and reasonable. Most trust departments give each trust officer a limit for discretionary requests made by their beneficiaries. Any requests beyond an officer's authority are presented to the trust administrative committee for approval.

### Executive and Administrative Officers

Most trust departments have one person in charge—a trust department executive who reports directly to the bank's chief executive or administrative officer. The trust department executive is assisted by key functional or product managers and the trust committee members selected by the board of directors. These individuals constitute the trust management team. As with most managerial positions, the primary responsibilities of a trust department executive and his or her chief administrative officers are *planning, organizing, leading,* and *controlling*.

In fulfilling its *planning* responsibilities, trust management establishes the trust department's mission; develops a strategic plan, including broad goals and strategies; and oversees the development and implementation of specific, measurable objectives to achieve each goal.

The *organizing* function entails developing a framework for coordinating the work of all trust employees to achieve departmental objectives. The organizational structure influences how effectively management can achieve the goals of the strategic plan.

In *leading* a trust department, management directs the ongoing responsibilities of supervision and staffing. Through person-to-person relationships with key subordinates, the trust department executive provides the guidance to integrate the employees' needs with the department's business objectives, thus propelling management's plans into action.

Trust management must also *control* operations by continually measuring actual progress against its strategic plans and taking corrective action when appropriate. By planning, organizing, leading, and controlling, trust management accomplishes the development and implementation of general policies to provide quality trust services with a reasonable profit to the bank.

## Marketing and Business Development

Although marketing and business development is a function common to all bank trust departments (see exhibit 12.1), in the past it has been underemphasized. Trust departments have traditionally downplayed aggressive marketing tactics and preferred to rely upon existing bank customers or referrals to supply the bulk of their new trust customers. Banks have come to recognize, however, that the financial services marketplace has changed, and a passive promotional stance is no longer acceptable. Competitors, such as investment counseling firms, are vigorously championing themselves as performance oriented, and for banks to succeed they must be as vigorous in their marketing. Consequently, the bank marketing and business development function has become increasingly important.

## Trust Administration

Another specific function within trust departments is trust administration. In medium-to-large trust departments, the administrative function is usually part of three separate organizational units for personal, employee benefit, and corporate trust clients. The personal accounts unit is often divided into separate subunits for estate settlement, trust administration, and administration of agencies (see exhibit 12.1). In a small bank, just one account administrator may be assigned to handle all types of accounts.

### *Personal Trust Account Administrators*

Personal and estate settlement administrative officers—referred to generally throughout this text as trust officers—spearhead the bank's delivery of personal trust services to the client. The primary responsibilities of the personal trust officer and the estate administrative officer are to exercise fiduciary discretion; interpret the will or trust agreement; exercise the powers and duties granted by the will, trust agreement, or applicable statutes; and provide personal services.

Generally, each trust or guardianship account is handled by one officer who has overall responsibility for the account. Because there are many different kinds of personal trust accounts, a trust officer's work varies. The tasks of a trust officer were covered in detail in section 2 of this text. To review, most trust officers are, at a minimum, responsible for answering their client's information requests, handling transactions (paying bills, buying or selling securities as directed by the client, removing or adding assets from the trust, and so forth), preparing reports, and monitoring accounts. In some trust departments, the investment and administrative functions are combined, and the officer often is referred to as the account officer. Now in some departments, the client's reason for buying trust services determines which staff officer will primarily work with the client. For example, an individual buying an investment management service would interact with the investment officer; a client wanting a custody account would see the support services officer.

Although a personal trust officer's duties vary from bank to bank, all work closely with their clients. The primary responsibility of a personal trust officer is, therefore, customer service.

### Employee Benefit and Corporate Trust Account Administrators

Administration of employee benefit and corporate trust accounts involves fewer personal contacts than individual accounts do. Nonetheless, the administrative officer works closely with corporate treasurers, actuaries, consultants, and other professionals and, as a result, an overriding function of the position is customer relations.

The specific responsibilities of the employee benefit and corporate trust account administrator were addressed in section 3 of this text. Some of the more common tasks of the corporate trust officer are to respond to information requests; manage corporate accounts (ensuring funds are available to meet dividend or interest payments, paying out funds to builders, performing securities transfers on time, presenting bond coupons for payment when due, and so forth); and carry out the trust department's fiduciary responsibilities that arise from the appointment.

As trust administrator, the legal responsibilities are substantial—a trust department can easily be held liable for any losses arising from a wrong investment decision, and a breach of fiduciary duty carries even stiffer repercussions, including possible civil or criminal sanctions. Consequently, all account administrators should ensure that everything done for a trust account complies with the laws and regulations that govern accounts and transactions. Furthermore, the agreement between the trust department and the client must be followed to the letter. Keeping abreast of all the legal and statutory requirements is a formidable task. For example, employee benefit account administration requires a detailed knowledge of ERISA; corporate trust administration requires knowledge of complex securities laws and industry standards. For these and other reasons, trust account administrators are often lawyers who have extensive legal experience.

In personal and institutional trust administrative functions, the administrative assistant plays a key role in helping the trust officer deliver the product to the customer. The assistant frees the trust officer to devote time to client communication and decision making. In a growing number of trust organizations, paralegals who have specific training in fiduciary matters fill the administrative assistant positions. As more qualifications are required of administrative assistants and the status of the position is enhanced, the assistants are more likely to have the opportunity to become trust officers.

## Investment Services

In the organizational structure of most trust departments, a separate unit is assigned for investment services. Investment services have assumed an increasingly important role in competing for and retaining trust customers. For institutional accounts, excluding the corporate trust business, investment service represents the client's primary motive for buying services. For most individuals who seek help with estate settlement and testamentary trusts, personal service is the key factor in their choice of trust departments. However, an increasing number of individual clients now establish trusts and investment management agencies by basing their decisions on the quality of the investment service.

As mentioned earlier, the trust committee often establishes one or more subcommittees to assist in the department's investment responsibilities. Two such groups are an investment policy committee and an investment review committee. The policy committee guides general investment policy, and the review committee considers the assets of individual accounts vis-à-vis the recommendations of the account's asset manager. A comprehensive look at trust investment management can be found in chapter 13.

### Portfolio Management

The investment department is often subdivided into smaller units that focus on portfolio management and investment research. The portfolio management arm of the investment services department makes the investment decisions for the trust account.

In managing trust assets, the investment officer looks at the needs of the individual client and establishes investment objectives and strategies that offer the greatest likelihood of fulfilling those needs. The investment strategy must be also in accord with the investment powers or limitations contained in the governing instrument and in statutes such as ERISA. With these considerations in mind, an acceptable risk-taking range can then be set.

*Research*

In most large trust departments, the portfolio management group is supported by an investment research staff. The research function is often further divided into subgroups responsible for following selected industries and preparing economic forecasts. For example, one or more persons might closely follow the automobile manufacturers, while others would concentrate on companies in the steel or computer industries. The research group is responsible for conducting studies to rank the expected return and risk characteristics of companies in an industry and to evaluate the prospects for the industry as a whole. The researchers also recommend securities suitable for the trust department's fiduciary accounts.

Many banks compile a list of recommended securities, which is commonly referred to as the **buy list.** Individual portfolio managers are constrained to buy securities on this list, unless they have a good reason not to. Depending on their economic prognostications, the researchers might suggest that it is better to have more money invested in short-term bonds than in equity funds. These recommendations are forwarded to the trust investment committee, which decides what are the best kinds of investments. These decisions become the investment policy of the trust department—general guidelines that are used by investment managers in determining which securities should be bought and sold.

## Support Services

Operational and support services form the foundation from which trust products or services are delivered. Traditionally, many trust institutions have gone to substantial expense to attract and retain the highest quality administrative, investment, and business development officers, only to see their success diminished by a failure to pay equal attention to the routine operational functions. Without proper management attention, including planning and organizing within the operations unit, the quality of service provided will be less than satisfactory, with a resulting detrimental effect on all product lines. Trust operations personnel should be made aware of the critical nature of their role as the support services arm of the trust department.

The primary function of the operations unit is to provide support services to the administrative, investment, and business development functions. In providing the support necessary to permit the account officer to deliver quality service to the customer, the support services unit is often organized into separate sections responsible for trust accounting, employee benefit operations, securities movement and control, tax, real estate, systems and project management, control, and corporate trust operations (see exhibit 12.1).

The trust operations group generally handles most of the clerical tasks associated with trust accounts—maintaining files, posting transactions, collecting income, disbursing funds, preparing and filing tax returns, executing trades, and calculating and collecting service fees. Major support services to bank trust departments and their functions are listed in exhibit 12.2. We will return to a comprehensive discussion of trust operations in chapter 14.

## ALTERNATIVE ORGANIZATIONAL STRUCTURES

The trust department organization discussed so far—presented in exhibit 12.1—developed along the traditional lines of functional responsibility. Other standard organizational structures are presented in exhibits 12.3 and 12.4. Exhibit 12.3 displays a product-line orientation, while exhibit 12.4 combines elements of both functional and product-line organization. All are typical organizational plans of medium-to-large trust departments.

## STRATEGIES FOR COMPETING IN TODAY'S TRUST SERVICES MARKETPLACE

When a trust department fails to consistently achieve adequate profitability, the problem can frequently be traced to poor marketing strategies or organizational shortcomings. One reason is that bank management often places comparatively less importance on its trust business. Consequently, it is common to find that the marketing budget for commercial or consumer lending products far outstrips that for trust services. Another result is that trust functions are often relegated to secondary status within the bank, viewed not as a promising source of earnings for the bank, but rather as something that is almost reluctantly proffered to a limited number of customers.

Not surprisingly, competitors have taken advantage of this situation. Investment counseling firms, for example, have been able through vigorous marketing efforts to portray themselves as active investors, placing banks in the light of conservative, almost stodgy, caretakers of trust assets. This perception is for the most part just that—perception, not reality—but nonetheless, it has caused many investors to shift their accounts to investment counseling firms, thinking that the returns are better there.

For these and other reasons, many banks are struggling to remain profitable while their market share is constantly eroded by competitors. In response, banks are reassessing their trust department operations and, in many cases, adopting a market-driven approach that gives more attention to service fees, cost analysis, cost reduction, and productivity improvement strategies.

EXHIBIT 12.2   Support Services to Bank Trust Departments

## Recordkeeping

- Transaction posting of assets and liabilities

- Income collection and posting
  Interest
  Dividends
  Rents
  Royalties
  Pensions and retirement benefits
  Mortgage payments

- Disbursements
  Beneficiary income distribution
  Real estate taxes and insurance

- Collective fund accounting
  Income calculation and posting
  Valuation of assets
  Posting of unit investment and redemption
  transactions
  Preparation of annual financial statements

- Employee benefit accounting
  Thrift/profit-sharing participant accounting
  Benefit payments to retirees
  Tax form preparation—W2P, 1099 R

- Trust fee income calculation and collection

- Customer reports preparation and mailing

## Asset Services

- Securities processing
  Asset safekeeping
  Settlement of securities trades

- Corporate actions
  Stock splits/stock dividends
  Tender offers
  Rights and warrants
  Asset conversions
  Securities spinoffs
  Called bonds
  Class action suits

EXHIBIT 12.2 continued

- Securities pricing

- Securities registration to nominee of trust department

- Redemption of matured debt securities

### Product Management for Custody and Recordkeeping Accounts

- Business development

- Client contact

- Trade execution directed by client

- Relationship with outside investment advisers

### Real Estate Management and Processing

- Property managementpurchase, sale, improvement, and lease negotiation

- Income collection

- Payment of taxes and expenses

### Tax Service

- Estate planning business development function

- Tax planning

- Final income tax returns for decedents

- Federal and state estate and inheritance tax returns

- Fiduciary tax returns

- Beneficiary tax letters

### Systems and Project Management

- Assessment of automated systems requirements

- Evaluation of systems alternatives

- Management of systems conversions

EXHIBIT 12.2   continued

- Training of department personnel in systems utilization

- Management of systems housed in trust department

- Liaison with bank data processing for systems shared with bank

- Provision of management information on special request

- Management of special projects such as
  Developing new product or new product features
  Developing procedures and personnel training to use new products or features
  Evaluating and recommending office equipment
  Evaluating requirements for physical quarters

## Corporate Trust Services

- Stock transfers

- Dividends and interest payments

- Dividend reinvestment services

- Shareholder inquiry responses

- Bond conversions, redemptions, and calls

## Control

- Development and management of quality assurance programs

- Management of accounting systems

- Development and maintenance of policies and procedures manuals

- Reconciliation of checks

- Review of compliance with policies and procedures

EXHIBIT 12.2 continued

- Liaison with internal and external auditors
- Development and maintenance of records management and disaster plans

**Financial Management**

- Financial planning and analysis
- Cost accounting and profitability measurement
- Productivity management
- Strategic planning facilitation
- Pricing strategy analysis and support
- New product evaluation

---

*Service Fees*

In a market-driven environment, banks have begun to recognize the importance of adequately pricing their services and, if necessary, to downplay or even drop services that offer little prospect for profitability. Trust business that a bank cannot handle effectively should be referred to another bank. A small bank, for example, may not have the operational capabilities to profitably handle the massive recordkeeping requirements of stock registration, transfer, or paying agencies.

In adopting a profit-oriented, market-driven approach for their trust departments, banks are also taking a hard look at the services they provide for free or little compensation. A trust department is frequently called upon to assist in tax return preparation, investment counseling, and other services that are often low volume and underpriced as well. A trust department may also be asked to handle, free of charge, much of the bank's own transactions, such as transferring securities, preparing dividend checks, and holding securities in safekeeping. While a bank should be able to call upon its own trust department for these services, a system of charge backs ensures that trust department personnel are not engaged in work for which there is no compensation.

There are several ways a trust department can price its services other than just assessing a flat fee. Often, bank trust departments charge their clients a **gross income receipts fee**—a percentage of income collected from interest and dividends. For example, if a trust department's fee is 5 percent and the gross

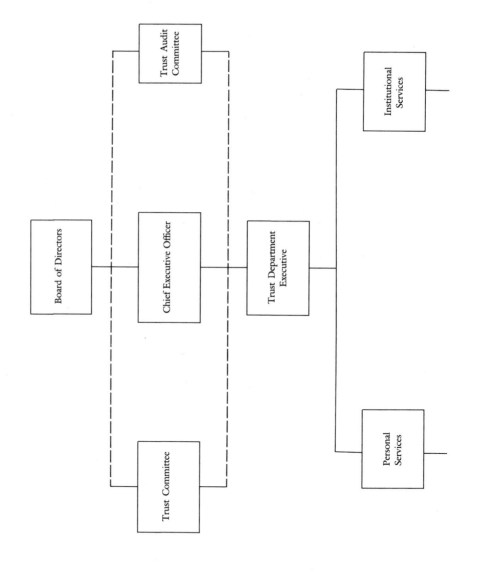

EXHIBIT 12.3 Trust Department Organization (by product line)

Board of Directors

Chief Executive Officer

Trust Department Executive

Trust Audit Committee

Trust Committee

Institutional Services

Personal Services

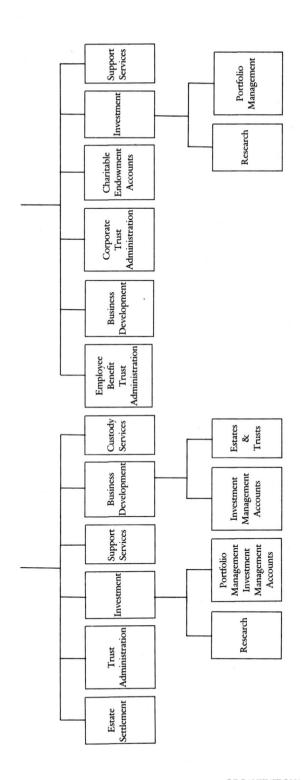

EXHIBIT 12.4   Trust Department Organization (modified product/functional)

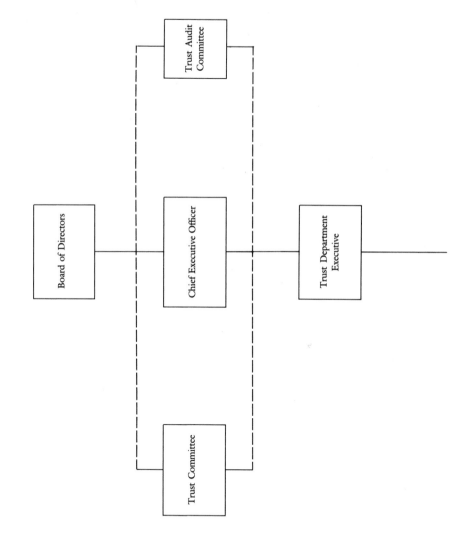

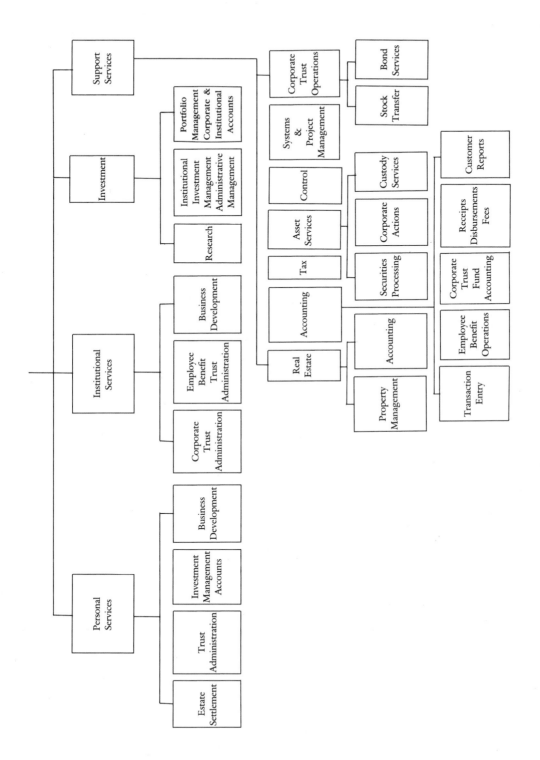

income earned from interest and dividends in one account totals $10,000, the bank would earn $500.

An alternative pricing schedule is a percentage of the market value of assets being managed in the account. Therefore, if the investment program is successful and the account is increasing in value, the bank will earn a higher fee. If the reverse is true, the bank will earn less. As an example, if the market value of an account is $100,000 and the bank's fee is one-half of 1 percent of the market value of the assets under management, the bank would earn $500 on this account.

Some trust departments use a combination of these fees for different types of accounts. Banks may also charge an annual minimum fee—for example, $750 to manage a trust account for a year. Finally, the trust industry is beginning to incorporate **activity fees,** usually in relation to custody accounts. For example, a fee of $25 might be charged for any transaction on the accounts. Fees should be clear to the client. The fee schedule should be established so that it provides enough income to support high quality administration, investment research, and support personnel for the trust department.

### Cost Analysis

Of course, to adequately price their services, banks must have a good understanding of what it costs to run their trust departments as a whole and administer different kinds of trust business and individual accounts. Most banks have implemented cost analysis systems for comparing departmental costs from year to year and with trust departments of similarly sized banks. The benefits of a cost analysis system include

- making personnel more cost conscious by impressing upon them the need for profit planning, expense reduction, and cost control

- establishing schedules for the pricing of trust services

- providing data to determine what types of trust accounts to accept

- determining trust service costs for purposes such as documenting to a court the justifiable fiduciary compensation when unusual or extraordinary services are performed

- providing cost figures in seeking adequate compensation for accounts in which the bank has been named as cofiduciary

- improving departmental procedures and techniques so that duplicate or unnecessary functions can be eliminated

## Cost Reduction

Banks have turned to rigorous cost reduction initiatives to improve the profitability of their trust departments. Many banks have established committees for the singular purpose of determining areas in which operational costs can be reduced. As salaries are one of the largest expenses, banks—particularly those with relatively small trust departments—are asking whether certain trust department tasks could be more efficiently and inexpensively handled by part-time personnel instead of the typical practice of having personnel wear several different hats. More banks are also turning to incentive compensation strategies as a way of attracting and retaining qualified trust officers, while linking the salary structure to productivity improvements.

## Productivity Improvements

Some of the greatest gains in profitability and competitiveness of bank trust departments are generated by improvements in productivity. The use of computers to perform most of the rote tasks that make up a considerable part of the trust business is a significant step forward. Modern computer systems maintain inventories of account assets, determine when and to whom disbursements are paid, calculate dividend payments, print checks, and so forth. Most securities processing activities—from trades to filing tax returns—can now be handled electronically, without the need for labor-intensive paper records. Again, this represents large productivity gains.

Many banks have also improved the productivity of their trust personnel without sacrificing the quality of service. As mentioned earlier, performance-based incentive compensation plans have been implemented. Many banks are giving their trust officers specific client-contact goals to encourage them to initiate calls and generate trust business, instead of waiting for customers to contact them. Likewise, banks are achieving productivity gains from investment officers by tying portfolio performance to incentive compensation.

Banks are also taking a hard look at the types of accounts they manage to see if productivity gains can be made through economies of scale. By grouping together accounts with similar objectives, trust departments can operate more efficiently and obtain leverage in their investment purchases and sales. While the very large and sensitive accounts are often handled by the most senior trust officers, smaller accounts are usually combined and invested in the bank's common trust funds to be managed by one or more junior officers.

There are, of course, many other strategies banks are pursuing to gain a large share of today's trust marketplace. For instance, the marketing, selling, and cross-selling of trust services have taken on renewed importance. Increasingly, customer-contact people on the commercial side of banks are being made aware of the products and services offered by their trust departments. Tellers, customer service representatives, loan officers, credit card personnel, and so forth are being trained to recognize the financial needs of clients and refer them to the appropriate departments.

Banks are also responding to their competitors by developing new trust products and modifying old ones as the marketplace and the needs of customers change. Future chapters in this book will explore these aspects of the trust business.

## SUMMARY

Although banks vary widely in size, type of customers they serve, and kinds of accounts they handle, all trust departments share a common purpose and exhibit many of the same functions and organizational structure. All trust departments are overseen by a board of directors who are responsible for setting overall operational policy and supervising the senior bank officers and department managers.

To help fulfill its trust oversight responsibilities, bank boards often appoint committees—the most common being a trust committee, a trust audit committee, a trust investment committee, and a trust administrative committee. Reporting to the board of directors or a committee of the board is the trust department executive, who is assisted by key functional or product managers. By planning, organizing, leading, and controlling they handle the day-to-day management of the trust department activities.

A traditional trust department, organized along the lines of functional responsibility, assigns separate units for marketing and business development, trust administration, investment services, and support services. These units are often subdivided into smaller groups to carry out specific responsibilities. For example, an investment department often separates the portfolio management and research functions. Another common organizational structure emphasizes a product-line orientation.

To compete successfully in today's financial services marketplace, many banks are finding that they must reevaluate their organizational and operational strategies. In the past, trust departments were not expected to be major contributors to a bank's bottom line. The promotion of trust services was often allowed to lapse, with the result that competitors have made inroads into banks' share of the trust market. Today, banks are responding by adequately pricing their trust services, performing detailed cost analyses, undertaking cost reduction initiatives, reorganizing their reporting lines, and constantly looking for ways to improve productivity.

## QUESTIONS FOR REVIEW

1.  Sketch the organizational hierarchy of your bank, beginning with the board of directors and continuing to the trust department and its units. Is it organized by function, product line, or a combination of both?

2.  Define the general responsibilities of the board of directors, the trust committee, and the trust investment committee.

3.  What are the duties of the portfolio management and research arms of the investment services unit?

4.  Identify some key support services for a trust department's accounting function, real estate management function, and asset services function.

5.  What are some of the benefits realized by implementing a cost analysis system?

6.  What steps has your bank taken to retain existing trust customers and attract new ones?

# CHAPTER 13 Trust Investment Management

## INTRODUCTION

While bank trust departments have always had the overriding responsibility of serving as custodians and safe depositories of assets, trust customers now expect good investment results as well. In today's financial services marketplace, trust beneficiaries look for investment performance and, consequently, are more aggressive in shopping around for the financial institutions and services that fulfill their investment objectives. To compete effectively, trust departments must deliver comparatively better investment results and provide better service, which includes satisfying customer demands for investment information.

Trust officers must, therefore, be well versed in the fundamentals of trust investment. To cross-sell services or, simply, to answer a client's questions requires an understanding of the bank's investment policy and practices. Today's trust customer can be expected to query the relative value and risk associated with a multitude of investment instruments, ranging from municipal bonds to repurchase agreements.

With this preoccupation on investment performance, a challenge confronting trust officers is explaining to customers that trust account management is not a "get-rich-quick" exercise. Trust customers should understand that the trustee is held to a different investment standard than the customer might follow in making personal investments. Meeting the fiduciary responsibility implicit in trust account management requires that the trustee act first to preserve assets and then to generate income.

This chapter explores the investment side of the trust business, beginning with an overview of the organization of the investment function in trust departments. This is followed by an analysis of the investment instruments, beginning with a look at the two principal types of securities—bonds and equities (stock)—and how they are bought and sold in the securities marketplace. Then we look at the basics of investing—how income is earned, how securities are valued, and how risk is measured. Once these variables are understood, a portfolio can be put together that best meets the client's investment objectives.

## ORGANIZATION OF TRUST INVESTMENT

In a properly administered trust department, a group of people set investment goals, analyze asset holdings, recommend asset changes, and review account investment performance. In a small bank, many or all of these tasks may be handled by the board of directors or by a board-appointed trust committee. As a trust department grows in size, these responsibilities are often delegated by the trust committee to subcommittees (such as an investment committee or an account review committee) or individual trust officers, who, for example, may be authorized to determine investment goals and make investments.

With larger trust departments there is further specialization; a common structural organization is to apportion the investment function among policy, research, trading, and portfolio management branches of the department. In some large trust departments, the investment function has spun off from the trust department and become a wholly owned subsidiary of the bank. The trust department is, of course, their major client.

## INVESTMENT INSTRUMENTS

Investments suitable for trustees are chiefly limited to marketable or publicly traded securities. In recent years, the number of investment alternatives has grown tremendously—one reason being the growing competitiveness in the financial marketplace that has spurred the creation of new investment instruments designed to meet specific investment needs. This chapter will consider the more common investment instruments. Before considering these instruments, though, it is important to understand how capital is raised, both in the public and private sector, through the issuance of stocks and bonds.

### Differences Between Stocks and Bonds

When stock is bought, the purchaser becomes a part owner of the company and receives stock certificates as evidence of that ownership. As ownership interest in a corporation is commonly referred to as equity, stocks are often called **equity securities.** It is important to note that investing in stock means acquiring ownership in a specific company. This ownership grants shareholders the right to participate in any future earnings of the company, both through dividends paid on the shares and through appreciation in the value of the shares (**capital gains**). Conversely, if the company performs poorly, shareholders also participate through a loss of dividends and a decline in the value of their shares. Because shareholders participate in the company's financial fortunes, there is some risk in selecting stocks as a trust investment.

The potential investment return of any particular stock is most closely tied to general economic and industrial conditions and to a lesser extent on the specific company. However, all things being equal, some stock issues perform better than others and some stocks are better suited to the investment needs of individual investors. Therefore, when investing in stock, specific factors, such as a company's earnings and financial position, warrant extensive investigation. The risk of investing in stock is mitigated somewhat by diversified holdings, and the stock in some companies—such as large, established "blue-chip" corporations—is less prone to price swings than stock in smaller "start-up" companies.

Stock is usually issued in one of two forms: common stock or preferred stock. Both are equity securities, but differ in several respects. As the name suggests, preferred stockholders enjoy certain preferences such as the right to receive dividends before dividends are paid on common stock. For example, dividends on common stock are generally paid only if a company has sufficient earnings; with some preferred stock (**cumulative preferred stock**), if the dividend is eliminated because earnings are insufficient, all missed preferred dividends must be paid before any dividends may be paid on the common stock. Preferred stock usually does not carry voting rights (whereas common stockholders are allowed to vote on all corporate matters), and preferred stock may have provisions for it to be called or retired after a period of time. In many respects, preferred stock and bonds share similar features.

Bonds are characterized as fixed-income investment instruments. That is, unlike equity securities, theoretically the return does not fluctuate, with payment coming from fixed payments of interest and a fixed payment of principal when the bond matures. Bonds are a type of debt security that represent a promise by the issuer to repay a specific sum of money at a particular time, with periodic interest payments made for the right to use the money. In other words, a bond is a loan that must be repaid; stock is a purchase of a portion of a company. Corporations, municipalities, state governments, the federal government, and federal agencies all issue bonds as a way of raising capital to finance their operations.

Interest payments on bonds are usually made semiannually or annually through the redemption of coupons. With bearer bonds, the owner's name is not imprinted on the bond certificate and ownership is only evidenced by physical possession of the bond. Interest payments are made when the holder of the bearer bond clips off the coupon and, on the appropriate date, presents it to the bond issuer's agent for payment. Registered bonds have the holder's name and address recorded in the issuer's books, and either the interest and principal payments, or both, are made directly to the registered bondholder. When one investor sells a registered bond to another, the bond must be reregistered in the name of the new owner. Most bonds issued today are in registered form, although some bearer securities (such as coupon Treasury securities issued before 1983) are still outstanding.

The principal value of a bond is also referred to as **par value,** which for most bonds is a multiple of $1,000. The **bond maturity** is the date the issuer will repay the principal. Bonds may be short term (maturity of less than 1 year) or long term (more than 1 year and typically 10 to 20 years or longer).

Most investors, including trust departments, invest in bonds for safety of principal and income. However, there is the potential loss of principal (market value) when interest rates rise or there is an impairment in the quality of the bond. As a consequence, bonds fluctuate in market value between issue date and maturity date. At maturity date, however, the investor will get the face value of the bond unless, of course, the bond defaults in the interim.

## Short-Term, Fixed-Income Investments

Among the instruments suitable for short-term, fixed-income investment needs are U.S. Treasury bills, repurchase agreements, certificates of deposit, bankers' acceptances, money market funds, commercial paper, and Eurodollar instruments. These instruments mature in one year or less and offer the investor a defined yield.

### U.S. Treasury Bills

**Treasury bills** (also known as T-bills) are short-term obligations of the U.S. government, with maturities of 13, 26, and 52 weeks. The minimum denomination of a T-bill is $10,000, and purchases over that amount must be in multiples of $5,000. To sell T-bills, the U.S. Treasury holds a public auction—usually once a week—where it receives competitive bids. The income earned on T-bills is exempt from state and local taxes, but is subject to federal income tax, and federal and state inheritance, estate, gift, and other excise taxes. As obligations of the U.S. government, they are considered the safest form of investment and, as such, generally have a lower yield than comparable investment instruments.

### Repurchase Agreements

A **repurchase agreement** (called a repo) involves the sale of securities to a customer, often a bank, with an agreement to repurchase them (hence the name) at a designated price at some future date—often the next day, although it may be for a longer period of time. In return for what is, in effect, a short-term loan, the purchaser of the securities collects a repo charge. The charge is usually collected in one of two ways. One approach is to sell and repurchase the securities at the same price, with an agreed interest fee to be assessed at the time of repurchase. The other is to repurchase the securities at a higher price than the sale, with the purchaser receiving the difference. The loan is collateralized by the securities, which the purchaser legally owns until repurchased.

Because repos are usually collateralized by U.S. government securities, the interest rate charged on a repo is lower than the interest on an ordinary commercial loan. Repos offer asset management advantages to the owner of the securities, while the purchaser realizes a safe return on a short-term investment.

### Certificates of Deposit

The **certificates of deposit** (CDs) used for investment in trust departments are short-term, often negotiable instruments that are typically issued in denominations of $100,000 or more. A CD is simply a written receipt given by the bank to the depositor. The certificate stipulates the amount borrowed, the date of maturity, the rate of interest, and the method of calculating the interest. Principal and interest are paid at maturity, which is a minimum of 14 days and usually 30 days to 12 months. Because CDs are highly liquid and offer a fixed return on a low-risk investment, these instruments are important components of institutional portfolios.

### Bankers' Acceptances

A **bankers' acceptance** is a time draft (bill of exchange) drawn on and accepted by the bank on which it was drawn. It is a securities instrument primarily designed to finance international trade transactions, in which the purchaser of goods guarantees payment to the seller at a future date. The bank accepting the draft assumes the obligation of making the payment at maturity (usually 6 months or less) on behalf of the buyer or the buyer's bank. Bankers' acceptances are negotiable instruments that are actively traded prior to maturity.

### Money Market Funds

**Money market funds** are mutual funds that are invested in high-quality, short-term notes, certificates of deposit, and acceptances of many corporations or governments. Money market funds sell shares to investors for a minimum initial investment that can range from $500 to $10,000. The comparatively low initial investment is attractive to small investors, who can obtain the same diversification of risk and competitive yields available to large investors. Money market fund participants receive regular income payments based on the interest earned on the investments and the expenses paid by the fund. Shares can be sold back to the fund at any time, with the investor receiving the original investment plus any accrued, unpaid interest. The high liquidity and competitive yield offered by money market funds make them popular investment vehicles for personal trusts and employee benefit accounts.

### Commercial Paper

**Commercial paper** is unsecured, short-term notes issued by major corporations, finance companies, and financial institutions. Commercial paper is sold at discount, usually in minimum denominations of $100,000, although more typical are notes of $1 to $2 million. Most paper is issued by large companies with excellent credit ratings, and as a result, the interest yield is slightly below prevailing bank loan rates. Investors tend to select commercial paper with a maturity that suits their needs and to hold it until the due date, which can range from a few days up to 270 days.

### Eurodollar Instruments

International securities offer another type of fixed-income, short-term investment. Two popular instruments are **Eurodollar certificates of deposit** and **Eurocommercial paper.** Eurodollar CDs are dollar-denominated certificates that are easily transferable to cash. Eurocommercial paper is similar to U.S. commercial paper, but issued by European corporations.

Eurodollar instruments typically pay a higher interest than domestic CDs because European banks are not required to hold as much money in reserve as U.S. banks, and thus can invest a larger proportion of their funds.

## Long-Term, Fixed-Income Investments

Bonds are long-term debt instruments that bear interest and promise repayment of the principal at maturity. Issued by governments, corporations, and municipalities, high quality bonds offer a relatively low-risk source of fixed income for the purchaser.

### U.S. Government Securities

Besides short-term T-Bills, the U.S. Treasury issues fixed-rate notes and bonds. The primary difference between **Treasury notes** and **Treasury bonds** is the length of maturity: notes mature in 1 to 10 years, while bonds typically have a life of 10 to 40 years. Treasury notes with a maturity of 3 years or less are issued in minimum denominations of $5,000, ranging upward to $1 million. Notes with a longer maturity have a minimum denomination of $1,000. Treasury bonds are issued in denominations of $1,000, $5,000, $10,000, $100,000, or

$1 million. All U.S. Treasury securities are now issued in book-entry form, with interest and principal payments made to the registered owner. Treasury securities issued before 1983 were often sold in bearer form; interest payments were made when coupons clipped from the certificate were presented for cash redemption.

For the investor, Treasury notes and bonds are deemed the most liquid and highest quality of fixed-income investment. And like T-bills, they are exempt from state and local income taxes, but subject to federal tax.

U.S. government agencies also issue bonds that are similar to Treasury notes and bonds. But unlike Treasury securities, these instruments are not guaranteed by the U.S. government and are somewhat more risky. The Federal Home Loan Bank, Federal Farm Credit Administration, Federal National Mortgage Association, Government National Mortgage Association, and Federal Housing Administration are among the issuers of government agency notes and bonds.

### Corporate Bonds

Corporations also issue bonds to raise capital. **Corporate bonds** are usually sold in denominations of $1,000 or more, and may be unsecured or secured (backed by such collateral as real estate, equipment, or a third-party guaranty). Most corporate bonds mature in 5 to 25 years, and most have a provision allowing the bonds to be retired prior to maturity. The conditions for repayment of the interest and principal are specified on the bond certificate. The quality of corporate bonds varies depending on the financial condition of the issuing corporation. Several services rate the quality of corporate bonds.

### Municipal Bonds

**Municipal bonds** are issued by state and local governments. Most municipal bonds are **general obligation bonds** or revenue bonds. General obligation bonds are backed by the "full faith and credit" of the issuing government, implying that all of its tax power will be brought to bear, if necessary, to repay the debt. Revenue bonds are issued by government authorities to finance various capital projects. Interest and principal on revenue bonds are repaid by revenues generated by users of the project and are not secured by the taxing power of the municipality. The credit risk on municipal bonds depends on the taxing capabilities of the issuing government in the case of general obligation bonds, and on the revenue-generating capabilities of the issuing authority in the case of revenue bonds. Maturities of municipal bonds range from 1 to 30 years, with the interest dependent to a large extent on the quality of the bonds. The interest earned on municipal bonds is exempt from federal income taxes and, if held by a person domiciled in the issuing state, from state tax as well.

# Equity Investments

As sources of fixed income, equity investments do not offer many of the advantages of bonds and other debt instruments. For instance, when stock is purchased, regular interest payments are not made to compensate for use of the owner's capital. However, dividends offer some substitute for the interest income earned on bonds, and there is the potential for greater investment returns if the stock increases in value. Furthermore, the risk of losing capital can be mitigated somewhat by diversifying stock holdings. The most common types of equity investment are common stock, preferred stock, and stock options.

## Common Stock

Common stock is an equity security that represents ownership in a company. As owners of the company, common stockholders have several rights, including the right to vote on company matters, the right to share in the company's profits through the issuance of dividends, and the right to inspect the corporation's books (financial statements, stockholder lists, and minutes of stockholder meetings). Earnings not retained by the company to finance its future activities are distributed as dividends among the company's stockholders. Dividends are calculated on a per-share basis and usually paid every quarter. Dividends may be accepted in cash or, in some cases, reinvested in the company, thus increasing the number of shares held by the stockholder.

Depending on the nature of the issuing company, common stocks can be characterized as income stocks, blue-chip stocks, growth stocks, or speculative stocks. **Income stocks** pay a large dividend relative to their market price. Utility company stock often yields large dividends. **Blue-chip stocks** are issued by large companies with long histories of consistent earnings and uninterrupted dividends. The stock of many Fortune 500 companies fall into the blue-chip category. **Growth stocks** pay relatively low dividends as the issuing companies retain most of their earnings to finance their development plans. Despite the negligible dividends, such stocks are attractive to investors looking for a high potential return realized through a significant increase in stock price. **Speculative stocks** offer a more risky investment. Stock that falls into this category includes that issued by small, newly formed companies and by companies that are struggling financially. If the company matures and becomes consistently profitable, the investor stands to realize a large return on investment; however, such companies are also much more prone to failure. Most speculative stocks offer little, if any, dividends. Speculative stock is not an appropriate investment for accounts over which the trust department exercises fiduciary control.

## Preferred Stock

Another equity security is preferred stock. Unlike common stock, the dividend rate of preferred stock is often fixed when the stock is issued. Consequently, preferred stock has fixed-income characteristics similar to debt instruments. Preferred stockholders enjoy several advantages over common stockholders—two of which are preference to dividends and to company assets in the event of liquidation. However, preferred stock often does not carry full voting rights, and in periods of high corporate profits, preferred dividends usually cannot increase above their fixed rate. Because preferred stock is—like most equity securities—more risky than bonds while subject to many of the same fixed-income characteristics, many trustees and fiduciaries do not recommend them for individual accounts.

## Stock Options

A **stock option** is a contract that gives the investor the right to buy or sell common stock at a certain price from the writer of the contract within a designated period. There are two types of options, **puts** and **calls.** A call option allows the investor to purchase the stock from the holder at a fixed price until the expiration date designated on the contract. A put option gives the investor the right to sell to the holder at a fixed price until the expiration date stipulated on the contract. In exchange for giving the investor this right to buy or sell securities, the writer of the contract receives a fee, called the premium, regardless of whether the option is exercised. The life of an option typically runs from a few days to 9 months. Most are written for 3 months.

Option contracts are written for several reasons. For the holder of stock, an option contract presents the opportunity to earn extra income on the stock investment, provided that the option is exercised and does not expire, worthless to the investor. Options can also be written as a hedge against the possible drop in the price of stock.

## Other Investments

In addition to bonds and stocks, many other investment instruments may be suitable for trust portfolios. In most instances, however, the market for these instruments is narrower and may be more risky.

One such investment is **futures contracts,** which call for the future delivery or receipt of a commodity such as grain, pork bellies, or foreign currency. **Interest rate futures** allow for the purchase of a short-term, fixed-income security (Treasury bills, notes, and bonds; CDs; or government agency bonds) at a specified rate. Since the interest rates on these instruments fluctuate, a futures contract is a way of obtaining a certain rate on funds to be invested at a later date.

In some instances, real estate, oil-and-gas partnerships, and other limited investment partnerships may also be acceptable trust assets. Again, such investments are not highly liquid.

## THE SECURITIES MARKET

When a trust investment officer purchases a stock or bond for a client's portfolio, the transaction is carried out in the securities marketplace. The securities marketplace serves as the mechanism for bringing together those seeking investment opportunities and those seeking investment funds. The securities that have been discussed in this chapter are bought and sold in primary or secondary markets.

### Primary Markets

New securities issues are bought and sold in **primary markets.** Basically, the process begins with the issuance of stock or bonds by a company, government agency, or other issuer to raise capital. Because these are initial offerings of new securities, no market already exists; the seller and buyers of the securities must be brought together. This is done through an intermediary—usually an investment banker—who provides the issuer with advice on the price, terms, and timing of the issue, and who then acts alone or as part of a syndicate to bring the securities to market. Under the Glass-Steagall Act, commercial banks are currently prohibited from acting as underwriters for all securities except general obligation municipal securities.

An investment banker or group may purchase the securities issue from the issuer and sell the securities to the investing public. If this course is taken, the investment banker's fee or commission is the difference between the price paid for the securities and the price received from selling them to the public. Alternatively, the investment banker may act as agent, selling the securities on a commission-per-share basis and assuming none of the marketing risk. The investment banker or group does not, therefore, underwrite or purchase the issue, but rather uses its best efforts to sell all of the issues at the agreed price. In both cases, the issuer absorbs all of the fees, commissions, or other markups. The investor pays only the stated price per share and does not incur broker's costs.

### Secondary Markets

Securities issues that are already outstanding are traded in the **secondary markets.** The secondary markets bring together buyers and sellers, thus easily effecting trades and helping define the value of securities issues. Many trades are carried out in **centralized trading exchanges**—most notably the New York Stock Exchange and the American Stock Exchange. At these centralized exchanges, investors, acting through brokers and dealers, meet at a common area—the floor of the exchange—to trade in listed securities. The exchange itself does not buy or sell shares, nor does it set the price of shares. Its primary function is to ensure fair and orderly markets.

Many types of securities are not listed on any organized exchange, instead they are traded in the **over-the-counter (OTC) market.** Corporate and government bond issues; equity securities of many smaller banks and insurance companies; foreign securities; and stock issued by small, local, or relatively new companies are all traded over the counter. Unlike centralized stock exchanges, there is no physical location for carrying out trades. Instead, transactions are made whenever a buyer or seller agrees upon the price for a particular issue. The OTC exchange is, in effect, a mass communications network linked together by telephones and computer terminals. The OTC market operates by brokers and dealers (both brokerage firms and individuals) for one buyer and one seller getting together and negotiating a price agreeable to both parties.

## INVESTMENT BASICS

The purpose of investing in an asset is to earn income in the form of dividends, interest, or capital gains. What constitutes an acceptable investment value is based on factors such as the length of time the funds are to be invested, the rate of inflation during the period of investment, and the risk involved. Bonds and equities have different investment characteristics and will be considered separately here.

### Investing in Bonds

As fixed-income investments, the return on bonds is preset, with regular payments of interest until the principal is repaid at maturity. Bonds differ, though, in investment characteristics, and gauging the value of bonds involves more than just determining their yield. For example, interest earned on T-bills is not subject to state taxes, while the interest realized on municipal bonds is exempt from federal taxes. Bonds also vary in quality, and risk factors must be taken into account when evaluating bonds in relation to other investments.

#### Yield

Most original issue bonds are sold at discount—that is, the ending value of the bond is known (usually in $1,000 increments), while the selling, or discount, price is somewhat lower than that amount. This difference provides the investor with an interest return on the asset. For example, a T-bill having a par value (the amount printed on the face of the certificate) of $1,000 with a one-year maturity might be sold at auction for $900; the $100 difference represents the income earned by the investor on the bond.

The yield on a bond can be expressed in several ways, each representing a different method of calculation. The **nominal yield** is simply the yearly interest rate stated on the face of the bond and is usually paid in equal, semi-annual installments. The total amount of annual interest income the investor receives is the nominal interest rate multiplied by the amount of the bond. For a bond with a par value of $1,000 and a nominal yield of 5 percent, the interest received would be $50 over the course of a year.

The **current yield** measures the return on the bond for the coming 12 months as it relates to the current market price of the bond. Assuming that the current market price of the $1,000 par value bond is $600, and the interest rate is 5 percent, then the current yield is as follows:

Current yield = Annual interest ÷ current market price

Current yield = $50 ÷ $600

Current yield = 8.33%

The current yield is shown in corporate bond market quotes. However, in referring to the current yield, it should be noted that it is the *current* yield, and like a stock price quote, represents the yield only at a specific point in time. It is not the yield over the time the bond is outstanding. The current market value of the bond, upon which the current yield is based, is constantly changing.

A more refined measure of yield, and one relied upon by institutional investors is **yield-to-maturity.** Yield-to-maturity offers a more representative picture of an investor's return and allows for comparison of the yield on bonds regardless of variations in maturity dates.

The formula for the yield-to-maturity is

$$\text{Yield-to-maturity} = \frac{\text{Annual interest} \pm \left( \dfrac{\text{Par value} - \text{Market value}}{\text{Number of years to maturity}} \right)}{\dfrac{\text{Par value} + \text{Market value}}{2}}$$

Referring to the bond with a par value of $1,000, an annual interest of $50, and a current market value of $600, which matures in 7 years, the yield-to-maturity formula reads:

$$\text{Yield-to-maturity} = \frac{\$50 \pm \left(\dfrac{\$1{,}000 - \$600}{7}\right)}{\dfrac{\$1{,}000 + \$600}{2}}$$

$$\text{Yield-to-maturity} = \frac{\$107}{\$800}$$

$$\text{Yield-to-maturity} = 13.38\%$$

The above calculation assumes that exactly one year's worth of interest payments are made. Because the purchase and sale of bonds rarely take place on the annual interest payment dates, the actual yield-to-maturity is often slightly lower or higher. More exact yields can be obtained from special tables available from bond dealers. Again, the basic utility of the yield-to-maturity is to compare bonds with unlike interest payments and maturities.

### Quality

Another factor in the valuation of bonds is their quality. Low-quality bonds are risky investments and, consequently, their yield should be higher to compensate for that risk. Of course, the argument can be made that unless the quality is sufficient, the yield is irrelevant. This is particularly true with the investment of trust assets, where the fundamental reason for purchasing bonds is to generate a steady stream of income and to ensure the repayment of principal at maturity.

For investors in bonds (both small and institutional), an essential tool is the rating services offered by Moody's Investor Service and Standard & Poor's Corporation. Using such criteria as the issuer's availability of credit and the issuer's ability to pay on time, these rating services evaluate the quality of corporate and municipal bond issues. (Bonds backed by the U.S. government are assumed to be of highest quality and are not rated.) Bonds rated Aaa by Moody's and AAA by Standard & Poor's are deemed to be of the highest quality (see exhibit 13.1). As bonds fall in quality, the risk increases and a correspondingly higher interest rate and lower price is necessary to offset the risk. In general, investment quality bonds are those with ratings of A or higher for Standard & Poor's and Moody's.

### Interest Rate Risk

Interest rates have a significant impact on the market value (as differentiated from the par value, which is usually $1,000) of bonds. When purchasing bonds, the prevailing interest rate determines the discount rate and the principal value of bonds. As interest rates rise, bonds sold at lower interest rates decline in

EXHIBIT 13.1   Bond Ratings by Moody's and Standard & Poor's

| Moody's | Standard & Poor's | Quality Indication |
|---------|-------------------|--------------------|
| Aaa | AAA | Highest quality |
| Aaa | AA | High quality |
| A | A | Upper medium grade |
| Baa | BBB | Medium grade |
| Ba | BB | Contains speculative elements |
| B | B | Outright speculative |
| Caa | CCC & CC | Default definitely possible |
| Ca | C | Default, only partial recovery likely |
| C | DDD-D | Default, little recovery likely |

*Source:* Douglas H. Bellemore, Herbert E. Phillips, and John C. Ritchie, Jr., *Investment Analysis and Portfolio Selection: An Integrated Approach* (Cincinnati, Ohio: Southwest Publishing Company, 1979).

market value. Conversely, falling interest rates increase the value of bonds sold under the older, higher interest rates.

Suppose, for example, that shortly after purchasing an 8 percent, 10-year bond, the market interest rate increases sharply and, consequently, the required return on 10-year bonds becomes 10 percent. When sold on the market, bonds earning interest at less than this higher, prevailing rate must be discounted to compensate for their lower interest rates, with a resultant loss of principal. For the 8 percent, 10-year bond, the loss of value approximates 10 percent. The loss of principal grows as the maturity lengthens—an 8 percent, 20-year bond loses over 15 percent of its value.

Choosing the right debt instrument requires a good understanding of what factors influence interest rates and an ability to predict how those factors will change. If the prognosis is that interest rates are going to rise, a bond investor may want to invest in short-term securities and avoid purchasing long-term bonds whose value will decline sharply if rates do rise. Alternatively, if interest rates are expected to fall, longer maturities are preferable because the higher investment return will continue for a longer period of time and the principal value of the bond will increase. Determining the future course of interest rates is an inexact science at best, and as the maturity of bonds lengthens so does the interest rate risk, which must be compensated for in bond pricing. For example, at the time of writing, a 6-month T-bill commanded a one-half of 1 percent higher interest rate than a 3-month T-bill.

# Investing in Common Stock

Investing in common stock means purchasing a stake in a company. The investment return on common stock is therefore directly tied to the financial performance of the company. A company that fares poorly will lose income for an investor through a decline in dividends and a drop in the market value of its stock. It is true that stock prices do move together, and the price of stock in an otherwise healthy company may fall when there is a general downward movement in the stock market as a whole.

However, regardless of general economic and market conditions, some stocks perform better than others, so the primary risk factor that must be evaluated when investing in stock is whether the earnings of the company under consideration will be sufficient to pay dividends and provide for the company's future growth. Investing in stock is therefore different from investing in bonds, in which the primary concerns are rising interest rates and the risk of default.

Bonds offer a fixed-income return from semiannual or annual interest payments that are set until maturity. The income from stock is uncertain and depends upon future dividend payments set by the company's management and the price of the stock when it is sold. The value of a stock is therefore the sum of all the dividends plus the increase in value of the stock over the period it is held. Obviously, if a stock falls in price, required return objectives will not be met. Because of this, it is particularly important to accurately assess the quality and risk of stock before investing in it.

## Quality

As with bonds, most common stock is graded by investment advisory services such as Standard & Poor's (see exhibit 13.2). However, bond ratings measure an absolute—the possibility of default. With stocks, the ratings are much more relative, and should be taken as a general guide to quality based on such factors as past earnings and dividend performance, and how the company fared compared with similar companies.

Many investors have their own criteria for valuing stock. An assessment of earnings, management quality, cash flow, return on assets, and other variables provide some insight into stock quality. One common measure is the price-to-earnings (P/E) ratio, which tells the investor how much the market is willing to pay for a share of stock relative to the company's earnings on a per-share basis. For example, if a stock is selling for a price of $50 per share and its earnings are $5 per share, then it has a P/E ratio of 10. This ratio can be compared with the company's historical ratio and the ratios of other companies in its market or

EXHIBIT 13.2   Ratings of Common Stock by Standard & Poor's Corporation

| | | | |
|-----|---------------|-----|-------------------|
| A+  | Highest       | B   | Below average     |
| A   | High          | B−  | Lower             |
| A−  | Above average | C   | Lowest            |
| B+  | Average       | D   | In reorganization |

industry. A company with a low P/E ratio may be undervalued and represent a good investment prospect. However, there may be underlying reasons for a low ratio, so, again, any specific rating of performance should be taken only as a general guide to stock quality.

Sifting through hundreds of specific issues to find the few that offer good investment opportunities presents practical problems. Therefore, most investors—including some of those responsible for stock investments in small banks—rely on brokerage firms, investment departments of large banks, and other financial institutions for information on what specific issues to buy or sell. For such investors, the investment strategy then becomes one of evaluating the sources of investment recommendations. It may be prudent to combine the recommendations of several sources to arrive at a small list of acceptable issues.

If various sources are used, it is not necessary to evaluate dividend payments, price-to-earnings ratios, and other criteria. However, it is of great importance to monitor the performance of the stocks recommended by investment services. Services that produce poor results should be discarded.

### Risk Factors

Several risks are involved in common stock investment. A major uncertainty that has already been discussed is whether earnings will be sufficient to pay dividends and support a company's growth, which is necessary for stock to increase in price over the long term. It is difficult to quantify this risk because numerous factors can come into play to depress the price of a stock, such as changes in management, the entry of a new competitor into the marketplace, obsolete products, labor problems, and so forth. General economic or industry conditions, such as a recession, will also have a bearing on a company's performance and the value of its stock.

The single most important source of risk for common stock is market risk—that is, the influence of market swings on the price of stock issues. Regardless of how well an individual company performs, the value of its stock is closely tied to the increase or decrease of stock prices in general. For example, when the stock market plummeted in October 1987, the fall in stock prices was across the board, irrespective of individual company performance.

Interest rates also affect stock prices. In general, stock prices and interest rates are inversely related. As interest rates rise, investors look to securities whose return is tied to interest rates—bonds, for example. As stocks are sold and the money is invested in the bond markets, stock prices fall. Conversely, when interest rates decline, money flows out of bonds and into the stock market, thus raising prices.

Because stock investment involves a large number of risks that can be difficult to anticipate, some trust investors have shied away from becoming heavily invested in common stocks. One way of mitigating some of these risks is to diversify stock holdings by investing in a mutual stock fund or purchasing stocks in several industries. Among individual issues, some stocks are less risky than others. Stocks classified as income stocks or blue-chip stocks may be more suitable for trust investment than stocks that are speculative in nature.

## INVESTMENT POLICY AND OBJECTIVES

In formulating investment policy, all trust investment departments take, as their starting point, the so-called prudent-man rule discussed in earlier chapters. Most state legislatures have adopted the prudent-man rule, which has provided a standard for trustees in considering their investment duties for more than 150 years.

A corollary to the prudent-man rule is that trust investments should be diversified. Putting "all of one's eggs in the same basket" by investing trust assets solely in common stock, for example, exposes the account to unwarranted risk, such as a 500-point fall in the New York Stock Exchange. In its *1981 Handbook for National Trust Examiners*, the Comptroller of the Currency provides guidance to trustees on quality of investments, stating that trustees must prohibit speculation, preserve principal, diversify portfolios, and optimize income. Thus every investment officer must, at a minimum, invest as a prudent person would in like circumstances and diversify assets to minimize risk.

Most banks have a formal investment policy—often developed by a policy committee—that establishes investment guidelines for the trust department and addresses variables such as asset quality, maturity, diversification, and risk. The policy prescribes objectives in each area and sets benchmarks for measuring how well those objectives are attained.

### Collective Investment

Asset diversification is more easily achieved when there are significant assets to invest. Consequently, banks often pool trust accounts into **collective** or **com-**

**mingled investment funds.** Often known as **common trust funds, pooled funds,** or **group trusts,** these commingled funds also provide an efficient way to invest the monies of many trust clients. Essentially, a collective investment fund is similar to a mutual fund that is managed by a bank trust department to pool the funds of trusts, estates, and guardianships for which the bank is acting in a fiduciary capacity.

Collective investment funds were originally developed to provide diversification for trust accounts that were too small to own more than a few individual securities. The advantages of these funds are now such that many trust departments' most valuable customers prefer them.

At first, bank trust departments designed their collective investment funds as balanced funds, which invested in equity and fixed-income securities in a predetermined ratio. Today, most collective funds in medium-to-large trust departments have specialized investment objectives. Typical among collective funds found in trust departments today are the following:

- growth-oriented equity funds

- long-term or intermediate-term fixed-income funds (primarily investing in bonds, either tax exempt or taxable)

- stable capital funds (primarily investing in certificates of deposit with 6- to 30-month maturities)

- short-term investment funds (similar to money market mutual funds)

- real estate equity funds

- venture capital funds

- international equity funds

- international bond funds

- special asset funds—precious metals, timberlands, and so forth

By combining otherwise small and disparate trust accounts, both the trust department and its clients benefit. Collective investment funds offer trust customers increased diversification and liquidity, greater asset management attention, and cost-effective management. Banks also realize cost benefits and, with fewer accounts to deal with, there is better management responsibility and more focused investment objectives. Collective investment funds are also effective marketing tools.

Plans for operating collective funds for trust accounts must be filed with the Comptroller of the Currency. Because of the fiduciary relationship involved, there are numerous regulations governing the operation of collective trust funds. For example, assets in the fund must be valued not less than quarterly, the fund must be audited at least once every 12 months, financial reports are required yearly, and investment in securities other than direct or guaranteed U.S. obligations is limited to 10 percent of the market value of the fund.

## Portfolio Management

Every trust client, whether individual or institutional, has certain investment objectives and constraints in areas such as risk, return, liquidity, and taxes. Understanding those needs is the first step in developing the right portfolio of assets for the investor.

### Return

While all trust customers want the highest possible return on their investment (assuming, of course, reasonable risk), investors differ on the type of return desired. For example, until recently, the tax treatment of income and capital gains differed, with the result that some investors preferred investments that offered the prospect of high capital gains (such as equity securities), while other investors leaned toward investments that offered good income (such as bonds). With the passage of the Tax Reform Act of 1986, capital gains are now treated as ordinary income and the distinction between capital gains and income is not as significant. Nonetheless, there are other good reasons why some investors prefer current income, while others prefer capital gains, and still others look for a combination of both—all of which has a bearing on portfolio management. If a client's investment objective is long-term growth, then a portfolio of growth securities that do not pay high dividends may be preferable to a portfolio of short-term, high-yielding securities.

### Risk

Although the goal of every investor is to achieve a high return with a minimum of risk, some investors are more tolerant of risk than others. A wealthy individual with substantial discretionary assets is more likely to accept the comparatively greater risk of investing in equity securities than a retired person with a small trust account whose overwhelming need is for a continual stream of risk-free, fixed income, which can be supplied by T-bills or other short-term bonds.

*Liquidity*

Liquidity is a measure of how quickly assets can be converted to cash. For instance, real estate is less liquid than marketable securities. Among investors, liquidity requirements differ. A young investor with sufficient earnings may be content to have the majority of his or her investments tied up in long-term investments. An older individual with no outside income has the potential need to cash in some assets to meet an unexpected contingency; consequently, that trust portfolio must be highly liquid. For minor beneficiaries of a trust, the trust must be able to meet living and educational expenses, which entails devising a portfolio with the proper liquidity to meet expenses as they arise.

*Tax Considerations*

Tax considerations are very important in portfolio management. Investments may be subject to federal, state, and local income taxes, and federal and state inheritance, gift, and estate taxes. As mentioned earlier, the tax treatment of capital gains underwent a major revision in 1986, which may affect the type of assets held in trust portfolios. The portfolio management process involves a constant effort to monitor the ever-changing tax rules for investments, individuals, and institutions.

An individual investor's tax circumstances and current tax rules may make it advantageous to develop investment portfolios that concentrate in T-bills, municipal bonds, real estate, oil-and-gas leases, or other securities instruments that are exempt from either federal or state taxes or offer tax advantages.

*Regulatory and Legal Considerations*

Regulatory or legal constraints may be imposed on investments by a governing instrument, such as a will or trust agreement. Some institutional trusts, for example, may be prohibited from holding investments in companies with holdings in South Africa. Other social goals may be similarly promoted by stipulations in trust documents. For a bank trust department, any legal or regulatory restriction should be clearly understood at the beginning of the portfolio management process. The trust department should also be aware of regulatory constraints that govern the banking institution itself.

## Devising a Portfolio Management Strategy

After evaluating the investor's unique investment objectives and constraints, a portfolio management strategy can be devised. The portfolio management process is, though, an ongoing process of assessing the social, political, and economic landscape, including factors related to the capital markets, the national and international economy, fiscal and monetary policies, interest rates, inflation, and so on. Expectational factors related to individual securities and their investment potential are also factored into the analysis, as are the changing circumstances and preferences of the investor.

## SUMMARY

Most trust investments are marketable or publicly traded securities, of which there are two principal types—stocks (equity securities) and bonds. Stock represents an ownership interest in a company, with investment income realized through the payment of dividends and appreciation in the value of shares. Because stockholders participate in company losses as well, there is more risk in selecting stocks as trust investments than in high-quality bonds. However, much of the risk can be minimized by diversifying stock holdings. Stock is issued in two forms: common and preferred.

Bonds are debt securities and are characterized as fixed-income investment instruments. Unlike equity securities, there are fixed payments of interest and a fixed payment of principal at maturity. Bonds can decline in market value, though, due to factors such as a decline in quality or a rise in interest rates.

Scores of investment instruments are available to meet the specific needs of investors. Popular short-term (with a maturity of one year or less), fixed-income debt instruments include U.S. Treasury bills, repurchase agreements, certificates of deposit, bankers' acceptances, money market funds, commercial paper, and Eurodollar instruments. Long-term (with a maturity of over one year), fixed-income debt instruments include Treasury notes and bonds, U.S. government agency securities, corporate bonds, and general obligation and revenue municipal bonds. Equity securities do not offer the same fixed-income advantages as bonds, but most stocks do pay dividends and there is the potential for greater investment returns when stock increases substantially in price. Common stock may be classified as income stock, blue-chip stock, growth stock, or speculative stock. Stock options also provide an opportunity to generate income on a stock investment.

Securities are bought on the primary and secondary markets. In the primary market, initial stock and bond offerings are brought to market through the assistance of an intermediary, usually an investment banker. Securities that are already outstanding are traded in the secondary markets—for example, the New York Stock Exchange, the American Stock Exchange, and the over-the-counter market.

Investing in bonds requires a comprehensive understanding of the concepts of yield, quality, and interest rate risk. The yield on bonds can be expressed in several ways—nominal yield, current yield, and yield-to-maturity are frequently cited. The valuation of bonds is directly affected by their rating, which is assigned by rating services such as Moody's and Standard & Poor's. Bonds of the highest quality (such as those backed by the U.S. government) generally pay less of a return than lower-rated, more risky bonds. Interest rate risk is also a factor. In periods of rising interest rates, the principal value of bonds falls, with long-term bonds suffering the most.

Investing in stock is more uncertain because it is harder to accurately assess such factors as quality and risk. Numerous indicators are used to judge stock value, including the price-to-earnings ratio and the dividend rate. Many investors prefer to leave stock purchase decisions to brokerage firms, large bank investment departments, and other financial institutions. Even if all the indicators predict future stock performance, the fact remains that stocks move in concert. A big slump in the stock markets affects almost all stocks, regardless of how financially strong individual companies might be.

The starting point for trust investing is the prudent-man rule, which stipulates that trustees should avoid taking unnecessary risks—the paramount concern should be the safety of the capital. Applying this principle, trustees should resist investing in speculative stocks and diversify holdings among several types of debt and equity instruments. Putting together the right portfolio of assets also entails evaluating the client's needs regarding return, risk, liquidity, and taxes. Once these needs are understood, a portfolio management strategy can be developed and revised as the client's preferences change and as social, economic, political, and other events warrant.

## QUESTIONS FOR REVIEW

1. Define some of the basic differences between a debt security and an equity security. Give examples of each.

2. What securities would you choose for a trust customer having a need for a low-risk, high-liquidity, fixed-income portfolio?

3. What are some differences between T-bills and Treasury bonds and notes? Assuming that interest rates are extremely volatile, which U.S. government security would you recommend to a trust customer?

4. Refer to New York Stock Exchange composite prices for stock issues in the financial pages of your local newspaper. What is the current price and the high and low prices for the year for Coca-Cola (CocaCl), General Motors (GMot), and IBM stock? How would

you classify these stocks? What is the percentage change between the high and low stock price for each of these issues? What implications do these price swings have for the need to diversify stock holdings?

5. Why are mutual funds attractive to small investors?

6. Referring again to the financial pages of your local newspaper, what is the yield on T-bills maturing in exactly 2 months from now? On Treasury bonds and notes maturing 2 years from now? Is the yield on Treasury bonds and notes generally increasing or decreasing over time? Why?

7. What is the current yield on a bond with a current market price of $800 and an annual payment of $75? What type of yield is commonly relied upon by institutional investors?

8. To develop a suitable portfolio of assets, what questions would you ask a client to ascertain his or her investment objectives?

CHAPTER  Trust Operations

## INTRODUCTION

As the preceding chapters demonstrate, the trust business is complex and difficult to administer. Every day, a trust department receives and distributes an enormous amount of money and is responsible for the assets of some of the bank's most valuable customers.

To carry out its responsibilities to its customers, a bank trust department must have operational systems for transaction processing and recordkeeping, asset control, income collection, income and asset distribution, securities movement and control, property management, tax preparation, corporate trust services, and auditing. The way a bank operates and manages these operations is unique and depends on characteristics such as its size, the types of customers it serves, the types of accounts it handles, and the services it provides.

Nonetheless, all trust departments share a common purpose and are similar in their basic operational tasks. This chapter presents the operational responsibilities of bank trust departments and examines how they are administered to meet the needs of trust customers and regulators.

## RECORDKEEPING

A key trust department function is accounting—maintaining and updating records of all accounts. Specifically, this involves recording assets, liabilities, and payments; posting and balancing transactions; and generating statements and reports. Once the transactions are entered, the bulk of the processing work is handled by computer, but even so bank personnel are needed to verify entries and check that the statements and reports are done correctly. Some of the major types of trust reports follow.

## Holding Reports

One type of record prepared by the trust department is often referred to as a **holding report** (or asset statement), which itemizes all the current assets and liabilities in a customer's portfolio. Assets are presented before liabilities, and both are denoted in order of decreasing liquidity. Cash or short-term T-bills would, for instance, be listed before common stock or long-term Treasury bonds.

In a holding report, each asset is described in detail and its assigned identification number is reported. Other information includes the number of shares of the asset held and their book and market values. Holding reports are used by trust administration and operations personnel to assist in account management, and periodic, formal reports are sent to customers.

## Transaction Reports

Similar to checking account or credit card statements, **transaction reports** disclose all transactions involving trust account holdings over a period of time—usually a month. Listings are chronological, with a brief description of the transactions, the cash or income received or expended, and the beginning and ending value of the account. For estates, guardianships, and other trust accounts under the jurisdiction of a court, a special accounting must be prepared periodically to show transactions that have occurred since the account's inception (or last accounting), current holdings, and current value of the account.

## Asset Records

Asset statements and transaction reports list asset holdings for individual trust accounts. However, because many accounts own the same security, trust departments maintain **asset records** that reflect the trust department's position in specific assets. For example, all accounts with holdings in Xerox common stock would be listed, with an itemized asset record showing the account name and, for each account, the shares held, the identification numbers, the book value, the location of the holding, and the registration or name in which the asset is held. Asset records are useful in balancing positions held at several custodial positions and for researching investment decisions.

## ASSET CONTROL AND PROCESSING

The asset control function within a bank trust department is responsible for holding, transferring, and processing assets. Specifically, asset control may include processing free receipts and deliveries, settling securities trades, processing miscellaneous asset transactions, and holding assets in the trust department's vault.

## Processing Free Receipts and Deliveries

Assets can be received for free or they can be bought. When assets are received for free (as when a trust account is opened or a gift is made to a current account), the transaction is called **free receipt.** Conversely, assets can be given away (as when an account is closed or a client makes or bequeaths a gift of trust account assets to someone else) or sold. Disposing of trust assets for free is termed **free delivery.** Both the movement and processing of free receipts and free deliveries of assets are typically handled by an asset control function within a trust department.

In posting free receipt transactions, several things must be done. If the assets are physically received, the account administrator should look at each asset closely and make a complete list of them, making sure all certificates (or separate stock or bond powers) are signed, and all legal papers are with the assets. After checking the assets, a receipt is given to the customer. The assets, legal papers, and list are then given to trust operations. If the assets are in book-entry form, only a statement of the assets is passed to operations. Once the physical assets are received, operations personnel check them against the list. For book-entry assets, the statement of assets is checked against the statement of the depository in which the assets are held.

For accounting purposes, assets are usually assigned an identification number. With stocks and bonds, the identification is often based on a unique number, called the **CUSIP** (Committee on Uniform Security Identification Procedures) **number** that is assigned to most securities issues. Assets that do not have CUSIP numbers (mutual funds, commercial paper, money market funds, and unique miscellaneous assets held by only one account) are often identified through a special property or asset number assigned by the trust department. Like CUSIP numbers, they assist trust operations in locating assets, tracking transactions, and generating reports.

## Processing Unique, Miscellaneous Asset Transactions

Miscellaneous assets—for example, insurance policies, certificates of deposit, real estate holdings, jewelry, gold, and coins—are also processed in the asset control area. Since most unique assets do not have a CUSIP number, they usually carry an in-house property or asset number. All assets are further identified by a complete description—for example, a description of real estate would include its address and jewelry might be described by its appraised value.

## Settling Securities Trades

Securities buys and sells are usually settled by the asset control function of trust operations. The processing of securities trades by trust operations involves five steps—order, execution, confirmation, settlement, and posting. A brief discussion of this process follows.

A **trade order** is an instruction to a securities broker to buy or sell a certain security at a designated price. Depending on the nature of the trust account (discretionary or nondiscretionary), either the customer or account administrator, portfolio manager, or other trust department personnel makes the final decision to place a trade order. Order information is recorded on a trust accounting or securities movement and control system, and includes the name of the broker, the trust account number, the security, the number of shares, the nature of the transaction, and the order date.

The trade order is executed when a seller (or buyer) is found for the security. Upon execution, a contract exists to buy or sell the security by a specified date, called the **settlement date.** Notification of the transaction is then passed to trust operations, where information pertaining to the order is recorded prior to the settlement date. A confirmation of the trade is then sent by the broker to trust operations. The **trade confirmation** provides all the details about the trade, including the broker's commission. Information on the confirmation is cross-checked with that on file with trust operations. Any discrepancies are immediately brought to the attention of the customer or the appropriate trust personnel.

**Trade settlement** occurs when the securities are exchanged for money. The actual certificate may be exchanged in the transaction, but it is becoming increasingly common for certificates to be kept at central depositories or immobilized under the Federal Reserve's book-entry system. Because funds are transferred only when the securities are delivered, it is essential that trust operations make delivery of sold securities on settlement date so that funds owed to the trust account can be promptly credited. Once the trade is settled, the final step is **posting** the trade to the customer's accounts.

## Vault Control

Once assets have been posted to an account, they are either put into a trust vault for safekeeping or maintained at a depository. Trust vaults are used to hold valuables—like jewelry and coins, and papers of importance such as stock and bond certificates, insurance policies, deeds and mortgages, and originals of wills and trust agreements.

To safeguard the customers' assets, vault control activities are based on the concept of **dual control.** That is, two people must be present at all times when moving assets and when verifying the accuracy of the actual asset against the accounting and control procedures. The people who work in the vault—often referred to as **vault custodians**—cannot even enter the vault area alone since the vaults have two locks that require separate keys or combinations for access.

## PROPERTY MANAGEMENT

Many banks have a sufficient number of trust accounts with real estate holdings to warrant a property management function of trust operations. Such properties include houses, apartment buildings, farms, office buildings, shopping centers, mineral leases, and exploration rights. As with other trust assets, information pertaining to real property is entered into the trust department's accounting system so that ownership, income, and expense records can be maintained. In managing real property for a customer, a trust department's responsibilities range from the simple to the complex. Often, all that is necessary is to pay the property taxes when due and to conduct a periodic inspection and appraisal. Caring for rental or commercial property, on the other hand, involves a variety of tasks, which may include the following:

- disbursing any interest or principal payments at the proper time

- inspecting the condition of the property and recommending whether any additional maintenance or repairs are needed

- appraising the current value of the property to determine whether existing insurance coverage levels are adequate

- maintaining appropriate insurance against personal liability, property damage, and any other insurable hazards

- maintaining appropriate property assessment and tax records and paying all taxes when due

- evaluating the property regularly to determine if it should be retained in its present form, sold, or improvements made

- arranging for repairs when necessary

- collecting rent

- renewing existing leases and executing new leases

- preparing income and expense statements and property status reports

From the preceding list, it is apparent that property management can be time consuming and requires well-trained personnel. Individual trust departments may decide to manage only certain types of real property or employ outside agents to perform such duties as rental collections and inspections.

## INCOME COLLECTION

An important responsibility of trust operations is to collect the income generated by assets in trust accounts. The complexity of the task depends on the type of asset and whether it is widely held.

### Securities

Bonds and other debt securities have income payment schedules that are established when the security is issued. Interest is collected periodically (for example, semiannually), with a final income payment made at maturity. The nature of the income collection task depends upon whether the securities are issued in bearer or registered form (see chapter 10). With registered securities, payment can be made directly to trust operations. Bearer securities involve detaching the appropriate interest coupon and forwarding it to the disbursing agent for payment.

Equity securities may or may not generate income in the form of dividends (either cash payments or additional shares of stock through automatic dividend reinvestment). The board of directors declares when dividends are payable (usually four times a year) and the amount per share. For equity securities that pay income only when publicly declared, trust operations must have a means of noting all such declarations. For widely held securities, this information is generally available and can be found in publications by Moody's, Standard & Poor's, and others. For other securities, the corporation may have to be contacted directly to determine when dividends are paid. On the due date, the dividend disbursing and transfer agent forwards the appropriate income payment or a statement notifying each investor of the shares earned through reinvestment.

Ensuring that income on securities is collected when due is an exacting task. Income payment information is entered on asset records of the trust accounting system and, from this information, **income anticipation reports** (sometimes called income maps or journals) are prepared. These reports are prepared in advance of payment date and identify all trust accounts that are to receive income for a specific asset. When payment is received, the amount is compared with the amount due as shown on the income map. Underpayments or overpayments must be reconciled by trust operations as soon after receiving payment as possible.

### Other Assets

The anticipation and collection of income on assets other than securities may be more difficult. This includes rent payments; interest or principal payments received on loans and mortgages; book royalties; income on mineral interests; and Social Security, retirement, and insurance annuity payments. For such assets, records should reflect what payments are due, when they are due, and who is obligated to make payment. For regularly occurring payments—such as rent on a dwelling—this may not be an arduous task. For other assets though, such as oil and gas leases, income payments are based on reports by the producer, which may be difficult to verify. Nevertheless, income control is an essential aspect of trust operations. Late or missed payments may result in losses for the trust department.

### ASSET DISTRIBUTION

Another function of trust operations is the distribution of trust assets. This happens for several reasons, such as when a trust account is terminated, a gift is made, or assets are transferred from one account to another.

When a trust account is terminating and assets are being delivered to the trustor or beneficiaries, title of the assets must be transferred to the appropriate parties. For instance, if the transfer involves registered bonds or stock, the trust account officer normally provides trust operations with instructions identifying the securities to be transferred, the name in which they should be reregistered, and delivery instructions. Operations then submits the securities to a transfer agent for reregistration, and when completed, the account officer is notified to make arrangements for final delivery to the recipient. When the asset is no longer in the possession of the trust department, it is removed from the department's asset records. The procedure for gifting assets is similar, as title to the assets must be transferred.

On occasion, assets are transferred from one account to another—for instance, when an estate is distributed and the assets are used to fund a testamentary trust. In such cases, it is usually not necessary to register assets. For assets held in the vault, the account officer simply instructs vault personnel to refile the certificates with the new account. All accounting entries must be made carefully to ensure that the correct registration and other information is reflected in the new account. And with all transfers, the orderly distribution of assets hinges on maintaining complete account records describing each asset and evidencing proof of ownership.

## TAX REPORTING

Most trust accounts, like individuals, are subject to a variety of taxes—income taxes, federal and state estate taxes, inheritance taxes, property taxes, and gift taxes, to name a few. This requires the preparation and filing of tax returns, a task that may be handled by the account officer, a separate tax department, or a tax group of trust operations. For tax purposes, a trust is considered a separate entity and must obtain a tax identification number from the federal government. Agency accounts are not separate entities for tax purposes, and information on these accounts is reported using the principal's tax identification number.

### Income Tax Returns

Income earned by a trust account is subject to federal and state taxes, and is reported on federal return 1041 and the appropriate state tax returns. The tax returns itemize the income received, the expenses paid, and the amount of tax owed. Taxable income received by trust accounts includes dividends, interest, rents, and royalties. Expenses that can be deducted from earned income include interest paid, property repair fees, personnel fees, and so forth. Capital gains or losses on assets sold are also reported as either income or deductions. Some large trust departments with separate tax departments have become so adept at preparing income tax returns that they offer this service to the general public.

### Estate Tax Returns

Trust departments also commonly prepare estate and inheritance tax returns. The IRS requires a federal estate tax return whenever an estate has a value of $600,000 or more, and a return must also be filed in states that assess inheritance taxes. These reports are used to report the value, deductions, and tax due on the estate of a person who has died. All the assets of the decedent are listed, along with deductions for doctors' and hospital bills, attorney's fees, trust department fees, funeral expenses, outstanding debts, and so forth. If the total remaining assets exceed the maximum allowable threshold, a tax is imposed and must be paid before distribution of assets.

## Information Returns

The IRS also requires that it be notified about certain income payments made by trust departments to their customers. Forms prepared for this purpose are called **information returns** and are sent to both the customer and the IRS. For example, when income is paid out of an employee benefit account to plan beneficiaries, the trust department must prepare and send information returns to the beneficiaries informing them of the total amount of income they received so that they can report it to the IRS and pay any income taxes that are due. A copy of the information return is also sent to the IRS. Information returns cover interest income, dividends, distributions from profit-sharing or retirement plans, lump-sum benefits, proceeds from broker transactions, and miscellaneous income.

## Tax Accounting Systems

Most trust departments have a tax accounting unit that is responsible for preparing all necessary federal, state, and local tax returns for each account. To facilitate this process, all account transactions with tax consequences are assigned a tax code. Entries are accumulated and stored in a tax history file and processed at the end of the calendar year. A tax administrator may add or modify transactions as necessary to aid in the preparation of returns.

A factor in preparing estate, inheritance, gift, and certain state tax returns is the market value of the trust's assets, which is arrived at through a separate valuation process. When the accounting process is completed, the tax accounting system generates the tax returns, which are sent to the federal and state governments and to beneficiaries of the trust. Beneficiaries may also receive tax information reports indicating the taxable income they received during the year.

## CORPORATE TRUST OPERATIONAL SYSTEMS

Chapter 10 considered the responsibilities of a trust department when administering corporate trust accounts and performing agency services. Here we will consider the basic operational aspects of transfer, registrar, and paying agencies.

## Transfer Functions

Much of the work arising from stock transfer agencies is shouldered by trust operations. One of the primary responsibilities of trust operations is to maintain stock ownership records. Another is transferring stock, either original issues or issues already outstanding, which includes canceling old certificates and issuing new certificates to reflect the change in ownership.

In maintaining stock ownership records, trust operations records the names, addresses, and tax identification numbers of all shareholders; the certificate numbers and dates of issuance to each shareholder; and the number of shares represented on each certificate issued, along with the total holdings of each shareholder. These records are constantly revised and updated as stock is transferred. Requests for transferring original stock are verified to ensure that all documents are properly prepared and signed by the appropriate parties—officers of the corporation, the transfer agent, registrar, and so forth. When there is a transfer in ownership of outstanding issues, the old certificates must be canceled when the new ones are issued. These changes in ownership must be reflected on the records maintained by operations. Once the transaction has been processed and the new certificates checked, they are sent to the address specified in the transfer instructions.

Other transfer agency functions handled by trust operations may include disbursing dividend checks, preparing lists of stock owners, taking surveys, and sending out financial information to shareholders. For example, corporate trust operations may have the responsibility of mailing proxy cards to all shareholders prior to their company's annual meeting. When the shareholders return their proxies, the corporate trust area counts the votes and notifies the corporation of the totals.

### Registrar Functions

The principal responsibility of a stock registrar is to make certain that the transfer agent does not issue more shares of stock than were authorized by the corporation. To do this, the registrar keeps a record of how many shares of stock are registered to all owners, and when stock is transferred, the registrar makes certain that the shares evidenced by the canceled certificates correspond to the number of shares on the new certificates being issued. The stock registrar and transfer agent therefore act as a check and balance for one another. The corporate trust operations area has the task of maintaining registrar records and checking stock certificates before they are sent out by personnel working in the stock transfer area.

### Paying Functions

Bank trust departments also assume the duty of making dividend, interest, and principal payments for the issuers of stocks and bonds. Because ownership records are used for this purpose, it is common for the transfer agent (who keeps the ownership records) to serve as the paying agent as well.

Dividends are paid to stockholders in the form of cash, stock, or stock splits. After a dividend has been declared by the issuer of the stock, the paying agent refers to computerized shareholder records to determine who is entitled to receive the dividend and in what form. The corporate trust operations group maintains the shareholder records, prepares the proper payments, and verifies that the payments are correct and sent out on time. Interest payments to holders of registered stocks and bonds follow a similar course.

The other kind of paying agency service involves bearer bonds, which are securities that are issued without the holder's name printed on them. Interest payments are made by detaching coupons and sending them to the paying agent for redemption. Whoever bears the coupons is therefore entitled to receive payment. Because of this feature, bearer bondholders must handle their coupons with care, usually taking the coupons directly to the bank rather than relying on the mail. The bank then records the name of the presenter, sends the coupons to the paying agent, and later receives the interest payment from the agent. The payment is then given to the bondholder, which usually means depositing it directly in the holder's checking or savings account.

For the bank serving as paying agent, its corporate trust operations division is responsible for verifying that the interest payment is actually due. Each coupon has a payable date and an identification number that can be checked against the issuer's records to see if the bond is still outstanding. The coupon is then canceled and a check issued to whoever sent in the coupon. Complete records must also be kept to ensure that the amount of checks issued matches the amount of coupons received and canceled.

## TRUST ACCOUNTING SYSTEMS

Before the advent of computers, trust departments were awash in paper documents and records. All transactions were posted to a ledger and laboriously checked and double checked by hand. Today, paper has given way to microfiche and computer tapes and disks, and the bulk of the recordkeeping, report generation, and transaction processing functions are computerized.

All trust departments now have automated trust accounting systems that provide information for individual and corporate trust customers and meet the data processing requirements of personal trusts, estates, employee benefit plans, and trust agencies. Specifically, a modern trust accounting system

- stores, classifies, and updates data

- calculates revenues and expenses

- provides reports to customers, management, and regulators

- assists in administrative functions

Often, a trust account is controlled by a main system that tracks all trust assets and liabilities. Predefined instructions, stored in each customer's asset file, are used to manage the assets.

A typical trust accounting system creates an administrative tickler file for use by the trust account administrator to manage the account. Customer instructions to issue beneficiary checks and make investment payments are stored in this file as well. Other miscellaneous transactions—for example, when supplemental funds are received by a trust—are entered into the system and stored on the customer's asset file. All expenses chargeable to the trust account are logged. Finally, the system creates reports, which are sent to customers and management informing them of the performance and status of the trust.

Most banks have subsystems that are linked to the main trust accounting system. One such system may control securities transactions, posting transactions that show additions or deletions to securities and cash holdings.

A tax accounting system prepares all calendar and fiscal year-end tax reports. To generate the reports, all transactions with tax consequences are coded, periodically transferred from the main trust accounting system to the tax history file, and processed. All reports are generated by computer and sent to the trust's beneficiaries and the federal government.

Another common subsystem is the master trust system, which tracks the assets and portfolios managed by each individual investment adviser, as well as the total portfolios owned by the bank. Reports are provided to trust department management that indicate how each portfolio or group of portfolios are performing. Additional reports generated may include cash flow, current account holdings, and current market values.

A performance measurement is often established in a trust department to calculate the return of a portfolio over time, comparing book value with the current market value. Some systems are even able to calculate the degree of risk in a portfolio by comparing its diversification and ratings with current averages.

## INTERNAL CONTROL AND AUDITING

Because the trust department handles a great deal of money and assets for an invaluable clientele, a system of continuous internal checks and periodic audits is essential. Quality of work begins with the trust employees themselves, but mistakes can happen and there is on occasion a person who is dishonest. Consequently, internal controls and audits are necessary to detect errors and deliver careful, accurate, and honest work.

Internal control is an ongoing job of checking, balancing, and reconciling to ensure that all procedures are performed correctly and all records are accurate. For example, someone independent of those responsible for issuing checks from a trust account would reconcile outstanding trust checks, thus ensuring that money is available to pay checks that have been written but not yet cashed.

The audit function is usually performed by a separate audit unit independent of other bank departments, which reports directly to the board of directors. All aspects of a trust department's operations—policies, procedures, internal controls, and compliance—are under the purview of the audit department. Specifically, an audit of trust department activities verifies that

- all banking laws and regulations are complied with

- all terms of the trust instruments are adhered to

- trust assets are protected by proper vault control procedures and by obtaining proper authority for the disposition of assets

- all trust investments were duly authorized and accurately reported to the proper account

- all trust income is collected in the correct amount and when due

- all account and asset reviews are conducted as required by banking regulations and bank policy

- all expenses were properly authorized and charged to the correct accounts

- all compensation is properly computed and charged or collected when due

To carry out its mission, the audit department continually reviews asset records, observes vault procedures, spot checks income postings and disbursements, confirms outstanding shares of stock with the corporation, reconciles paying agencies, and so forth. It also has the responsibility of bringing any apparent weaknesses to the attention of the board and suggesting remedial procedures.

### SUMMARY

Many trust department tasks—from transaction processing and recordkeeping to income collection and distribution—are handled by trust operations. One key operational function is maintaining and updating records of all accounts. Holding reports and transaction reports show customers their current asset and liability holdings and their account transactions over a period of time. Asset records reflect the trust department's position in specific assets, with a breakdown by individual trust account.

Asset control and processing is another important function and includes processing free receipts and deliveries, settling securities trades, processing miscellaneous asset transactions, and holding assets in the trust department's vault. Trust vaults are used to hold valuables and papers of importance. These assets are safeguarded by a system of dual control in which all asset movements and verifications are performed by a minimum of two people.

For banks with trust accounts that have real estate holdings, a property management function is necessary. Tasks range from the simple (paying property taxes and conducting periodic inspections) to the complex (collecting rent, having repairs made, renewing leases, and so forth). Many of these responsibilities may be assigned to outside agents.

Income collection, like most other operational procedures, depends upon complete records and accurate accounting procedures. Securities income is in the form of dividend and interest payments. To ensure that income is collected when due, operations departments prepare income anticipation reports. These reports identify all trust accounts that are to receive income for specific assets.

Trust operations is also responsible for distributing assets when an account is terminated, a gift is made, or assets are transferred from one account to another. This usually requires transfer of the title to the assets. For instance, if the transfer involves stocks or bonds, the securities must be reregistered in the new owner's name.

Preparation of income tax returns, estate and inheritance tax returns, and IRS information returns may be assigned to trust operations or performed by a separate tax department. To facilitate this process, all trust account transactions with tax consequences are assigned a tax code. Entries are accumulated and stored in the department's accounting system, and processed at the end of the year.

Another function of corporate trust operational systems includes most of the recordkeeping, reporting, and paperwork requirements associated with transfer, registrar, and paying agencies.

Finally, operations plays a major role in internal control and auditing. Internal control consists of ongoing checking, balancing, and reconciling procedures to ensure that all operational tasks are performed correctly. The audit function encompasses periodic, in-depth evaluations of all aspects of a trust department's operations—policies, procedures, internal controls, and compliance with laws and regulations. Audits are conducted independently of any bank department, and the findings are reported directly to the board of directors or an appointed committee.

## QUESTIONS FOR REVIEW

1. Identify some of the operational tasks involved in running your trust department.

2. What is typically shown on the asset statement? List five different types of trust assets and liabilities in order of decreasing liquidity.

3. Define free receipts and deliveries.

4. Briefly explain how a securities trade is settled from the time an order is placed to its posting.

5. What operational tasks may be required of a trust department when managing an apartment building as an account asset? Assume you are preparing an income tax return for such an account. What is one source of taxable income? Name five potential sources of expense deductions.

6. What are some operational tasks associated with serving as a transfer agent?

7. How does internal control differ from auditing?

## INTRODUCTION

The financial services marketplace of today bears little resemblance to the marketplace of 20, or even 10, years ago. Before the 1970s, banks enjoyed unchallenged dominance in many areas, one of which was trust services. Since then, however, deregulation has opened the door to legions of new competitors. Competition is coming from brokerage houses, the insurance industry, money market funds, and investment counseling firms. Conglomerates are also venturing into the financial services marketplace—for example, Sears has entered into the brokerage and insurance business.

These competitors have spawned a variety of services to attract consumers, and as a result, money that ordinarily would have been placed with trust departments is flowing into accounts managed by these new competitors. Adding to the competitive challenge facing banks is the fact that they are still prohibited from engaging in certain insurance, real estate, and securities activities. For instance, banks cannot sell most forms of insurance nor can they distribute mutual funds without going through an intermediary, although the latter restriction may soon be lifted. Consequently, banks are precluded from providing the full range of financial services offered by their competitors.

It is unclear what effect these regulatory constraints and the recent explosion of new financial providers will have on bank trust departments. It is certain, though, that banks must seriously assess the services they provide from the viewpoints of clients and prospective clients. The banking industry can no longer afford to ignore the importance of vigorous marketing and selling efforts, which for so long were considered incompatible with the genteel atmosphere of providing services to wealthy clients. Waiting for customers to call or relying solely on referrals is a losing strategy in today's marketplace.

This chapter looks at how banks are revamping their marketing and sales efforts to compete for trust business. We begin by considering some inherent difficulties in marketing and selling trust products. Next, each stage in the marketing and sales cycle is explored, beginning with planning and research and continuing through to the sales and follow-up monitoring. The chapter closes with a look at some of the ways banks are adjusting to the new competition and consumer demands of today's trust marketplace.

## WHY MARKETING AND SELLING
## TRUST PRODUCTS IS DIFFICULT

Marketing and selling trust services is a challenge for several reasons.

*Trust services are intangible.* The first difficulty in marketing trust services is that they must be marketed as services, which are intangible, instead of as products, which are tangible. For too long, the trust industry has conceived its function as providing products, when it actually offers services. Clearly, some tangible items are involved in providing trust services, such as account statements and correspondence. Nonetheless, the basic services consist of a series of processes handled by a trust officer.

*The value of trust services is not easily defined or compared.* The second marketing problem involves a client's perception of value. Some services, such as hair styling, are so routine that it is easy to establish standards by which the services can be compared. Consumers maximize money and time by patronizing services that meet their individually perceived standards. However, trust services are so seldom used by the general public that they have had no opportunity to establish standards and values for the services.

Ancillary to that is the difficulty of comparing the value of trust services among financial institutions. For example, investment performance is a notoriously tricky thing to measure. What may look like good investment performance at one financial institution may, in fact, not be the case if the risk was higher than normal. Furthermore, investment performance figures can be taken over any period of time. A better-than-average investment return achieved over several years is preferable to a high investment return realized over one or two quarters. Nonetheless, a financial institution may be quick to proclaim a record of superior investment performance that is based on short-term results.

*Personal trust services are often viewed in a limited context.* A third difficulty in marketing trust services is the common perception that trust services involve unpleasant subjects, namely death and incapacity. For years, trust departments have concentrated their marketing efforts on estate planning and minimizing taxes at death to generate interest in their services. If these were insufficient inducements, the possibility of the client's potential incapacity could be emphasized. Frequently, the advantages of trust services to normal, healthy individuals are not promoted energetically enough.

*Trust services often have a lofty image.* Finally, to market trust services effectively, trust officers have to learn to fight their way out of the ivory tower. Since banks once offered trust services to the wealthy free of charge or for a negligible amount, trust executives never thought of themselves as other businesspeople do—that is, offering a service for a profit. The self-perception that trust services involve an exclusive preserve far above the need to make a profit still persists in some places.

However, with the challenge from new competitors and with new market demands, this lofty attitude could easily make bank trust services obsolete. Trust managers and trust personnel are increasingly aware that the trust department must become an independent profit center of its bank. Trust people must recognize that they are operating a business for profit, and that they are now a part of a competitive business environment.

This metamorphosis may necessitate wholesale changes in the way a bank approaches its trust business. Banks must adopt an innovative approach to investment services, using as their guideposts good business sense and a sensitivity to the customer's needs.

## STAGES IN THE MARKETING CYCLE

To be successful in a competitive business environment, banks must formulate clear and effective marketing and sales strategies. This involves planning, product research and development, promotion, sales, superior service, and constant monitoring of results. Let's examine each of these stages in the marketing cycle.

### Planning

Planning is a new concept to the trust industry. By planning for the future—which includes setting defined goals and objectives—organizations avoid drifting along the path marked "status quo." For example, in a departure from traditional practices, many banks have looked into the future and decided to reorganize their trust departments along product lines. Related product lines can be grouped for maximum efficiency and costs can be allocated to each product, allowing trust departments to make better business decisions about which product lines to promote and which to deemphasize or drop. By planning for the future, rather than just continuing with "business as usual," trust departments can respond better to the competitive challenges that await them.

One aspect of planning is to establish long-range organizational goals that set the direction for the trust department. Planning for an intermediate period involves exploring various alternatives—potential objectives—that the organization could choose to achieve as long-range goals. Selecting objectives to implement from among these alternatives is the short-range planning dimension, which is usually done every year.

Good planning requires

- analyzing the trust department's current situation—its strengths and weaknesses, its problems and opportunities

- understanding the organization's basic role—its reason for being

- formulating management, operational, and marketing strategies to achieve long-range goals

- initiating tactical action plans that are achievable, measurable, and specific in terms of responsibility and target dates

- determining the impact of such plans on the organization's success and progress toward its goals

## Product Development

To build a successful sales program, a trust department must have the right products to sell. In the past, banks provided a few core trust services. However, following an easing of regulations, product offerings have become more diversified, and banks have had to develop new products of their own. Furthermore, trust customers have become more active in deciding how they want their money invested and often opt for banks that meet their particular investment needs. For example, one bank now offers a customized, short-term, cash-management account specifically designed for the beneficiaries of corporate mergers or acquisitions or other people who have come into a tremendous amount of cash. With such innovative services, banks can tap a market that would otherwise invest its money elsewhere.

Product development begins with the question: What does the client want? Often the answer comes through personal contact with existing customers. Marketing research is also essential, both to determine what new services are needed and to avoid costly mistakes by testing the acceptability of a new service before it is made available to the public.

## Promotion

In the past, trust departments obtained new customers mainly through referrals. For example, a lawyer who has handled the legal paperwork for establishing a guardianship may direct his client to a specific bank to administer the guardianship. Recognizing the importance of these referrals, trust departments devoted much of their promotional resources on direct contacts with professionals to inform them of the high-quality trust services available at the bank. Banks also printed notices and brochures that detailed their trust services, but for the most part, this kind of literature was designed to inform the inquiring customer rather than to attract new business.

### Advertising

While these low-key initiatives are still necessary today, banks have become more aggressive in their promotion of trust services. Many banks now advertise in magazines or newspapers, an approach that was once considered unwise because trust departments sought a select clientele, not the general public that was reached through the mass media. However, with the introduction of common trust fund investments and other products aimed at people who are not necessarily affluent, advertising has become more cost effective.

Advertising trust services is a challenging undertaking because they offer an intangible benefit to consumers and are often complex, which makes it difficult to differentiate the benefits of the bank's trust services from that of its competitors. Consequently, advertising is primarily used to build awareness and interest in trust services.

### Publicity Initiatives

Promotion includes publicity as well as advertising. Publicity is promotion that is not paid for, such as an article or photograph that is published in a newspaper or magazine. Since the trust business is by nature private and confidential, publicity has not been particularly easy to achieve. However, opportunities for favorable publicity occur with, for example, the development of new services or the attainment of good investment performance results.

Some banks have gone one step further and hired public relations firms to achieve favorable press coverage. Used correctly, the press can often be a forum for announcing a new product or emphasizing the bank's expertise in areas such as investment and tax and financial planning. Other promotional strategies include establishing a speakers bureau for talking to groups and the press, producing and distributing newsletters on such topics as taxes and personal financial planning and investment, holding tax and investment seminars, providing a telephone hotline for information or advice regarding trust services, and offering free or low-cost portfolio analysis.

## In-Bank Referrals

Trust departments have an extraordinary source of built-in prospects—those who use the bank's commercial services. Yet, in most banks, the trust department's role and the services it offers remain a mystery to many bank employees. To remedy this situation, banks are concentrating on what has been termed internal marketing—that is, marketing directed at employees in other bank departments. To explain what a trust department does, its services, and its performance record, trust representatives are making presentations before commercial banking officers and other bank personnel and are circulating literature throughout the bank. Banks are also creating incentive programs to reward employees for referring new accounts to the trust department and are setting specific goals for referrals.

## Selling

In the highly regulated, noncompetitive trust services marketplace of the past, selling was essentially synonymous with order taking. A customer came to the bank, conferred with a trust account officer, and purchased the trust services that best met his or her specific needs. Sales skills were unknown to most bankers, and in fact, this deficiency was a point of pride to many, who considered selling unnecessary and beneath them.

Of course, nothing could be further from the truth. In today's environment, selling is essential. The trust customer has a myriad of financial products to choose from and institutions willing to provide them. Banks whose trust employees are mere order takers will not be taking orders for long.

Banks are investing considerable resources to train employees in sales skills, beginning with a new look at the professional salesperson. Professional sales-people listen, clarify, advise, and package. By identifying the services that best fit the client's needs and encouraging him or her to purchase them, bankers serve in the capacity of partner, not peddler. For example, one bank encourages its portfolio managers to contact their clients whenever a manager sees a bro-kerage report on an asset important to a client's account. A sale might result, but regardless, the manager is serving the client. Similarly, banks are establishing client-contact goals that encourage trust account officers to initiate calls, write letters, and hold seminars. The alternative is waiting for the phone to ring.

To improve selling techniques, trust departments are holding training pro-grams that show account officers how to communicate effectively (questioning, listening, displaying empathy and interest, probing, and paraphrasing con-cerns); sell to prospects (identifying prospects, recognizing financial needs, planning and making calls, and following up on contacts); and manage account relationships (monitoring and identifying potential needs, and staying in touch).

Another initiative offered by an increasing number of trust departments is incentive compensation. Instead of compensating employees for "time in grade," many trust departments are rewarding their trust officers for performance—whether based on referrals, sales, investment performance, or some other measure. Again, this instills a service- and performance-oriented approach in trust employees, which in turn increases sales.

### Fulfillment

At the core of the marketing cycle is the quality of service that is provided. Once the bank has the customer, it is service that keeps him or her loyal. Again this entails more than just delivering existing services with a high degree of professionalism. The trust officer must constantly seek to fulfill needs, whether the customer recognizes them or not. This requires an understanding of the bank's trust products and the ability to package them to suit the client's needs. Defined in this way, high-quality, personalized service instills confidence in clients, who in turn come back for additional services and refer new customers to the bank.

### Monitoring

Monitoring occurs throughout the marketing cycle and includes following up on the plans that are agreed to, verifying and updating research, testing new services, assessing the effectiveness of publicity programs and advertising campaigns, and ensuring that services are being delivered as promised. To stay competitive, trust departments must continually take stock of their situation, adapting their services as the marketplace and needs of their customers change.

## STRATEGIES FOR COMPETING IN THE TRUST MARKETPLACE

The trust business is being rapidly reshaped as the marketplace changes from regulatory and insular to entrepreneurial and expansive. To compete effectively, bank trust departments are having to devise new strategies that represent a departure from traditional trust practices. Three strategies for attracting new business are creating a sales culture, cross-selling, and relationship management.

### Creating a Sales Culture

In the change to an intensely competitive trust marketplace, banks are finding that an aggressive, professional sales program is a necessity. This entails more than just voicing a commitment to an abstract sales philosophy. To be truly successful, a pro-selling attitude must pervade the entire bank, from the board of directors down to trust account officers and support staff. In other words, a **sales culture** must be created.

Building a sales culture in an industry where bankers have not had to sell until recently can be a difficult enterprise. It can involve fundamental changes—restructuring departments, redefining goals and objectives, retraining employees, instituting a system of performance-based incentives, and instilling pro-selling attitudes and behaviors in all employees. Trust officers need to change their thinking from "I carry out fiduciary responsibilities," "I handle estate settlements," or "I am an account administrator," to a more positive attitude of "I serve the client by identifying and fulfilling needs." This change in approach requires an overall sense of the market and the need to sell services.

Leonard L. Berry, Charles M. Futrell, and Michael R. Bowers, in *Bankers Who Sell*, state that banks with a strong sales culture all exhibit the following characteristics.

*Customer orientation.* Selling is viewed as a way to satisfy the client's needs, as a way to serve the customer. For example, all customer inquiries and complaints are handled promptly.

*Pervasive selling attitude.* Everyone in the bank—from top management to supervisors and staff—believe that selling is both legitimate and important. In a shared sense of purpose, staff are encouraging the bank to go after business, not wait for it.

*Sense of teamwork and institutional pride.* Banks with the strongest sales cultures foster the feeling among their employees that they are on a shared mission to promote the bank and its products. By imparting institutional pride, employees are inclined to sell the bank and sell for the bank.

*Visible top management commitment.* At banks with a strong sales culture, top management executives demonstrate their commitment to selling. They make calls themselves, set and insist that sales performance criteria are met, and commit the necessary resources to make the sales effort work.

*Faith in employees.* A final characteristic of sales culture is that top management has faith that employees can and will sell if given encouragement and the proper tools. The common perception is that most bankers are not sales-minded people (unlike, for example, those in the insurance or securities brokerage business) and consequently cannot be expected to become sales-oriented.

## Cross-Selling

Recognizing that the most promising prospect for a new bank service is a current customer, banks are exploring ways to expand existing account relationships by cross-selling bank services. This strategy takes advantage of banks' long record of good, reliable service. If customers are pleased with the service they have received to date, the odds are good that they will purchase additional services from the bank. It is certainly easier to make a sale this way than it is to woo a customer away from a competitor.

Cross-selling is the natural result of a sales culture in which everyone is actively involved in selling the bank and its services. As banks become more sales-oriented, various divisions cooperate with each other, rather than act independently. Information is exchanged, files are shared, and referrals made. For example, a personal trust officer would not only alert clients to the bank's investment management services but would also be on the lookout for the possibility that they might need a safe deposit box or certificate of deposit. Similarly, an account officer for a charitable trust should be alert for ways his or her bank might serve the personal and commercial financial needs of the trust's board of directors, whether or not those needs are trust related.

One way banks are actively promoting cross-selling is by rewarding employees for referring new accounts. An incentive system is often instituted at the departmental level, with the benefiting department paying the selling department a finder's fee for revenue received as a result of the referral. To promote better communication with other areas of the bank, trust departments are publishing and circulating literature within the bank that describes the trust department's services and performance record.

## Relationship Banking

The trend toward more complex and varied financial services has spawned a new innovation—relationship banking. The objective of relationship banking is to satisfy a client's total financial service needs with a minimum of inconvenience to the client. In a sense, the client is guaranteed a "one-stop" quality banking service—that is, a client is often assigned one banker who becomes intimately familiar with the client's financial service needs, takes a genuine interest in fulfilling those needs, assembles the right package of services, and continually monitors the account after the sale is made.

The personalized service of relationship banking requires a sizable commitment in personnel time and resources. For example, account officers must have the necessary training to understand what products the bank has to offer and when to take the client to someone else. The realities of competition make it necessary for banks to establish long-term, multiple-service relationships. Relationship banking can only work, though, if a bank and its employees are committed to selling, rather than just taking orders.

# SUMMARY

Faced with stiff competition in the trust marketplace, banks are placing more importance on their marketing and selling efforts. Marketing and selling trust products is difficult for several reasons. First, trust services are intangible. Second, their value is not easily defined or compared with those of competitors. Third, trust services are often viewed in a limited context and therefore promoted as such.

To be successful in the trust business, banks must formulate an effective marketing and sales strategy that encompasses planning, product research and development, promotion, selling, fulfillment, and monitoring.

Planning includes setting defined goals and objectives so that the trust department is positioned for the future rather than just adhering to the status quo. Product research and development is essential to provide customers with new and innovative services and to avoid the costly mistake of marketing unacceptable services.

Promotion of trust services once consisted primarily of referrals and brochures. Today, banks are becoming more aggressive and turning to such promotional efforts as advertising campaigns, press releases, speakers bureaus, newsletters, seminars, and telephone hotlines.

Internal marketing—educating employees in other bank departments about trust services—is also important to creating new accounts. Selling trust services is vastly different today than in the past. Instead of merely serving as order takers, trust officers must listen, clarify, advise, and package. To develop these skills, trust departments are holding training programs and instituting incentive compensation programs. Once the sale is made, the service must be delivered with a high degree of professionalism and the relationship continually monitored to ensure that the client is satisfied.

To compete successfully in the financial services marketplace, banks are devising new strategies, among which are creating a sales culture, promoting cross-selling services, and emphasizing relationship banking. In a bank with a strong sales culture, there is a customer orientation, a pervasive selling attitude, a sense of teamwork and institutional pride, visible commitment from top management, and a faith that, if given the opportunity, bank employees can and will sell. Cross-selling offers an opportunity to expand existing account relationships and sell additional bank products and services. Relationship banking provides clients with a "one-stop" quality banking service that satisfies all of their financial service needs.

Although the trust business is centuries old, by adapting to the needs of the marketplace it can enjoy a renaissance as restrictions on banks' abilities to compete are eased. Working from a foundation of experience and probity, trust officers will be able to develop creative solutions to clients' needs, as new opportunities arise in the future for banks.

## QUESTIONS FOR REVIEW

1. Why are trust services a challenge to market and sell?

2. Is your trust department organized along product lines? What products has your bank developed to attract trust customers?

3. How has the promotion of trust services changed over the last few decades?

4. What are some of the measures banks have taken to promote their trust products? How does your bank advertise and publicize its trust products?

5. What is entailed in selling trust products in today's marketplace?

6. What characteristics are evident in banks exhibiting a strong sales culture?

7. Identify some nontrust products that might be of interest to a client with a personal trust account at your bank.

8. Define relationship banking.

# Glossary

**active trust.**   A trust in which the trustee is required to perform some duty.

**activity fee.**   A fee charged for each account transaction.

**administrator.**   A personal representative appointed by a court to settle the estate of a person who died intestate, or whose will did not name an executor who was able to serve.

**agency.**   A relationship in which a client (the principal) engages a bank (the agent) to perform specific services. The distinguishing characteristic of an agency is that title to the property involved does not pass to the agent.

**agency house.**   A service that developed in India in the eighteenth century to transact business between trustees and individuals, such as receiving money on deposit and administering estates.

**agent.**   A person who acts on behalf of another (the principal) with the principal's authority and subject to the principal's control. Title to property does not pass to the agent, and the agent's fiduciary responsibility is that of obedience to the principal's wishes.

**American depository receipt (ADR).**   A negotiable, registered receipt for foreign stock held by a depository bank or correspondent bank in the country that issued the stock. Similar to regular stock certificates, holders receive dividends after the depository's charges have been deducted.

**asset record.**   A statement that reflects the trust department's position in specific assets, which may be used to balance positions in several custodial accounts and research investment options.

**attesting witness.**   A person who witnessed the signing of a will and can attest to its authenticity.

**bankers' acceptance.**   A negotiable time draft (bill of exchange) drawn on and accepted by the bank on which it was drawn. The bank assumes the obligation of making the payment at maturity.

**bearer bond.**   A bond that does not have the owner's name on it, so interest is paid by clipping coupons from the certificate and presenting them to the paying agent.

**beneficiary.**   The person for whose benefit a trust is created.

**blind trust.**   A trust that holds a separate estate in which property is invested and managed without the trustor's knowledge. Often used by public officials who enjoy the benefits of the trust but can avoid conflict-of-interest charges.

**blue-chip stock.**   Stocks issued by large companies with long histories of consistent earnings and uninterrupted dividends.

**blue-sky laws.**   State laws concerning the issuance and registration of securities. They may differ from federal regulations.

**bond maturity.**   The date when the issuer will repay the principal.

**bond registrar.**   An agent that performs registration and transfer functions for bond issues and maintains ownership records.

**buy list.**   A list compiled by a bank of recommended securities.

**call option.**   An option that allows an investor to purchase stock from the holder at a fixed price within the time specified on the contract.

**canons of descent.**   Laws that governed the distribution of real property when a person died intestate. Many states have passed new probate codes that eliminate the distinction between real and personal property.

**capital gains.**   The amount by which shares appreciate in value.

**centralized trading exchange.**   An exchange, such as the New York Stock Exchange, where dealers and brokers trade securities. The exchange itself does not buy or sell shares or set their prices.

**charitable foundation.**   A trust, created for charitable purposes, that usually has a connection with the group or person who established it, such as medical foundation established by a state medical society.

**charitable remainder annuity trust.**   A trust created to provide an annuity for the beneficiaries during the life of the donor or the beneficiaries, which cannot be less than 5 percent of the asset value at the time the trust was established. The remainder interest—the property in trust—goes to the named charity at the annuitant's death.

**charitable remainder trust.**   A trust that pays an income or annuity to the beneficiaries. The property in trust goes to charity upon the death of the beneficiaries.

**charitable remainder unitrust.**   A trust that provides the lifetime beneficiary with a fixed percentage of the net market value, which is determined annually. At death, the property in trust is distributed to the named charity.

**chattel.**   Any kind of personal property.

**Chinese Wall.**   A policy barrier between the trust and commercial departments of a bank that prevents the sharing of material inside information in making investment decisions. The Glass-Steagall Act requires the separation of investment and commercial banking activities.

**closely held stock.**   Stock held by an individual, family, or a few holders.

**codicil.**   A legal amendment to a will.

**collective investment fund.**   Accounts pooled together to provide a diversified portfolio of investments and improve earnings. Also called a commingled fund.

**commercial paper.**   Negotiable, unsecured, short-term notes issued by major corporations and finance companies. Generally sold at a discount.

**common stock.**   An equity security that entitles the holder to receive dividends and to vote.

**common trust fund.**   A pooled fund for the collective investment of funds.

**community foundation.**   A trust set up by a city or town for charitable purposes.

**community property.**   Property in which a husband and wife have an undivided one-half interest, which is recognized in all civil law countries and in some southwest and Pacific Coast states of the United States.

**conservator.**   A term applied in some states to the individual or institution appointed by a court to protect the estate of an incapacitated person.

**conservatorship.**   A court-appointed arrangement to protect the estate of an incapacitated person.

**constructive trust.**   A trust imposed by a court of equity on persons who had no intention of creating a trust, but where one was necessary to preserve justice.

**convertible bond.**   A bond that gives the holder the right to exchange it for another type of security, usually the common or preferred stock of the issuing corporation.

**corporate bond.**   A long-term bond issued by a corporation to raise outside capital.

**corporate trust indenture.**   An agreement in which a bank agrees to act as an intermediary between a corporation offering securities and the purchasers of those securities. As trustee under the indenture, the bank is obligated to protect the investors' interests.

**cumulative preferred stock.**   Preferred stock that pays at a later date the dividends that are missed during profitless years.

**current yield.**   The current yield of a security, expressed as a percentage by dividing the annual interest by the current market price.

**CUSIP number.**   The 9-digit alphanumeric code that uniquely identifies a security issue.

**custodianship (custodial agency).**   A service that provides safekeeping of the customer's securities and collects the dividends and interest. May buy, sell, receive, and transfer securities upon the instructions of the customer.

**debenture.**   An unsecured bond or promissory note backed only by the general credit of the issuer.

**debt capital.**   Capital supplied by a corporation's creditors, such as a bank loan.

**decedent.**   A deceased person.

**decree of distribution.**   Authorization by a probate court after the final accounting that directs the personal representative to distribute the estate.

**defined-benefit plan.**   A pension plan in which a predetermined amount will be paid to participants at retirement. If returns on the funds invested by the plan are poor, or if employees retire sooner or live longer, the employer has to contribute more to the plan.

**defined-contribution plan.**   A pension plan in which the employer contributes a set amount of money on behalf of each employee. The amount received by each participant at retirement depends on the return realized on the money invested by the plan.

**devise.**   A gift of real property established by a will.

**dispositive provision.**   A clause in a trust agreement that states how income earned by the trust and the property in trust are to be disposed.

**distribution committee.**   A group of people who decide how funds from a charitable trust will be allocated to the community.

**domicile.**   The place regarded as permanent home and principal establishment of a person, which may differ from that person's residence.

**donor.**   A person who gives a gift.

**dual control.**   A process of using two people to safeguard assets when they are being moved and to verify the accuracy of the actual assets against accounting and control procedures.

**ecclesiastical registrar.**   A public official given the legal authority to settle the estates of British subjects in India in the eighteenth century.

**employee benefit trust.**   A trust account in which money is contributed by the employer, employees, or both, for the future benefit of the employees, such as at retirement or in case of disability.

**Employee Retirement Income Security Act of 1974.**   A federal law governing the management of employee benefit plans. The act's regulatory reach extends to most aspects of employee benefit trust administration.

**employee stock ownership plan (ESOP).**   A plan in which the employer or employee makes contributions to an account so that the employee may purchase stock in the company.

**endowment fund.**   A fund arising from a bequest or gift, in which the income generated by the assets goes for a specific use, such as a cultural or educational program.

**equipment trust bond.**   A bond secured by a corporation's equipment.

**equitable ownership.**   The right to enjoy the benefits of real or personal property in which the legal ownership is held in trust.

**equity.**   An ownership interest in a corporation equal to the difference between its total assets and total liabilities.

**equity capital.**   Capital supplied by stockholders.

**equity securities.**   Stock certificates that evidence ownership in a company.

**escheat.**   The reversion of property to the state when there are no heirs, next-of-kin, devisees, or legatees.

**escrow.**  An agency service that holds assets or documents on behalf of two or more persons to be delivered on a specific contingency or a certain occurrence.

**estate.**  The right, title, or interest in property, as distinguished from the property itself.

**estate settlement.**  The process of distributing a decedent's property. If the decedent died testate, specific legal steps must be taken before the property can be disbursed. If the decedent died intestate, the state imposes a law of succession on the distribution, which may not reflect the decedent's wishes. If there are no heirs or beneficiaries, the estate may revert to the state.

**estate tax.**  A tax imposed on a decedent's estate and not on the distributive shares of the estate.

**Eurocommercial paper.**  Similar to U.S. commercial paper but issued by European corporations.

**Eurodollar CD.**  A highly liquid, dollar-denominated certificate of deposit that frequently pays a higher interest rate than U.S. CDs.

**exchange agent.**  An agent that receives one or more kinds of securities of a company and, by previous arrangement, delivers other securities in its place. Often used during a merger or acquisition, when stock of the acquired company is replaced with stock of the new company.

**executor.**  A personal representative named in a will to settle the decedent's estate.

**express trust.**  A trust, either oral or in writing, in which the parties to the trust were aware of their intent to create a trust, and the terms of which were prescribed.

**fee simple.**  The highest form of ownership in real property, that of owning the property outright. If the owner dies intestate and without heirs, the land reverts to the state.

**fee tail.**  An estate limited to a person and the offspring of that person. If there are no descendants of the owner, the estate reverts to the original grantor of the property.

**fiduciary.**  An obligation of a person or trust institution to act in the best interests of the client on issues within the scope of their relationship.

**fiduciary income taxes.**  Taxes levied during probate.

**final accounting.**   An accounting to the court that supervises the guardian's performance—of the property and any capital changes, receipts, and disbursements—when the guardianship is terminating.

**first mortgage bond.**   A long-term debt secured by a mortgage on land, buildings, or equipment that is not subordinate to any other claim.

**foundation.**   A permanent fund established for charitable, religious, educational, or other benevolent purposes. None of the trust's net earnings may go to private shareholders or individuals.

**free delivery.**   A term describing assets that are given away, such as when an account is closed or a client gives or bequeaths trust account assets to someone else.

**free receipt.**   Assets that are received for free, such as when a trust account is opened or a gift is made to the account.

**fully trusteed plan.**   An employee benefit plan in which the contributions to the plan are invested and administered by a trustee. As each participant retires (or becomes disabled), the trustee begins paying him or her an annuity out of the trust estate.

**futures contract.**   A negotiable contract to buy or sell commodities, securities, or financial instruments at a set price on a future date.

**general agency.**   A complete, general authorization through a power of attorney to act on behalf of the principal in all transactions.

**general obligation (GO) bond.**   A municipal bond backed by the "full faith and credit" of the issuing authority.

**Glass-Steagall Act.**   A portion of the federal Banking Act of 1933 primarily concerned with the separation of commercial and investment banking.

**gross income receipts fee.**   A fee charged on an account based on a percentage of interest and dividend income.

**group trust.**   Pooled accounts to provide a more diversified portfolio of investments and a better rate of return.

**growth stock.**   Stocks that pay relatively low dividends because the issuing company retains most of its earnings to finance development plans. Their attraction lies in the potential return realized when the stocks are sold.

**guardian.**   An individual or trust institution appointed by a court to protect the estate, or in some cases the physical well-being, of an incapacitated person.

**guardianship.**   Known as a conservatorship in some states, it is a court-appointed arrangement to protect the estate of an incapacitated person. Also called a guardianship of the estate to distinguish it from a guardianship of the person, which involves the physical protection and well-being of an individual.

**guardianship in chivalry.**   A seventeenth-century practice in which the guardian's interests were put before the ward's, often resulting in the ward being sold in marriage to the highest bidder.

**holding report.**   A statement of all assets and liabilities in a customer's portfolio, including the number of shares held and their book and market values. Also known as an asset statement.

**incapacity.**   A legal term for a person's ineligibility to act on his or her own behalf by reason of minority, medical cause, or senility. Other forms of incapacity include mental illness, addiction to drugs or alcohol, incarceration, detention by a foreign power, or disappearance.

**income anticipation report.**   A report used by trust departments to track when payments are due on a specific asset and identify which accounts are affected. When payment is received, it is compared with the amount shown as due and reconciled on the statement. Also known as an income map or journal.

**income stock.**   Stocks that pay a large dividend relative to their market price.

**indenture.**   An agreement that stipulates reciprocal rights and duties.

**information return.**   A form notifying the customer and the IRS of income generated by a customer's accounts.

**inheritance tax.**   A tax on inherited property.

**institutional trust.**   A trust account established by a large investing body, such as an insurance company, pension plan, or charity.

**intangible property.**   Property that gives evidence of a value or right, such as a stock certificate.

**integrated retirement plan.**   A pension plan that calculates the total retirement benefit by combining the funds received from the plan and Social Security.

**interest.**   A share, right, or title in property.

**interest rate futures.**   A contract that gives the investor the right to buy a fixed-income, short-term security, which locks in a certain rate of interest on funds to be invested at a later date.

**intestate.**   Having died without leaving a will.

**irrevocable trust.**   A trust in which the trustor does not have the power to terminate the agreement. A trust may be irrevocable for a given time and then become revocable, or may be revocable for a stated period and then become irrevocable.

**joint tenancy.**   Ownership of property by two or more people, each having full right of usage, that passes to the survivor(s) when one tenant dies.

**leasehold.**   A tenancy for years in real property for a specified consideration.

**legal ownership.**   The right, title, and interest in real or personal property that is enforceable by law. A trustee has legal ownership of the assets held in trust for the beneficiaries (equitable owners).

**legatee.**   A person receiving a gift of personal property by will who is not a blood relative or next-of-kin.

**letter of guardianship.**   A document issued by a court that authorizes a guardian to act on behalf of a protected person.

**letter testamentary.**   A certificate issued by a probate court authorizing the personal representative to settle the decedent's estate.

**life estate.**   An estate for the life of the person holding the estate (the tenant) or for someone other than the tenant. Can refer to a person's interest in tangible personal as well as real property.

**living trust.**   An express trust operative during the life of the trustor.

**management agency.**   A service account in which the agent has managerial duties and perhaps even discretionary responsibilities, depending on the terms of the arrangement.

**money market fund.**   A mutual fund that is invested in a variety of short-term, high-quality notes, CDs, and acceptances. The low initial investment makes them particularly appealing to small investors.

**municipal bond.** A bond issued by state and local governments. Their credit risk depends on the reliability of the issuing authority. Maturities range from 1 to 30 years.

**negotiable certificate of deposit (CD).** In trust departments, short-term instruments usually issued in denominations of $100,000 or more.

**nominal yield.** The rate of return on an investment not adjusted for inflation.

**nominee ownership.** Ownership designated to a person, partnership, or corporation to hold title to securities, which will facilitate the management of such securities.

**obligor.** One who has an obligation to discharge, such as a corporation that issues bonds.

**over-the-counter market.** A market for trading securities that are generally not listed on a national exchange. Dealers and brokers negotiate an acceptable price through a mass communications network of telephones and computer terminals.

**participant.** An employee who takes part in a benefit plan.

**par value.** The face value of a security.

**passive trust.** A trust that requires the trustee to serve only as titleholder, without any specific duties.

**paying agency.** A service in which the bank pays dividends to stockholders and interest and principal payments to bondholders when due.

**pension plan.** An employee benefit plan in which employees receive reduced salaries at retirement, or upon disability, for the rest of their lives.

**pension portability.** The right of employees to take their vested pension benefits with them if they change jobs.

**personal representative.** A party that carries out the terms of a will. See also executor and administrator.

**personal trust.** An account in which an individual puts assets in the care of a trustee for the use of beneficiaries.

**pooled income fund.**   A charitable fund that provides donors with income interest on their gifts during their lifetime, with the gifts passing to the charity at their death.

**posting.**   The recording of a securities trade to a customer's account.

**pour-over will.**   The will of a person with a trust account who leaves all property to the trust; so-named because all assets outside the trust pour into the trust after probate.

**power of attorney.**   A witnessed document authorizing an individual to act as attorney-in-fact for the signer of the document. The powers may be general or specific.

**preferred stock.**   An equity security that has a prior claim to dividends and certain other rights, but does not entail a voting right.

**primary market.**   The market in which an issuer sells newly issued securities to an investor using the services of an underwriter, broker, or investment banker.

**principal.**   A person who appoints another party to act on his or her behalf.

**probate.**   The process of establishing the validity of a will so that the decedent's estate may be disbursed to the heirs and beneficiaries.

**profit-sharing trust.**   A trust established by an employer to share the company's profits with the employees. A type of employee benefit plan often administered by the trust department.

**proxy.**   A paper that evidences a shareholder's right to vote.

**prudent-man rule.**   A term coined from a judicial decision in 1830, which obligates a fiduciary to act as a prudent investor and maintain the safety of the capital above all.

**put option.**   An option to sell an asset at a specified price within a specified time.

**real property.**   Land and anything attached to the land that can be considered fixed, permanent, or immovable. Real property includes buildings, minerals, and other products of the soil, including air space above the land.

**registered bond.**   A bond that has the owner's name imprinted on it.

**relationship management.** The concept of having an experienced professional who assumes overall responsibility for a client by bringing together whatever specialists are needed to ensure the client is well served.

**remainderman.** The beneficiary of an estate after the prior estate has expired, who will ultimately receive the principal assets.

**repurchase agreement (repo).** The sale of securities (often to a bank) in which there is an agreement to repurchase them at a later date, typically the next day.

**resulting trust.** A trust created when the parties involved are unaware that their actions constitute a trust, yet the nature of the transaction establishes a trust relationship.

**revenue bond.** A bond issued by a state, municipality, or public or quasi-public authority to finance an income-producing project such as a sewage plant or road and secured by the income that will be generated by the project.

**revocable trust.** A trust in which the trustor reserves the power to alter or terminate the trust. The trustor may assign this right to someone else.

**right.** A just claim or privilege, such as that reserved by a trustor to amend or revoke a trustee's powers. Note that some trusts are irrevocable.

**right of survivorship.** The interest in real property that is conveyed, at death, by certain forms of tenancy (joint tenancy and tenancy by the entirety) to the surviving tenant(s) and not to the heir(s) or devisee(s).

**rule against perpetuities.** A rule of common law that voids any estate or interest in property that will not take effect within a given life or lives existing when the trust was created, plus 21 years and the period of gestation. Many states have modified the rule by statute.

**safekeeping agency.** An agency account that safeguards documents and securities, and occasionally jewelry, coins, stamps, or other collectibles, and delivers them on demand to the principal.

**sales culture.** An atmosphere and attitude that promotes the commitment to sell to and serve the customer.

**savings plan trust.** An employee benefit plan in which an employee contributes a specific amount to a retirement plan, which is matched in part, or in all, by the employer. Often administered by a trust department.

**secondary market.** Any market that deals in the resale of securities.

**secured bond.**   A bond issued under a trust indenture that is guaranteed by the pledge of collateral.

**Securities Act of 1933.**   Sometimes referred to as the "truth in securities" act, it safeguards the public from misrepresented and fraudulent securities issues by requiring that all new securities are fully and clearly described in the offering literature and sales presentations.

**Securities Exchange Act of 1934.**   An act that created the Securities and Exchange Commission for the purpose of regulating the issuance of securities by corporations.

**settlement date.**   When a securities trade has been negotiated, this is the date specified on the contract when the exchange will take place.

**Simplified Employee Pension.**   A tax-deferred account that allows a self-employed individual to deposit a stipulated amount of income tax free into an account to be withdrawn at retirement, when presumably it will be taxed at a lower rate.

**speculative stock.**   Stocks, issued by companies that are small, new, or struggling, that are a risky investment but may realize a significant return if the companies mature and become profitable.

**spendthrift provision.**   A clause in a trust agreement that limits the right of a beneficiary to dispose of his or her interest in the trust property and protects that interest from legal claims by creditors.

**sponsor.**   An employer who sets up a benefit plan.

**sprinkling trust.**   A trust in which the income or principal is distributed among members of a designated class, in amounts determined by the trustee.

**standby trust.**   A trust in which the trustor retains control over the property in trust until a specific event, such as the trustor's incapacity or death, when the trustee assumes management of the assets.

**Statute of Uses.**   An English statute of 1536 that provided that the legal as well as the beneficial title to land held for the use of a person be vested in that person.

**statutes of distribution.**   Laws that governed the distribution of personal property from an intestate's estate. Now superseded in many states by probate codes that do not distinguish between real and personal property.

**stock option.**   A right to buy or sell common stock at a specific price within a specified time. May be traded like other securities.

**stock registrar.**   An agent with the primary function of preventing the over-issuance of stock by keeping records of outstanding stock and the number of shares canceled and reissued.

**tangible property.**   Property of physical substance, such as an automobile.

**Tax Reform Act of 1986.**   Major legislation that overhauled the U.S. tax system. Some significant implications for trust institutions were the abolition of Clifford and spousal remainder trusts and federal estate tax on estates less than $600,000.

**tenancy by the entirety.**   Tenancy by a husband and wife in which neither has a disposable interest in the property during the lifetime of the other, but which passes to the survivor when one spouse dies.

**tenancy in common.**   The holding of property by two or more people in which each has an undivided interest that, at death, passes to the heir(s) or devisee(s) and not to the surviving tenant(s).

**testamentary capacity.**   The capacity to make a valid will. States vary in their requirements but most require a person to be at least 18 years of age and of sound mind.

**testamentary trust.**   A trust established by a will and inoperative until the death of the trustor.

**testate.**   Having made and left a valid will.

**testator.**   A person who has died leaving a valid will.

**thrift trust.**   Another name for a savings plan trust.

**title.**   The legal right to or evidence of ownership of real or personal property.

**trade confirmation.**   A confirmation of a securities trade containing every detail of the transaction, including the broker's commission.

**trade order.**   An instruction to a securities broker to buy or sell a security at a certain price.

**trade settlement.**   The exchange of securities for money.

**transaction report.**   Usually a monthly report generated by a trust department detailing all transactions and the beginning and ending value of each account.

**transfer agent.**   An agent retained by an issuer to maintain records of share ownership.

**Treasury bill (T-bill).**   A short-term obligation of the U.S. government.

**Treasury bond.**   A long-term (typically 10 to 40 years), fixed-rate investment backed by the U.S. government.

**Treasury note.**   An intermediate-term (typically 1 to 10 years), fixed-rate investment backed by the U.S. government.

**trust.**   An arrangement in which one person (the trustor) transfers legal title to property to another (the trustee) for the benefit of others (the beneficiaries).

**trust agreement.**   A written agreement containing the terms of the trust. Also known as the trust instrument.

**trust company.**   A corporation that acts like a bank by engaging in the trust business for individuals and businesses.

**trustee.**   A person or institution that holds legal title to property for the benefit of one or more people.

**Trust Indenture Act of 1939.**   A landmark act that represented the federal government's first attempt to regulate corporate trust indentures. The act requires that trust indentures and the accompanying registration statement be submitted to the SEC for approval.

**trustor.**   A person who creates a trust. Also called grantor or settlor.


**Uniform Commercial Code.**   A code of laws, adopted in various forms by all states except Louisiana, that governs commercial credit transactions.

**unsecured.**   Not backed by collateral.

**use upon use.**   The practice of giving property to one person for the use, or benefit, of another, which was a means of evading debt.


**vault custodian.**   A person who has a safekeeping responsibility in the vault of a bank.

**vested interest.**   A nonforfeitable right to benefits in an employee benefit plan.

**vesting.**   The attainment of a participant's right to benefits in an employee benefit plan.

**ward.**　A person who by reason of minority, mental incompetence, or other incapacity is under the protection of a court, either directly or through a guardian.

**warrant.**　A certificate that gives the holder the right to purchase shares of securities at a set price within a specified time.

**will.**　A legally enforceable declaration of a person's wishes and disposition of property upon death, which is inoperative until death. May be amended or revoked by a codicil.

**yield-to-maturity.**　The rate of return on an investment, including all interest payments and the difference between the market price and face value, if held to maturity.

# Index